DAILY READINGS

From
Quaker Writings
Ancient & Modern

Edited by
LINDA HILL RENFER

DAILY READINGS
FROM QUAKER WRITINGS
ANCIENT & MODERN

by Linda Hill Renfer, Ed.

Published by:

Serenity Press
131 Meadow Lane
Grants Pass, Oregon
97526 U.S.A.

Copyright© 1988 by Linda Hill Renfer
First Printing November 1988, First Edition
Second Printing October 1990
Third Printing April 1992
Fourth Printing August 1996

Printed in the United States of America
Library of Congress Catalog Card #: 88-62203

ISNB 0-9620869-0-8   Hardcover

Additional copies of this book may be ordered from the publisher at US $31.95 plus shipping and handling, or at bookstores.

TABLE OF CONTENTS

Author Index
Preface
Acknowledgements

AUTHOR INDEX

PREFACE

On the journey to convincement, I found Quaker literature to be of remarkable quality—direct, questioning, challenging, insightful— and impressively well written. As going to meeting meant a hundred-mile trip, much of my spiritual journey was accomplished through reading. Those writings frequently had the ability to put a confusing day in perspective. It wasn't long before the habit was formed of reading some sort of pamphlet or booklet nightly.

Sometimes a paragraph or passage would be so powerful, so rich, it would almost stand out from the page, and there would be the need to underline it, the desire to keep it, and wistfully hope to remember it always. It wasn't long before a notebook was necessary for the copies of pages made from borrowed materials. Sometimes there was the feeling of being on a critical threshold of spiritual insight, a sense of identity and oneness with Friends of centuries past, a moment that wanted to be preserved. The writings, regardless of the time written, carried similar messages to be gentle, be plain, be honest, and walk with God.

Sometimes the reading would consist of accounts of courage during critical times of history, sometimes they were confessions in a jour- nal—they were all inspirational in their own way. I found that comprehension difficulties sometimes experienced when reading 17th and 18th century literature vanished and the writer's meaning became perfectly clear, if I just read it aloud.

There was never any intention of compiling an inspirational book— certainly there are those among us who are far more qualified than I to sift through the stirring and jewel-like passages that we are so fortunate to claim as our own. And certainly I was content to continue my private reading. Then one day I came upon a remark- able little book published in 1869, DAY BY DAY, BEING A COMPI- LATION FROM THE WRITINGS OF ANCIENT AND MODERN FRIENDS, edited by Wm. H. Chase. As I held the worn little green volume in my hand, I knew why that notebook of mine was started many years ago. It was an odd feeling—perhaps the reader will identify. Several entries from that book have been included in this volume. This has been a singular experience and a labor of great satisfaction.

A word of explanation seems in order. The reader may notice that there is little, if any, description of the author beyond their name and the date written, when known. This is in keeping with Friends' tradition that the message is of greater importance that the individual giving it. A more thorough acknowledgement is given in the back of the book.

But there is no denying we are blessed with people with special gifts and writers of great insight and sensitivity, and we all have our favorites. It is hoped that the reader's favorites are here as well and they will perhaps discover additional ones.

Linda Hill Renfer
Grants Pass, Oregon
1988

ACKNOWLEDGEMENTS:

To properly acknowledge the people who helped make a book as far ranging as this is a very formidable task, and undoubtedly will be inadequate. In some respects, the search for the whereabouts of living authors for permissions at times required a detective's training, and were it not for an effective Quaker "underground", I am sure this book would not have been printed.

I am especially grateful to my husband for his steady encouragement and his willingness to do seemingly endless proofreading.

I am grateful to Marjorie Kellogg, for her encouragement and suggestions and reading of many rough drafts, to the members in my monthly meeting in Ashland for the use and temporary absence in our lending library of many books...to Barbara Mays of Friends United Press for her help and permission to quote from their publications and QUAKER LIFE...to Vinton Deming of FRIENDS JOURNAL...to the London Yearly Meeting for permission to use passages from the CHRISTIAN FAITH AND PRACTICE IN THE EXPERIENCE OF THE SOCIETY OF FRIENDS...to Rebecca Kratz Mays of Pendle Hill Publications for her advice and encouragement and permission to quote from their publications...to Douglas V. Steere for the use of several of his works and his kind words...to the library staff at George Fox College for the use of the special Quaker Collection...to Quaker Home Service for permission to include extracts from some of their Swarthmore Lectures, and for their assistance in locating several British Friends, Elizabeth Watson for her assistance and for permission to quote from GUESTS OF MY LIFE and other fine writings...to Mary Hoxie Jones for granting permission to quote from several writings of her father, Rufus Jones...to Margaret Hope Bacon, whose book THE QUIET REBELS was the first Quaker book I read...to Elizabeth Gray Vining, whose "Beauty from Ashes, Strength and Joy from Sorrow", forever touched my life...to Betty Stone, whose advice was invaluable...to Richard Hall, Stuart Banister, and Susan Smith for sharing a part of their lives and enriching mine...to and for the design of the cover, I owe thanks to my mother, who had never done one before....

The editor gratefully acknowledges the use of material from the following books:

A TESTAMENT OF DEVOTION by Thomas R. Kelly. Copyright 1941 by Harper & Row, Publishers, Inc., renewed 1969 by Lois Lael Kelly Stabler. Reprinted by permission by Harper and Row Publishers,

FINDING THE TRAIL OF LIFE by Rufus M. Jones. Copyright 1926 by Macmillan Publishing Co., Inc., renewed 1954 by Mary Hoxie Jones. Reprinted with permission of Mary Hoxie Jones.

THE ETERNAL PROMISE by Thomas Kelly, Copyright 1966, Friends United Press edition published in 1977. Reprinted by permission.

JOHN GREENLEAF WHITTIER: A PORTRAIT IN PARADOX, By Edward Wagenknecht, New York Oxford University Press.

BARCLAY'S APOLOGY: In Modern English, edited by Dean Freiday.

Additional acknowledgements appear in the chapter on Sources and References.

But most of all I wish to thank Friends everywhere, who took the time to write it all down, so from the inspiration of their lives, the insightfulness of their books, articles and their journals, we may benefit from their spiritual journeys.

Linda Hill Renfer
Grants Pass, Oregon

DAILY READINGS
FROM QUAKER WRITINGS
ANCIENT AND MODERN

by Linda Hill Renfer, Ed.

AND WE ARE UNHAPPY, uneasy, strained, oppressed, and fearful we shall be shallow. For over the margins of life comes a whisper, a faint call, a premonition of richer living which we know we are passing by. Strained by the very mad pace of our daily outer burdens, we are further strained by an inward uneasiness, because we have hints that there is a way of life vastly richer and deeper than all this hurried existence, a life of unhurried serenity and peace and power. If only we could slip over into that Center!...We have seen and known some people who seem to have found this deep Center of living, where the fretful calls of life are integrated, where No as well as Yes can be said with confidence. We've seen such lives, integrated, unworried by the tangles of close decisions, unhurried, cheery, fresh, positive. These are not people of dallying idleness nor of obviously mooning meditation; they are busy carrying their full load as well as we, but without any chafing of the shoulders with the burden, with quiet joy and springing step. Surrounding the trifles of their daily life is an aura of infinite peace and power and joy....they are so poised and at peace.

If the Society of Friends has anything to say, it lies in this region primarily. Life is meant to be lived from a Center, a divine Center. Each one of us can live such a life of amazing power and peace and serenity, of integration and confidence and simplified multiplicity, on one condition— that is, if we really want to. There is a divine Abyss within us all, a holy Infinite Center, a Heart, a Life who speaks in us and through us to the world...— *Thomas R. Kelly, 1941.*

HE THAT easily credits an ill report, is almost as faulty as the first inventor of it: for though you do not make, yet you commonly propagate a lie. Therefore never speak evil of any upon common fame, which for the most part is false; but almost always uncertain whether it be true or not.

*   *   *

Let us accustom ourselves to pity the faults of men, and to be truly sorry for them, and then we shall take no pleasure in publishing them. This common humanity requires of us, considering the great infirmities of human nature, and that we ourselves also are liable to be tempted.

Whenever we hear any man evilly spoken of, if we know any good of him, let us say that. It is always the more humane and the honorable part, to stand up in the defense and vindication of others, than to accuse and injure them.

That you may not speak ill of any, do not delight to hear ill of them. Give no countenance to busy-bodies, and those that love to talk of other men's faults.

And lastly, let us set a watch before the door of our lips, and not speak but upon consideration; I do not mean to speak finely, but fitly; especially when thou speakest of others, consider of whom, and what thou are going to speak; before thy words slip from thee, which when they are once out of thy lips, are forever out of thy power.— *Wm. Crouch to his children.*

I THOUGHT back on the inspiration that came to me in the Lenten series from the speakers of different religious traditions who were attempting to share with the rest of us the highest that they knew. Their expressions may have varied, but we were on a common quest, on different trails up the same mountain. There was unity in the motives that had set each of us on this course, and even greater unity at its end. I felt this undergirding unity very strongly, aided by much practice in our meetings for worship in sensing our basic oneness through our diversity. What is primary for Friends is our direct experience of the Divine. How one may be moved to bespeak this in ministry is secondary.

Trying to know God experimentally, to be in touch with an infinite power of love and goodness that pervades our universe and our very being, we know that any attempt to define God in words, including this one, must fall short. As we try to contemplate God's infinite qualities, we are like the blind men and the elephant. In all humility we are aware that we can know God only partially.

Moreover, in our ministry we speak each in our own tongue. Even the words of those most clearly "in the Spirit" are culture-bound, limited by background and vocabulary. It is the Spirit, not the words, that touches our hearts and draws us together and upward.

In a word, the essence of Quaker spirituality is right listening.— *Irwin Abrams, 1987.*

CONVICTION about eternal life dispels much of the fear and sadness of life. I might even welcome death and seek it, if convinced that an eternal life of fulfillment awaited me. Yet, I don't long for death, and am grieved at someone's death, as long as it seems that more fulfillment was possible in that person's life. We would not want our children to grow up too quickly; even if we knew that a glorious adulthood awaited. Why not? Childhood is not just preparation for adulthood, it has its own value. The same is true of all of life, it is no unimportant stepping stone; it is where wonderful values can be fulfilled.

No matter how convinced we are about the validity of a glorious eternal life, it can never be as real to us as this life. That is as it should be. Jesus said that to love Him was to do good to others. This is the way of demonstrating that people are the most tangible evidence of God's kingdom and most deserve our attention. Life, then, is not to be dishonored or made unimportant, just as old works of art are not to be denigrated because greater ones came after. As Jesus said, we gain life if we lose it, because we can best fulfill values in this life when we are not afraid.— *Arthur Rifkin, New York, 1987.*

IN THE MONTHS of my recovery a new "opening" came to me. It was simple. Like most young people, I had always thought of my life as my own. Now I saw my life differently, a gift from God to be used for other than a selfish purpose, no matter how acceptable such a purpose was in terms of definition by normal society. I didn't consider myself a reformed sinner, for I was "straight" by the standard of society at that time. Rather, I saw the need to dedicate my life to purposes for which I felt God would lead me. And this developed over a period of time.

In my developing understanding of Quakerism, I saw more clearly what being "born again" means, at least to me.

It is an adult understanding and acceptance of our divine responsibilities as children of God. It comes to each individual who accepts it in terms of one's own condition and need. It may not properly be circumscribed by any outward orientation. And it should be evident in one's own life rather than through vocal pronouncements, except as such quiet statements make clear where one stands on issues such as war and peace and the place to which one feels led by that commitment.

Nor should we presume to stand in judgment of those who offer no vocal or verbal evidence of being "born again." Of all issues, this is most private and not subject to some kind of "grading system" by human beings. Jesus made perfectly clear he felt relations between persons and God were essentially a private matter.— *Cecil E. Hinshaw, 1982.*

IN THE YEAR 1803, probably in the Eighth or Ninth Month, I was one day alone in the fields, and observed that the sun shone clear, but that a mist eclipsed the brightness of its shining....And I heard a voice from heaven say, "This that thou seest, which dims the brightness of the sun, is a sign of the present and coming times. I took the forefathers of this country from a land of oppression; I planted them here among the people of the forest. I sustained them, and they became a numerous people: but they have now become proud and lifted up, and have forgotten Me, who nourished and protected them in the wilderness, and are running into every abomination and evil practice of which the old countries are guilty; and I have taken quietude from the land, and suffered a dividing spirit to come among them. Lift up thine eyes and behold."

And I saw them dividing in great heat. This division began in the Church upon points of doctrine. It commenced in the Presbyterian Society, and went through the various religious denominations, and in its progress and close, the effect was nearly the same; those who dissented, went off with high heads and taunting language; and those who kept to their original sentiments, appeared exercised and sorrowful. And when this dividing spirit entered the Society of Friends it raged in as high a degree as any I had before discovered, and as before, those who separated, went with lofty looks and taunting, censuring language; those who kept to their ancient principles, retired by themselves.— *Joseph Hoag.*

[Continued next page]

[Continued]

IT next appeared in the Lodges of the Free Masons, and it broke out in appearance like a volcano, inasmuch as it set the country in an uproar for a length of time. Then it entered politics throughout the United States, and it did not stop until it produced a civil war, and an abundance of human blood was shed in the course of the combat. The Southern States lost their power, and slavery was annihilated from their borders. Then a Monarchical power arose— took the Government of the States— established a national religion, and made all societies tributary to support its expenses. I saw them take property from Friends to a large amount. I was amazed at beholding all this, and heard a voice proclaim, "This Power shall not always stand, but with this Power I will chastise my Church until they return to the faithfulness of their forefathers. Thou seest what is coming on thy native land for their iniquity, and the blood of Africa; the remembrance of which has come up before me. This Vision is yet for many days."

"I had no idea of writing it down for many years, until it became such a burden, that for my own relief I have written it."— *Joseph Hoag (1762-1846).*

"Vision" Joseph, as he later became known, was a recorded minister, and traveled extensively. First actively preaching against slavery, he later warned the Society of Friends of the danger of the divisive potential of the testimonies of Joseph John Gurney and Elias Hicks. He later supported John Wilbur.

THE SECRET of finding joy after sorrow, or through sorrow, lies, I think, in the way we meet sorrow itself. We cannot fight against it and overcome it though often we try and may seem at first successful. We try to be stoical, to suppress our memories...to kill [the pain] with strenuous activity so that we may be too tired to think. But that is just the time when it returns to us in overwhelming power. Or we try to escape from it— to run away through travel, books, entertainment, study. But when the trip is over, the book closed...the research accomplished, there is our sorrow waiting for us, disguised perhaps, but determined. We do worse sometimes. We don't try at all but fall into a lethargy and despondency saying it is the will of God and saying it accusingly as if God's will were always the most disagreeable thing possible....

What we must do...with God's help, is to accept sorrow as a friend, if possible. If not, as a companion with whom we will live for an indeterminate period, for whom we have to make room as one makes room for a guest in one's house, a companion of whom we shall always be aware, from whom we can learn and whose strength will become our strength. Together we can create beauty from ashes and find ourselves in the process.

We do not have to foresee the whole course of the way when we start out with sorrow as our companion. All we have to do is to be genuinely willing to accept his company for as long as he shall stay with us, to learn from him all that he has to teach us, to live our life quietly and steadily in these new circumstances. We do not do it alone. We do it with God's help.— *Elizabeth Gray Vining, 1979.*

IF WE ARE TO OBEY this Supreme Light, we must of course learn to recognize it; and in order to do so we must be quiet. True inward quietness is not that which may be produced by shutting out all outward causes of distraction— a process which, when carried out too severely, may intensify the inward ferment of the mind, especially in the young. It is rather a state of stable equilibrium; it is not vacancy, but stability— the steadfastness of a single purpose.

Inwardness and true quietness indeed appear to be but two aspects of the same thing— of a "truly centered" life. In the innermost region of life there is perpetual calm; perturbations and excitements belong to the comparatively superficial part of our natures. In cleaving to the Centre we cannot but be still; to be inwardly still is to be aware of the Centre. This may be mystical language, unfamiliar to those to whom it has not occurred that all parts of our nature are not on one level, and do not respond to the same plane in our environment; but it is also the language of hard common sense. The Centre means whatever is most unchangeable, most real, most truly important. Notwithstanding all possible dangers from perversion or exaggeration in the teaching of quietness, the need for it lies too deep in human nature to be forgotten while the search after Truth and the God of Truth holds its place among us.— *Caroline Stephen (1834-1909).*

THE COMFORTABLE reflection, that a watchful Providence regulates every event, and that nothing happens to us but for wise and good ends, greatly tends to alleviate every earthly care, and prevent that anxiety which would otherwise be the portion of mortals.

If sickness or even death approach us in our near connections, if prospects of various sorrows present themselves to our view, how calm is that mind whose dependence is on the Lord, who considers all the evils of this life as things that endure but for a moment; and that they may work "for us a far more exceeding and eternal weight of glory!"

If we feel that all is right within, why should outward events disturb our repose? If the afflictions we meet with are not judgments for past transgressions, and to rouse us more to a performance of duty in future, yet the sorrows that encompass us may be designed to wean us from this sublunary world, and engage us to fix our affections on heavenly objects, and lay up for ourselves treasures where no thief can steal.

However discomposed, however afflicted we may be, yet this hope still remains, a never-failing source of peace; and the mind that sincerely desires so to overcome every propensity to evil, as to be accepted in the sight of the most holy God, will feel a renewal of strength to get the better of all those passions which war against its peace.— *Margaret Woods, 1774.*

I HAVE FOUND that the more I enjoy living— the more I learn to lift up my heart— the easier it is to accept life cheerfully, because it means living from the deep joy of inward peace. But the price is to feel the pain of the world more acutely. But if we live in the flow of balanced inbreath and outbreath nothing is too difficult. That is why much of the teaching of the New Age is so rewarding to study. It is towards balance and must be studied from known truths so that unknown thoughts can be tested by wisdom.

How to distill this outpouring of wisdom into a working blueprint? The following have become my basic essentials;

There has never been a time in human development when so many paths, and so many truths, have been so freely available.

There will be no one, as David Spangler reminds us, "suddenly appearing and saying, this is the right path".

We must each of us define our own path out of the truths which we have been exposed to and follow it in practice, never forgetting that we must be open to change.— *Margaret E. Wilkinson, Australia, 1978.*

Because of her seriously defective eyesight Margaret E. Wilkinson did not commence her formal education until the age of twelve, and discontinued study after five years on the advice of a specialist.

Unable to take up any academic profession, she worked with children, and for the next thirty-five years was involved in their care— in charge of a Children's Home— nursing victims of poliomyelitis— and assisted in the rehabilitation of the victims of the great bushfire disaster in Tasmania in 1967.

(With difficulty and potential danger, Rufus Jones, accompanied by Robert Yarnall, and George A. Walton, traveled to Berlin and presented this statement to Reinhard Heydrich inside the Gestapo in 1938 in hopes of facilitating emigration of the Jews, as well as other relief measures.)

"WE HAVE COME to Germany at this present time to see whether there might be any service which American Quakers could render, and to use every opportunity open to us to understand the present situation. Those whom we are to meet and with whom we are to consult should clearly understand that we have had close and friendly relations with the German people throughout the entire post-war period. We represent no governments, or international organizations, no parties, no sects, and we have no interest in propaganda in any form. We have always been concerned over the conditions of the Peace Treaty and in spirit opposed to these conditions.

"We came to Germany in the time of the blockade; organized and directed the feeding of German children, reaching at the peak no less than a million two hundred thousand children per day. We were first to arrive in Vienna after the war where we brought in coal for the fires in the hospitals. After the different revolutions in Austria, we gave relief to the families of those who suffered most in these collisions, always having permission from the existing government to do so. And at the time of the "Anschluss" we were distributing food to a number of the Nazi families." *— [Continued next page]*

[Continued]

"IN ALL THIS work we have kept entirely free of party lines or party spirit. We have not used any propaganda or aimed to make converts to our own views. We have simply, quietly, and in a friendly spirit endeavored to make life possible for those who were suffering. We do not ask who is to blame for the trouble which may exist or what has produced the sad situation. Our task is to support and save life and to suffer with those who are suffering.

"We have come now in the same spirit as in the past and we believe that all Germans who remember the past and who are familiar with our ways and methods and spirit will know that we do not come to judge or criticize or to push ourselves in, but to inquire in the most friendly manner whether there is anything we can do to promote life and human welfare and to relieve suffering."

In immediate, practical terms, they had got permission for two Quaker commissioners to go to Germany to oversee the disbursement of Quaker relief funds ... to assist with the emigration of individuals. This short reprieve meant the difference between life and death to some families, at least.

In the light of subsequent history, it seems unlikely that the Nazi hearts were touched by the unexpected encounter with a different way of life, though Rufus Jones to the end of his days believed that there had been a softening and a moment of vision. What is perhaps of lasting significance is the sheer fact that three Friends— modern, practical men— faced enormous forces of evil and directly and quietly offered an alternative, the way of love. — *Elizabeth Gray Vining, 1958.*

IT WOULD SEEM important at this stage of the development of our Religious Society that all of us became more liberated both to evangelize and to be evangelized. For there is no doubt that we have much to gain from and to give to each other if we carry this out in a good spirit.

We, as evangelists of each other, must have it as our first duty not to preach but to listen. We must practice an open and sensitive awareness which allows us to listen not merely to each other's theology but to what the other person is. By doing this we will begin to live in such a way that we neither crush nor dominate nor entangle our companions, but rather help them to be themselves, and bring them to fulfilling service for the benefit of the larger Society of Friends. We will aim for transparency of heart; we will never manipulate each other's consciences, or try to force other members of our Religious Society into our own scheme of things. No one will seek a procedural victory, or a formulation for faith and practice, or the advancement or postponement of a concern, which leaves someone else defeated.

Above all, everyone will understand that true spirituality is that which succeeds in bringing one to inner transformation, a process which cannot be forced by external pressure, but can only be elicited through kindness, much the way we share an enthusiasm. True evangelism understands that people always benefit more from what they themselves discover and from what they are led to from within, than from what they are told from without. — *Daniel E. Seeger, 1985.*

HOW BEAUTIFUL, how glorious a sight it is, to behold the sun in the morning when it issues from its bed of crimson hue, when it gradually ascends the horizon, dissipating the dusky gloom of fading night, and tingeing every object in nature with its golden rays. And Oh! may I not say, that through the blessing of a gracious Creator, I am enabled almost daily to witness the spiritual arising of the "Sun of Righteousness with healing in his wings." Surely the day-spring hath visited and is visiting me, and assuredly the end and purpose of his light is the same that it was formerly, even "to give light to them that sit in darkness and in the shadow of death, to guide their feet into the path of peace." I think I say not amiss, when I declare my belief, that the light within me seems to get brighter, and fire to remain in the refiner's fire, that so I may become purified and refined from everything evil.

I have been long in much trouble and difficulty about changing my dress, as well as adopting those other distinctions and testimonies which Friends uphold and practice; and my anxiety respecting these things has been, lest I should take them up without good ground, and without being clearly and indubitably sensible that these sacrifices are called for. Indeed I have gone mourning on my way, day after day, and night after night. — *John Barclay, 1816.*

THERE IS A SPIRIT which I feel, that delights to do no evil, nor to revenge any wrong, but delights to endure all things, in hope to enjoy its own in the end. Its hope is to outlive all wrath and contention, and to weary out all exaltation and cruelty, or whatever is of a nature contrary to itself. It sees to the end of all temptations; as it bears no evil in itself, so it conceives none in thoughts to any other: if it be betrayed it bears it: for its ground and spring is the mercies and forgiveness of God. Its crown is meekness, its life is everlasting love unfeigned, and takes its kingdom with entreaty, and not with contention, and keeps it by lowliness of mind. In God alone it can rejoice, though none else regard it, or can own its life. It's conceived in sorrow, and brought forth without any to pity it; nor doth it murmur at grief and oppression.   It never rejoiceth but through sufferings; for with the world's joy it is murdered. I found it alone, being forsaken; I have fellowship therein with them who lived in dens and desolate places in the earth, who through death obtained this resurrection and eternal holy life.— *James Naylor, 1660.*

His last testimony, said to be delivered hours before his departure out of this life; several Friends being present.

WILLIAM PENN furnishes a remarkable instance of the acquisition of solid and durable fame, by means which in their commencement appeared totally destructive of that end. When, upon arriving a man's estate, he embraced the religious principles of a new and despised Society, he must have considered himself, and been considered by others, as giving up all his prospects of eminence in the world. The mortification which his father experienced, upon discovering the choice he had made, unquestionably arose from a belief that he was renouncing the path of eminence and fame for one of obscurity and reproach. To see his only son, the heir apparent of his fortune and fame, instead of pursuing the brilliant career which was opened before him, associating with a self-denying people, who were considered as the offscourings of the earth, was more than his philosophy could patiently bear. The pacific principles of the Society to which he was united, as well as the uncourtly character of their peculiar doctrines, must have formed, in the view of Admiral Penn, an insuperable barrier to the advancement of his son. He did not perceive that the magnanimity displayed in that very renunciation of eminence and fame, that inflexible adherence to the path of apprehended duty,...would assign him a station in the temple of fame incomparably higher than that which the admiral had attained with all his heroism.— *Enoch Lewis, Philadelphia, 1852.*

WHEN WE, with our limited human intellect, see only more calamity, death, and destruction in our personal, community, or national life, when all we have lived for and attempted to do leads nowhere, turns to dust and ashes, and the future looks hopelessly bleak, Pentecost tells us that the bleakness is of our own imagining, that our intellect and our fears blind us to deeper layers of reality.

John Woolman called on us "to turn all that we possess into the channels of universal love," and by possessions he meant not only material possessions but also our skills and our mental abilities.

The call to us is to sense the future possibilities and be ready, to have prepared ourselves physically to the extent our bodies allow, to have our minds trained and to be spiritually alert and sensitive to the deep layers of our being where the divine spirit and ours touch.

May God imbue our hearts with the hope, the faith, and the love that will prepare us spiritually, mentally, and physically for tasks as yet unknown or only dimly sensed, in a world which when looked at objectively and analytically seems quite doomed, with no sign of redemption or hope for improvement. And may we have the courage to take on the tasks chosen for us and to carry them out in God's companionship and service.— *O. Theodore Benfey, 1986.*

ELIZA GURNEY wrote President Abraham Lincoln during the Civil War in 1883, saying,

"Many times, since I was privileged to have an interview with thee, nearly a year ago, my mind has turned towards thee with feelings of sincere and Christian interest, and, as our kind friend Isaac Newton offers to be the bearer of a paper messenger, I feel inclined to give thee the assurance of my continued hearty sympathy in all thy heavy burdens and responsibilities and to express, not only my own earnest prayers, but I believe the prayers of many thousands whose hearts thou has gladdened by thy... efforts "to burst the bands of wickedness, and let the oppressed go free" that the Almighty Ruler of the universe may strengthen thee to accomplish all the blessed purposes, which...I do assuredly believe He did design to make thee instrumental in accomplishing, when He appointed thee thy present post of vast responsibility as the Chief Magistrate of this great nation.— *Eliza Gurney", 1863*

He replied:

"Your people— the Friends— have had and are having a very great trial. On principle, and faith, opposed to both war and oppression, they can only practically oppose oppression by war. In this hard dilemma some have chosen one horn and some the other. For those appealing to me on conscientious grounds, I have done, and shall do, the best I could and can, in my own conscience, under my oath to the law. That you believe this, I doubt not; and, believing it, I shall still receive, for our country and myself, your earnest prayers to our Father in Heaven.

Your sincere friend, Abraham Lincoln."

— Daniel Bassuk, 1987.

"WE UTTERLY deny all outward wars and strife, and fightings with outward weapons, for any end, or under any pretense whatever; this is our testimony to the whole world. The Spirit of Christ by which we are guided, is not changeable, so as once to command us from a thing as evil, and again to move us unto it; and we certainly know, and testify to the world, that the Spirit of Christ, which leads us unto all truth, will never move us to fight and war against any man with outward weapons, neither for the Kingdom of Christ, nor for the kingdoms of this world ... Therefore we cannot learn war any more."— George Fox and Others. A declaration from the Harmless and Innocent People of God, called Quakers, presented to Charles II, *1660.*

*   *   *

I told them that I lived in the virtue of that life and power that took away the occasion of all wars.

*   *   *

For all dwelling in the light that comes from Jesus , it leads out of wars, leads out of strife, leads out of the occasion of wars, and leads out of the earth up to God, and out of earthly mindedness into heavenly mindedness.— *George Fox, 1657.*

THOUGH CONSCIENCE is an imperfect instrument for transmitting the Light, its claims are absolute and must always be obeyed, for conscience gives us the highest knowledge of the Light that we have at any one time. Because clearer and clearer knowledge may be progressively attained as the virtue of obedience grows, Friends have never declared any doctrine to be a final and unalterable creed.

An important question which must be faced by every pacifist is this: Is it better to take an absolute, uncompromising stand, far beyond the reach of an average man or is it better to compromise, keeping ahead of the average man but not so far ahead as to get out of touch with him? Friends have usually aimed at the first position, believing it not so far beyond that "average man" as is generally supposed, though they have acknowledged that those who take the second often accomplish much that is good. When Joseph Hoag in 1812 was pleading his peace principles a man in his audience said, "Well stranger, if all the world was of your mind, I would turn and follow after." Joseph replied, "So then thou hast a mind to be the last man in the world to be good. I have a mind to be one of the first and set the rest an example." (Hoag's JOURNAL, 1861, p.201.)— *Howard H. Brinton.*

THE BELIEF that the Light is within all men means that every person is capable of taking an advanced position and can be appealed to on these grounds. The same identical Light shines in every heart however obscured by selfishness and greed. Hence the non-violent method of good-will and confidence will sometimes produce unexpected results because it reaches something in the other person which responds in similar fashion. That of God in one person arouses similar capacity in the other. Men tend to rise to what is expected of them. No human being is so depraved that nothing but force can appeal to him. There are many extraordinary instances in Quaker history in which an evil doer has been suddenly halted and transformed by the power of non-resistance combined with good will. These methods sometimes fail, but so also does the method of violence.

The Quaker has often been asked whether, if he were attacked by another person, he would defend himself. There have generally been two types of reply. Either he has said that, rather than use violence, he would meekly suffer in the hope of persuading his assailant to desist or he might reply that he would use violence if it did not involve taking life. Some would use only such violence as would inflict no serious injury.— *Howard H. Brinton.*

RELIGIOUS PACIFISM as a positive way of life rather than as a negative attitude toward fighting can be considered to be a direct derivative from worship. True worship which pierces through the surface of the mind where multiplicity lies, finds in the depths...what George Fox called "the hidden unity in the Eternal Being." Here the worshipper feels as a present experience rather than as abstract theory his kinship with his fellow men in God....Out of this felt unity there comes a sensitizing of the soul, a feeling of oneness with all men which rules out conflict. A new and positive word for pacifism is community. This signifies the union of men from within enabling them to work together, rather than external coordination produced by authoritarian means or by the threat of violence.

In meetings for conducting the business of the Society, a decision can be made only when those present reach a state of unity. No vote is taken. a vote might represent the coercion of a minority by a majority. It may take weeks or even years to attain such unity. If a group has achieved a truly non-violent frame of mind, unity is eventually possible because every member has access to the same Light of Truth. This Light is not divided, it is One. This peculiar method, while slower than the process of voting, is more creative for it gives time for new points of view to arise out of the syntheses of old ones. It is more durable for the very reason that it represents a greater degree of convincement on the part of the group as a whole. It seeks for the solution of conflict not by the ascendancy of one faction nor even by a compromise which is often a meager selection of common elements.— *Howard H. Brinton.*

BENEATH ALL overt acts and decisions the immense subconscious forces, charged with emotion, have been slowly pushing toward this event. There are no words which can express the gravity of the tragedy. It is one of those appalling events which test to the bottom our central faith in God, in human goodness, in cosmic rationality and in onward progress. But we must not let our cable slip in the storm. The supreme faiths of humanity have always had their births and their baptisms in baffling mysteries and in the deeps of tragedy and suffering....We shall come out of this crucible with a new and finer temper at the heart of our faith.... Out of this very flood that seems to mock at ideals of peace and brotherhood new forces will appear.

*   *   *

Whatever may be the "causes" that have led to this cataclysm, our main problems just now must be: How to keep our faith in God and the coming of His Kingdom; how to interpret our ideals of love and peace; how to suffer patiently and loyally where our ideals collide with systems and requirements that are "survivals" from the past."— *Rufus Jones, 1914, upon the declaration of world war.*

THE LIFETIME wellness plan of Moses Bailey, in his tenth decade:

"Keep the desire for knowledge burning strong. Appreciate what you know and marvel at all that's left to learn.

Read the Bible again and again. Take what is helpful to you.

Choose lifework that you enjoy. Figure it out and don't settle for less.

A steady correspondence with friends old and new provides stimulation and satisfaction.

Eat vegetarian. A visit to a slaughter house will provide motivation. Eat only when hungry, and befriend yogurt.

Read two new books a month for a lifetime. Build a tower of knowledge, book upon book.

Be a lifetime athlete. In early years jog from village to village in Palestine. After 50, take long walks and do daily floor exercises.

Avoid all advertising. It'll rile the blood.

In the Quaker faith, with its simplicity, harmony, equality, and community, there is great power. Only living the faith releases that power.

Pause before speaking— to ensure that mind and mouth are connected.

When someone learns that you are a Quaker and begins to lift you up on a pedestal, resist it. Friends don't belong on pedestals. In truth they are found moving forward, standing still, or sitting on their backsides."— *Larry Cargill, 1986.*

SILENCE is the inaudible echo of the voices of God which is heard with the ears of the heart. It is not simply the absence of speech but a state of being. It is a universal language that speaks and comprehends all, contains all languages and all accents, tolerates and absorbs all. The paradox of the silence is that one can never say enough about it since it is inexhaustible by its very nature.

The silence of a wise person is not the same silence as that of a beginner. In other words, there is an ignorant silence as there is a knowing silence, and finally there is the silence of the dead who have merged with the Infinite. Many of those who are not present with us anymore have left some of their silence with us.

Silence can spill over into our speech as our utterances can spill over into the silence. When the silence penetrates the words with its own quality it enhances them, but when words spill into the silence they may diminish it unless they are truly inspired and give it new meaning the moment they are uttered...

Silence enables us to escape the prison of words. As long as we respect it we can neither err nor offend. The implicit message in meeting is our silent presence, the explicit in our verbal statements. Silence creates its own tensions, it fluctuates like waves; after every high there is a low, even soft murmurs as its waves dissipate toward the shore. You may step into the pool of silence denuded and in pain but you will emerge from it restored in truth and peace. — *Peter and Carole Fingesten, 1987.*

ONE DAY, being under a strong exercise of spirit, I stood up and said some words in a meeting; but not keeping close to the Divine opening, I said more than was required of me. Being soon sensible of my error, I was afflicted in mind some weeks, without any light or comfort, even to that degree that I could not take satisfaction in anything. I remembered God, and was troubled, and in the depth of my distress he had pity upon me, and sent the Comforter. I then felt forgiveness for my offence; my mind became calm and quiet, and I was truly thankful to my gracious Redeemer for his mercies.

About six weeks after this, feeling the spring of Divine love opened, and a concern to speak, I said a few words in a meeting, in which I found peace. Being thus humbled and disciplined ...my understanding became more strengthened to distinguish the pure spirit which inwardly moves upon the heart, and which taught me to wait in silence sometimes many weeks together, until I felt that rise which prepares the creature to stand like a trumpet, through which the Lord speaks to his flock...

All the faithful are not called to public ministry; but whoever are, are called to minister of that which they have tasted and handled spiritually. The outward modes of worship are various; but whenever any are true ministers of Jesus Christ, it is from the operation of his Spirit upon their hearts, first purifying them, and thus giving them a just sense of the conditions of others. This truth was early fixed in my mind and I was taught to watch the pure opening, and to take heed lest, while I was standing to speak, my own will should get uppermost....— *John Woolman, 1742.*

THE LIFE of faith requires that we have vision, that we be attentive and obedient to revelation. It requires that we have a sense of the potential for God's work to take place in an through us— the capacity to apprehend the ideals which we can grow to embody and personify in our lives. It also requires an awareness that much of what we must do to live life fully in faith has been revealed and is to be heeded— a commitment to being mindful of what Friends have long called Truth and right order in our lives...

In some places one see Friends who with some justification, have taken pride in their Quaker heritage, but who now are content merely to abide comfortably in their familiarity with other members of the meeting and their versions of the Quakerly way of doing things. One finds Friends basking in the reputation of Quakers as good people, and resting on their or their ancestor's laurels...

Our religious life becomes little more than a maintenance project where we strive to uphold lifeless forms of an ancient and honorable, but increasingly empty, tradition....

We must be cognizant of how much God has already shown us and our ancestors about what it means to be in harmony with divine purpose. These revelations are available to us in the Bible, in the journals of our Quaker forbears, in the devotional literature, and in the rich and varied record of human history...It is the challenge to become a people with a vision...so that Truth might flourish in our lives for the benefit of all. It is the challenge to become the people God wishes us to be.— *Thomas H. Jeavons, 1987.*

IN THE BEGINNING of the day it ought certainly to be our care to lift up our hearts to God as soon as we awake; and on rising from bed to endeavor to have our minds brought into seriousness and stillness; to thoughtfulness as in the Divine presence; for this is a season when there are many considerations which may, or ought to, suggest a variety of pious reflections...which are so obvious that a mind inclined to piety could hardly forget or miss them. The cheerfulness natural on our first waking; the refreshment we have found from sleep; the security we have enjoyed during that defenseless condition; the enjoyment of witnessing once more the reviving influence of the sun; the recollection of the many comforts and conveniences which we have enjoyed or received, and are surrounded with, so graciously provided by the great Author of our mercies.

And now having the prospect of one day more, not only to see our dear connections, but to serve our Heavenly Father, whose service is freedom and whose labor is love; and continued opportunity for the improvement of our minds; and above all, cherishing a lively hope of finally witnessing a perfect resurrection to an eternal day of happiness and glory.

The exercise of private devotion in the morning, I hope you will, my children, engage in as the first work of the day, yet I cannot prescribe a particular method to any of you. Consult the witness for God in your own hearts.— *David Sands, 1795.*

I MAY HERE MENTION a remarkable circumstance that occurred in my childhood. On going to a neighbor's house, I saw on the way a robin sitting on her nest, and as I came near she went off; but having young ones, she flew about, and with many cries expressed her concern for them. I stood and threw stones at her, and one striking her, she fell down dead. At first I was pleased with the exploit, but after a few minutes was seized with horror, at having, in a sportive way, killed an innocent creature while she was careful for her young.... I beheld her lying dead, and thought those young ones, for which she was so careful, must now perish for want of their dam to nourish them. After some painful considerations on the subject, I climbed up the tree, took all the young birds, and killed them, supposing that better than to leave them to pine away and die miserably. In this case I believed that Scripture proverb was fulfilled, "The tender mercies of the wicked are cruel."

I then went on my errand, and for some hours could think of little else but the cruelties I had committed, and was much troubled. Thus He whose tender mercies are over all his works hath placed a principle in the human mind, which incites to exercise goodness towards every living creature; and this being singly attended to, people become tender-hearted and sympathizing; but when frequently and totally rejected, the mind becomes shut up in a contrary disposition.— *John Woolman, 1743.*

CHRIST'S major point throughout the Sermon on the Mount is to get rid of fears and anxieties. It might almost be said that the substance of his mission as a teacher was to set men free from the slavery of fears. "Why are ye so fearful?" he keeps saying. Stop your unnecessary worries. Cut out your excessive anxieties. It has been well said that the most ruinously expensive of all our emotions is fear. It is that very emotion of fear that has thrown our world out of joint and brought us to this unspeakable calamity...

Be not anxious for your life. He is not against ownership as such, only against excessive worry over things that moth and rust corrupt and thieves and depressions sweep away...The real issue which Jesus is discussing here is: in what does your life really consist?...

He is making a powerful plea for clarity of vision, for a place for inspiration in our lives, for insight of real values. If your eye is single you can find your way to life, but if you see double and are clouded in your estimate of true values your whole life will be full of darkness.

What matters most is the recovery of the radiance of life. We need to have buoyance and radiance in place of worry and anxious care. That is the substance of the great sermon of the man who, in two years, was going to be crucified and who has strangely been called "the man of sorrows."— *Rufus Jones, written between 1939-1942.*

FOR EACH and all the silence and stillness are needed. It is not that the worshipers wait for something to happen, for the service to begin. That would be like the hush before a storm, when no leaf or twig dares to stir. That is not the waiting in a Friends' Meeting. Think rather of the high noon of Summer, or of the stillness of a snow-covered country, how the heat or lightness everywhere gives an intense sense of overflowing and abounding life, making a quietness of rapture rather than of fear. Such, only of a deeper and far more intimate kind, is the atmosphere of waiting souls.

It may be that words will spring out of those depths, it may be that vocal prayer or praise shall flow forth at the bidding of Him Whose presence makes worship a communion, but whether there be speech or silence matters not.

Gradually, as mind, soul, and even body grow still, sinking deeper and deeper into the life of God, the pettinesses, the tangles, the failures of the outer life begin to be seen in their true proportions, and the sense of Divine infilling, uplifting, redeeming Love becomes real and illuminating. Things are seen and known that are hidden to the ordinary faculties. This state is not merely one of quiescence; the soul is alive, active, vigorous, yet so still that it hardly knows how intense is its own vital action."—*J. M. Fry, 1911.*

WHEN I SIT down by the fireside in my own room to take a short repose in the afternoon, the thought often arises whether I am not getting into habits of too much self-indulgence. Threescore and ten years of age may afford some plea for an increase of those indulgences that are within our reach; but I think it requires watchfulness, that they do not extend too far, lest we should begin to think ourselves of most consequence when we are in reality in the least. Yet many things conspire to promote self-importance. Our friends and relatives, perhaps perceiving some increasing debilities and infirmities, are careful respecting us; they prompt us to take care of our selves, and withdraw from everything that may fatigue or trouble us; and I believe we sometimes give way to their apprehensions, lest we should in any respect become burdensome to them.

When I have been comtemplating the happiness of my own situation respecting temporals, and comparing it with those of inferior classes, I have felt my heart touched with compassion. But when, on the other hand, I have looked at the situation of those much above me, and considered how unhappy they would think themselves if reduced to mine, it has led me to the conclusion that there is a more equal distribution of happiness than one might, at a casual glance, imagine. — *Margaret Woods, 1818.*

"Remove me far from vanity and lies: give me neither poverty nor riches; feed me with food convenient for me."— Proverbs 30:8.

IT IS A STRIKING feature of each of [the] Beatitudes*
that the blessedness inherently attaches to the trait of
character itself.   The quality of spirit is good, not
because it will some day win a much desired reward—
it is good because blessedness is essentially conjoined
with that trait of character, with that kind of person.

The beatitude-trait that has perhaps most puzzled
this strenuous and militant world is meekness.   The
very law of survival seems to refute its worth.

I believe, however, that the method of modern science
has given us a fresh revelation of the worth of meekness.
The most elemental qualities of fitness for true
scientific, or historical research are traits of meekness:
utter absence of bluster and assertiveness, restraint of
mind which will not go beyond the facts, unwearied
patience in the effort to find what is actually there, and
readiness to be merely a humble and submissive
reporter of things as they are.

Christ's meek man is, in the same way, a person who
has calm and absolute confidence in the eternal nature
of things, in the moral and spiritual laws of the universe
and in the goodness of the divine Heart.   He will not
strive or cry, he will not storm or rage or become
hysterical.   He expects God to work all things up to
better.   He will mainly endeavor to get into parallelism
with celestial currents.   He will show endless patience
and   noble   restraint,   and   he   will   confine   his
proclamation to what his soul's sight and his heart's
deepest experience augustly affirm to be real.— *Rufus
Jones, late 1920's. *Matt. 5:5*

I KEPT STEADILY to meetings; spent first-day afternoons chiefly in reading the Scriptures and other good books, and was early convinced in my mind that true religion consisted in an inward life, wherein the heart doth love and reverence God the Creator, and learns to exercise true justice and goodness, not only toward all men, but also toward the brute creatures.

That, as the mind was moved by an inward principle to love God as an invisible, incomprehensible Being, so, by the same principle, it was moved to love him in all his manifestations in the visible world. That, as by his breath the flame of life was kindled in all animal sensible creatures, to say we love God as unseen, and the same time exercise cruelty toward the least creature moving by his life, or by life derived from him, was a contradiction in itself.

I found no narrowness respecting sects and opinions, but believed that sincere, upright-hearted people, in every society, who truly love God, were accepted of him.

As I lived under the cross, and simply followed the opening of truth, my mind, from day to day, was more enlightened, my former acquaintances were left to judge of me as they would for I found it safest for me to live in private, and keep these things sealed up in my own breast...My heart was tender and often contrite, and universal love to my fellow-creatures increased in me. This will be understood by such as have trodden in the same path.— *John Woolman, 1720-1772.*

OUR IMPACT on others, our evangelism in the larger world, will come not from what we say but from how we live. "Let your lives preach," said George Fox.

A few years from now, if the WALL STREET JOURNAL does a follow-up article on the Religious Society of Friends, perhaps it is doubtful that they will find a much greater degree of doctrinal conformity among us than they saw a few months ago. They will not be able to write that this small spiritual fellowship has at last settled into agreement about some portion of the doctrinal agenda— about the atonement, or the Virgin birth, or about the absolute identicalness of the Christ within and the historical figure of Jesus of Nazareth. But whatever else a hypothetical reporter of the future may find when exploring the condition of the Religious Society of Friends, let us pray that she or he will be overwhelmed by the evidence that all Friends, whatever their background or theology, practice toward each other nothing but a constant and mutual charity so striking that when the feature story is written it exclaims, "This is what the whole world should be like!" For what Babel has dispersed, love can gather in. That one people, one family, became many was the work of human pride. We should not wonder, therefore, that when many peoples become one family again it will be the result not of doctrine, not of debate, not of triumphalism of any sort; rather, such unity will be the fruit only of humility, and of love.— *Daniel A. Seeger, 1985.*

MEISTER ECKHART wrote, "As thou art in church or cell, that same frame of mind carry out into the world, into its turmoil and its fitfulness." Deep within us all there is an amazing inner sanctuary of the soul, a holy place, a Divine Center, a speaking Voice, to which we may continuously return. Eternity is at our hearts, pressing upon our time-torn lives, warming us with intimations of an astounding destiny, calling us home unto Itself. Yielding to these persuasions, gladly committing ourselves in body and soul, utterly and completely, to the Light Within, is the beginning of true life. It is a dynamic center, a creative Life that presses to birth within us. It is a Light Within which illumines the face of God and casts new shadows and new glories upon the face of men. It is a seed stirring to life if we do not choke it. It is the Shekinah of the soul, the Presence in the midst. Here is the Slumbering Christ, stirring to be awakened, to become the soul we clothe in earthly form and action. And He is within us all.

You who read these words already know this inner Life and Light. For by this very Light within you, is your recognition given. In this humanistic age we suppose man is the initiator and God is the responder. But the Living Christ within us is the initiator and we are the responders. God the Lover, the accuser, the revealer of Light and darkness presses within us. "Behold I stand at the door and Knock." And all our apparent initiative is already a response, a testimonial to His secret presence and working within us.— *Thomas Kelly, 1939.*

SILENT worship being the most sublime part of our religious performances, how important it is not to interrupt the silent travail, or conclude our meetings before experienced minds have time to dig to the spring of life in themselves, witness the gradual arising thereof as high as the great Feeder and Waterer of his people designs. This she (Mary Griffin) had a deep sense of, and her public appearances in the meeting to which she belonged were not generally lengthy, nor very frequent, sitting generally in silence when other ministers from abroad were present, preferring others to herself, speaking lightly of none, and very tender towards the young or inexperienced; careful not to stir up or awake her beloved until he pleased, nor rise above or go beyond the pure leading of truth. Her language was correct and copious, well adapted to her subject. Her matter was plain to be understood by all, not necessarily branching out into words, but kept to the life and marrow of things, tending to center the minds of hearers in the fear and love of God.— *Joseph Talcot, 1812.*

Why is my mind with sorrow thus opprest?
Where shall I go to find the balm of rest?
There is nothing in this world can give relief,
For all is mingled with the cup of grief.
Then may my soul retire unto that power.
Which calmed the tempest in a trying hour,
The wind and sea obeying His command,
The raging storm became a quiet calm!
— Sarah Talcot, 1810.

I WENT to another ancient priest at Mancetter in Warwickshire and reasoned with him about the ground of despair and temptations, but he was ignorant of my condition; and he bid me take tobacco and sing psalms. Tobacco was a thing I did not love and psalms I was not in an estate to sing; I could not sing. Then he bid me come again and he would tell me many things, but when I came again he was angry and pettish, for my former words had displeased him.....

I brought them Scriptures, and told them there was an annointing within man to teach him, and that the Lord would teach his people himself....

Now after I had received that opening from the Lord that to be bred at Oxford or Cambridge was not sufficient to fit a man to be a minister of Christ, I regarded the priests less, and looked more after the dissenting people. And among them I saw there was some tenderness, and many of them came afterwards to be convinced.... But as I had forsaken all the priests, so I left the separate preachers also, and those called the most experienced people; for I saw there was none among them all that could speak to my condition. And when all my hopes in them and in all men were gone, so that I had nothing outwardly to help me, nor could tell what to do, then, Oh then, I heard a voice which said, "There is one, even Christ Jesus, that can speak to thy condition", and when I heard it my heart did leap for joy. Then the Lord did let me see why there was none upon the earth that could speak to my condition, namely, that I might give him all the glory.... Thus, when God doth work who shall let [prevent] it? And this I knew experimentally.— *George Fox, 1647.*

WE are all suffering from a sense of pressure. Feeling that our ancestors had ways of meeting the pressures of their day, we sometimes imagine that we might imitate their ways with profit. But it may be that their situation was so different from ours that we cannot imitate them....

Busyness, restlessness, the desire for activity is a form of escapism; we are trying to escape from ourselves. Not being able to face our own inner lives with all their stresses and strains....., we occupy ourselves as much as possible with what is outward. We do not like our own company so we feverishly seek the company of others. We compensate for inner weakness by seeking outward sources of strength. We are continuously in motion because we do not know what to do when we are still...

There is a partial explanation of our inner disorder which is based on the fact that our interests are spread out over a number of fields in which the standards of behavior are not consistent with one another. Our home creates one set of requirements, our social club another, our meeting for worship another, our business... In each case we attempt to fit ourselves into the code of behavior of a certain group of persons and this code may be and often is different from the code of other groups...... The result is an inner strain. Our ancestors were better integrated within themselves because their lives were better integrated without, they belonged to fewer different kinds of groups. In early Pennsylvania.....everything centered in the Quaker meeting, a condition which made possible an inner life in which there were few conflicting interests. — *Howard H. Brinton, 1948.*

THE ACTIVIST who seeks explanations based on outer facts declares that our restlessness is due to the terrible state of the world at present. If we could just get the outer world in order we could then feel inward peace. But perhaps...the more fundamental difficulty is with our inward world. As long as there is inward chaos, all outward actions will be contaminated by this chaos. In such a case all that we do will promote rather than allay confusion. We seek to bring peace in the world when there is no peace in our hearts and as a result we infect the outer world with our inner conflict. As an old Chinese saying has it, "The right action performed by the wrong man is the wrong action."

[Jesus] had little to say regarding better laws, better governments, better agreements between nations to keep the peace, better organized relief work....and such inward emphasis is the principal characteristic of Quakerism....

The Quaker way is so to order the inner life that outer pressures can be adequately met and dealt with. This is not the method of the ascetic who conquers his sensual desires by violence toward himself, nor of the hermit who avoids his fellow men, nor of the stoic who makes himself independent and indifferent to the world around him. It is rather an ordering of the inner life, so there will be a proper balance of inner and outer, the inner holding first place. In one sense we become independent of outer tumults and conflicts, but in another sense we are not independent because we must seek to reproduce in the world around us the inner peace created within ourselves. If we do not seek to reproduce our inner peace it will become lifeless and static. — *Howard H. Brinton, 1948.*

LET ALL PROMISES and obligations for payment of just debts be truly kept and performed; and due care taken that all offenses, trespasses, and differences be speedily ended and composed, in God's wisdom, according to gospel order among us, either by mutual forgiveness, Christian counsel, or just arbitration, as the case may require, and safely admit or allow; and the choice of arbitrators and umpires be of such just impartial men, as neither party can justly except against.

* * *

As our Lord and Saviour Jesus Christ exhorted and warned to beware and take heed of covetousness (which is idolatry), we are concerned that all professing Christianity among us may take heed of pride, covetousness, and hastening to be rich in the world, which are pernicious and growing evils; let them be watched against, resisted, and suppressed, in the fear and dread of Almighty God, and have no place or countenance in his camp. O ye grave elders, both men and women! pray be careful and watchful against these evils, and over the youth in these cases.

It is also seriously advised that no Friends suffer romances, play-books, or other vain and idle pamphlets, in their houses or families, which tend to corrupt the minds of youth; but instead thereof, that they excite them to the reading of the Holy Scriptures and religious books. — *London Epistle, 1720.*

IN THE LONG PULL of yielding ourselves to God, of coming under the guidance of the inward Christ, there can be no standing still. The religion of Jesus Christ is not a holding operation. In the flyleaf of Oliver Cromwell's Bible was penned, "He that is not getting better is getting worse." What we secretly long for is to grow into the men and women that God in his infinite yearning means us to become. We are not content, like a local car-ferry, to hug the shallows and to shuttle safely back and forth across a comfortable narrow strait. We secretly long for God's seaway, and we have hints that he is calling us into a real discipleship and that, in our prayerlessness, we are not responding.

We know what the late Marius Grout, a contemporary French Quaker servant of God and his fellows, meant when he wrote, "I believe in the influence of silent and radiant men and I say to myself that such men are rare. They, nevertheless, give savor to the world....Nothing will be lost here so long as such men continue to exist. If there is a wish we should make today, it is that we might see in ourselves the beginnings of contemplation."

In religious circles we find today a fierce and almost violent planning and programing, a sense that without ceaseless activity nothing will ever be accomplished. How seldom it occurs to us that God has to undo and to do all over again so much of what we in our willfulness have pushed through in his name. How little there is in us of the silent and radiant strength in which the secret works of God really take place! How ready we are to speak, how loath to listen, to sense the further dimension of what it is that we confront.— *Douglas V. Steere, 1962.*

MY EMPLOYER, having a negro woman, sold her, and desired me to write a bill of sale, the man being waiting who bought her. The thing was sudden; and though I felt uneasy at the thoughts of writing an instrument of slavery for one of my fellow creatures, yet I remembered that I was hired by the year, that it was my master who directed me to do it, and that it was an elderly man, a member of our Society, who bought her; so through weakness I gave way, and wrote it; but at the executing of it I was so afflicted in my mind, that I said before my master and the Friend that I believed slave-keeping to be a practice inconsistent with the Christian religion. This, in some degree, abated my uneasiness; yet as often as I reflected seriously upon it I thought I should have been clearer if I had desired to be excused from it, as a thing against my conscience; for such it was. Some time after this a young man of our Society spoke to me to write a conveyance of a slave to him, he having lately taken a negro into his house. I told him I was not easy to write it; for, though many of our meeting and in other places kept slaves, I still believed the practice was not right, and desired to be excused from the writing. I spoke to him in good-will; and he told me that keeping slaves was not altogether agreeable to his mind; but that the slave being a gift made to his wife he had accepted her. — *John Woolman, 1743.*

"And we have known and believed the love that God hath to us. God is love; and he that dwelleth in love dwelleth in God and God in him."—John 4:16.

HOW CAN WE be sure that God is real, and not just a creation of our wishes? We have disquieting desires for a God, for a real God. There come to us times of loneliness when we seem to have a premonition of a deep vastness in ourselves, when the universe about us, gigantic as it is in all its starry depths, seems cramped and narrow for our souls, and something makes us long for an abiding Home. We have times of fatigue, of confusion, of exhaustion, of utter discouragement, when we long for a serene and everlasting Bosom on which to lay our heads and be at peace. But how can we be sure that what we call God is not a product of our wishful thinking, a self-delusion we create, a giant shadow of our longings flung up against the sky and asserted to be real?

We have moments when we long, not for freedom and yet more freedom, but for self-surrender, self-dedication, self-abandonment in utter loyalty to an Overself. If I could find an Object worthy of my utmost allegiance, if I could find a Mark worth to be the aim of the bow of my life, I should gladly pull the arrow back to its head and let all fly upon a single shot. I should be integrated, freed from internal conflicts, those confusions and tangles within which make me ineffective, indecisive, wavering, half-hearted, unhappy. I should gladly be a slave of such a being, and know that I am truly free when I am His utter slave. But I see men and women, my brothers and sisters in Germany and Italy and Russia, who joyfully commit their all to the State, to an earthly State, to a state which to them seems noble, glorious and ideal. They seem to get integration and joy in enslavement similar to that which my religious friends get from commitment to an invisible, spiritual world.— *Thomas Kelly, 1941.*

BUT THERE IS a wholly different way of being sure that God is real.   It is not an intellectual proof, a reasoned sequence of thoughts. It is the fact that men *experience* the presence of God. Into our lives comes times when, all unexpectedly, He shadows over us, steals into the inner recesses of our souls, and lifts us up in a wonderful joy and peace. The curtains of heaven are raised and we find ourselves in heavenly peace in Christ Jesus. Sometimes these moments of visitation come to us in strange surroundings— on lonely country roads, in a classroom, at the kitchen sink. Sometimes they come in hour of worship, when we are gathered into one Holy Presence Who stands in our midst and welds us together in breathless hush, and wraps us all in sweet comfortableness into His arms of love. In such times of direct experience of Presence, we know that God is utterly real. We need no argument. When we are gazing into the sun we need no argument, no proof that the sun is shining.

This evidence for the reality of God is the one the Quakers primarily appeal to. It is the evidence upon which the mystics of all times rest their testimony. Quakerism is essentially empirical; it relies upon direct and immediate experience. We keep insisting: It isn't enough to believe in the love of God, as a doctrine; you must experience the love of God....To be able to defend a creed intellectually isn't enough; you must experience as reality first of all what the creed asserts. And unless the experience is there, behind it, the mere belief is not enough.— *Thomas Kelly, 1939.*

WHEN I WAS eight years old, I read the Psalms entirely through. Much of it was over my head and I missed its meaning but the exalted nature poetry thrilled me as it would any boy who loved the outdoor world. I could feel the difference between that written by the scribe and that written by the true poet and prophet, though I could not tell what made the difference.

The scribe is legal. He glorifies the past and wants to preserve what has been. The prophet is always seeing new dawns, new sunrises, new hopes and new worlds. He opens the gates to the future.

There is very much of this note of the prophet in the Psalms. The sense of wonder— Selah! You find this note of the prophet where you would least expect it in Psalm 119. It was too long and too legal to suit a boy of eight. But all of a sudden in the thirty-second verse you find in modern translation these great words: "I will obey thee eagerly as thou dost open up my life."

Our great slogan today is self-expression, and in the right sense of the word it is a genuine aim. But it is useless to talk about self-expression until we have got a self to express and we are all the time confronted by the question, which one of our thousand possible selves shall we express? In order to do that....you must discover what you want most.

The primary issue after all is how to get a rightly fashioned life that is truly worth expressing. That is what this Psalm is talking about. How to open out the possibilities of life. There are many things religion does for us, but this is one of the most striking ministries its brings to us. It opens up life.— *Rufus Jones, 1933.*

IN THE MOMENT that we sense in prayer the sweep of God's love, a light is cast upon our own condition revealing us to ourselves as no amount of introspection can do. No amount of considering what we think of ourselves, or what our friends think of us, or what our enemies say of us, is even faintly comparable to this self-revelation that comes from prayer. It is this chamber of loving scrutiny that Pascal speaks of when he says that all the troubles that come to men in this world come from their not being willing to stay in their own chambers. If we dare to stay in this chamber— aware of our shortcomings in the Light of God's loving presence— both the revelation of what must be put right and the strength to put it right are given to us. "He who shows a man his sin is the same that takes it away," declares George Fox. Both the pain and the healing are ministered to us within those chamber walls. But chambers are not all alike.

I recall an elderly woman telling a group, at the opening of a religious retreat, of her impressive apartment which looked so elegant and orderly and well kept in the parts where guests were permitted to circulate. "But," she confessed, "I've got a room in my apartment which I lock up and permit no one to enter, and it is in the most frightful state of confusion and disorder and chaos." A look of understanding spread over many faces...for they, too, had a "room," often more than one, that would not stand scrutiny...But [being willing to enter] the chamber of prayer...we are brought with...clarity to see. To come near to a God of revealing love is to change.— *Douglas V. Steere, 1962.*

THIS PEACE-MAKING is excellent work, and a blessed calling; what a pity it is, that there are not workmen in the world who would set themselves heartily to it, which if they did in a right spirit, God would certainly prosper the work in their hands, and plentifully reward them with his own peace, which passeth the understanding of the natural man. If our ingenious men, our men and women of skill and good natural parts, would take a little pains, nay, when the case requires it, a great deal, the Almighty would richly reward them. This work is not too mean even for princes and nobles; no, not even the greatest monarchs on earth, unless it be too mean for them to be called the children of God.

*   *   *

Wherefore, we should seek peace with all men, and ensue it, or sue for it, by our continual seeking of it, being a precious jewel, when found; and though this office may seem a little unthankful at first, yet in the end it brings forth the peaceable fruits of righteousness, as many so laboring have witnessed. And Christ, to encourage the work, says, "They shall be called the children of God;" which are the words of the King of kings; and if the princes of this world would promote this work among themselves, it would save a vast expense of treasure and of blood; and as these peace-makers are to be called the children of God, they who are truly concerned therein are not only so called, but are so in deed and in truth.— *Thomas Chalkley (1675-1741)*.

"Blessed are the peace-makers, for they shall be called the children of God."— Matt. 5:9.

I SHALL..state only one more effort to prove the objective reality of the spiritual world. For, honestly, all these arguments leave me cold. Even if they were sound—and none of them is watertight—they would only quiet my intellectual questionings. They would never motivate me to absolute dedication to Him for whom I yearn. But religious men are dedicated men, joyously enslaved men, bondservants of God and of His Christ, given in will to God. Arguments are devised subsequent to our deep conviction, not preceding our conviction. They bolster faith; they do not create it.

The...argument is this: Here is a world, amazingly complex, astonishingly interknit. Here are flowers, depending upon bees for pollination, and bees dependent upon flowers for food. Yonder are the starry heavens, adjusted, maintained, wheeling their way through staggering spaces in perfect rhythm and order. Whence comes it all, if not from God? And here am I, a complex being, of amazing detail of body and astounding reaches of mind. Yet my parents didn't *make* me; they are as incapable of being my true cause as I am incapable of being the true cause of my children. This whole spectacle is too vast, too well articulated to be caused by any single thing *in* the world. There must be a cause outside and beneath the whole, which I call God, Who creates, maintains, and preserves the whole world order.— *Thomas Kelly, 1939.*

WHEN I WAS A BOY the man who influenced me most was a schoolmaster. I don't remember his preaching pacifism; but he lived it, and many boys of my generation became pacifists as a result.... I saw the same thing, on a bigger scale, with Gandhi. What Gandhi wrote and what he said in his many speeches could have been unimportant, but for what Gandhi was and what he did....

I remember how, when I was in India in 1930, the doctrine of non-violence had an unexpected success among the warlike Pathans... and they began demonstrating in support of Gandhi and the Congress. It was a double shock to the British Government, because these Pathans are all Moslems. According to British propaganda all Moslems should have been against Gandhi, because he was a Hindu....... Two platoons [of a Hindu regiment brought into Peshawar] refused to fire [upon the Moslems]...

Twenty-two years later I was speaking at a meeting... when at the back of the hall a man rose to his feet— tall, grey-haired, with the carriage of a soldier...speaking slowly and deliberately. I knew from the first, and I think everybody in that hall knew, that he was speaking from experience...He was the British officer who had given the order to fire at Peshawar, when those two platoons had disobeyed. God through Gandhi had touched the hearts of the wild Panthans. Their courage and the miracle of their non-violence had moved the hearts of the Hindu soldiers. This change in the soldiers, willing to face death rather than kill unarmed men, had deeply affected a British officer— one, at least... We do not need to go back to the First Century to find that light on the road to Damascus. It is here. It is all around us.— *Reginald Reynolds, 1956.*

AMONG HER MEMORANDA are inserted the following queries and observation, which she was careful often to answer according to the testimony of the faithful witness in her own conscience.

Have I studied the Scriptures diligently?
Have I said anything to the disadvantage of another?
Have I indulged vain thoughts?
Have I profitably employed my time?
Have I checked all improper thoughts and feelings?
Have I in all cases kept strictly to truth?
Have I done good to any one?
Have I gained any useful knowledge?
Have I endeavored to live in the fear of the Lord?

If I have been enabled to pass a day in a manner which my conscience approves, oh! may I not feel on this account any self-complacency; but rather deep humiliation under a sense of my entire unworthiness of the assistance thus mercifully afforded me: and when, through unwatchfulness, I have erred, let not this too much discourage me, but stimulate me to renewed diligence, and render me more sensible of my entire dependence upon a merciful Creator.— *Ann Backhouse, aged 18.*

"Search me, O God, and know my heart: try me, and know my thoughts: and see if there be any wicked way in me, and lead me in the way everlasting."— Psalm 139:23,24.

ALL PRAYER reaches plateaus where it loses the initial exhilaration of climbing. These are the times when a consolidation of our commitment may be taking place. In such times the testing of our real loyalty is in process. Anyone can pray when the heart is bubbling over; no loyalty is needed then. But when the spirit is dry and all surface desire gone, then is the time when we learn to whom we really belong. No one has expressed this better than Francois de Sales who insists that when we cannot give God fresh roses, we give him dry ones for "the dry have more strength and sweetness."

It should be clear to us that we are in this business for the long pull, for fair weather and foul, through sickness and health, and that it is perfectly natural that we should run into these rough patches... and that then, as never before, our prayers are needed.......

It is here that our faithfulness will tell who it is we mean to serve. It is only the sentimentalists who depict prayer as a perpetual April. A good deal of prayer is framed in fall and winter, and much of the real work of prayer is best done in these very seasons. Does a painter stop painting when the exhilaration palls? Does a writer lay aside his book on which he is working if he is not in a glow of creativity? An Indian man of prayer notes that, "In spite of monsoon or summer heat, the Ganges never stops, so why should I?" There is a line in the Book of Ecclesiastes which says, "He who observes the wind will not sow; and he who regards the clouds will not reap....In the morning sow your seed" (Ecc.11:4-6,). This speaks the right word for dealing with times of dryness in prayer.— *Douglas V. Steere, 1962.*

WHEN I VIEW my steps in life, and reflect how greatly deficient I have been I am humbled, and have cause to admire the great compassion and long-suffering kindness of a gracious God, and with abasement acknowledge it will be of his mercy if I am saved. If I have been helped at times to be found faithful, it has been, and is, through the efficacy of grace, and therefore no room to boast. My failure in duty and watchfulness has been great. Through the religious care of pious parents when young, and an early sense of the Divine fear, I was and have been preserved from the gross evils of the world to this day, which is a great mercy and favor. But I have often passed under many hidden conflicts for disobedience and failure in duty, and have at times been ready to despair; yet I have had to acknowledge the Lord is righteous, whatever might be my portion; and after days of sorrow, and nights of deep exercise, he has been pleased to renew light and favor; under a sense of which, I desire to be found more attentive, diligent, and faithful, the residue of my days, esteeming the light of the Lord's countenance, and the evidence of his peace, beyond all terrestrial enjoyments.—*John Pemberton, aged 67, 1794.*

"Blessed is the man that walketh not in the counsel of the ungodly, nor standeth in the way of sinners, nor sitteth in the seat of the scornful. But his delight is in the law of the Lord; and in his law doth he meditate day and night."—Psalm 1:1,2.

HOW MANY...women or men have come to Quakerism for its historic and contemporary support of the equality of all persons is hard to judge. The Quaker stress on individual responsibility and individual faithfulness makes it a demanding religious path. Friends do not expect to become a mass movement in the foreseeable future.... [There is] a long parade of Quaker women who have acted on the basis of the Light, sure that more light will come. It is a strengthening and liberating belief. From Margaret Fell to Mary Fisher, Mary Dyer, Elizabeth Haddon, Susanna Morris, Charity Cook, Rebecca Jones, Angelina and Sara Grimke, Sarah Douglass, Abby Kelley Foster, Lucretia Mott, Elizabeth Comstock, Hannah Bean, Rhoda Coffin, Emma Malone, Susan B. Anthony, Ann Branson,Mary Meredith Hobbs, Sybil Jones, Hannah Whitall Smith, Alice Paul, Emily Green Balch, Kay Camp, Elise Boulding, Kara Cole, and Mary Ann Beall, the parade continues, bring to each generation the same message. that in Christ there is neither male nor female, and in souls there is no sex.— *Margaret Hope Bacon, 1986.*

"Even them will I bring to my holy mountain, and make them joyful in my house of prayer: their burnt offerings and their sacrifices shall be accepted upon mine altar; for mine house shall be called a house of prayer for all people."— Isa. 56:7.

IT SEEMS more than probable my time will not be protracted very long in this probationary state; and through redeeming love and mercy I am enabled to anticipate the close without dismay; fully believing that through the efficacy of the merits and mediation of a crucified Lord, death will have no sting, nor the grave any victory. I mention this in the deepest humility, to satisfy thee on a point in which I know thou wilt feel a deep and lively interest, shouldst thou survive me in the journey through time. I remain unmoved in all points of Christian doctrine as held by our early Friends, and by faithful brethren since their time.

*   *   *

May the feeling of infirmity quicken my diligence in the great work of the day, so that when the solemn period arrives in which I must bid a final farewell to all visible things, I may, through divine mercy, be enabled to adopt the language, "Although the earthly house of this tabernacle be dissolved, I have a building of God, a house not made with hands, eternal in the heavens." There, with the collected just of all generations, I shall be forever with the Lord, employed in the unceasing song of thanksgiving and praise to him who is the author and finisher of our faith, and who wrought all our works in us.— *George Withy.*

HAVE WE SET ASIDE the query: do you make time in your daily lives to wait upon God in prayer that you may know more of God's presence? Dear Friend, do you come to meeting prepared in mind and heart to worship God in spirit and in truth? Have we lost track of the promise of heaven: "Seek ye first the kingdom of heaven, and all these things shall be added unto you"?

It is not that we do not value the spiritual blessings of our faith; it is rather, I believe, that we take them for granted. Because we are Quakers we are content to believe that we may continue to come to meeting—as a sort of come-as-you-are-affair—and confidently expect to be blessed with the Spirit and strengthened, ipso facto. How many of us know and heed the injunction "worship is work"? How many of us take to heart Rufus Jone's definition: "The worship of Almighty God is the single most exalted exercise of which the human mind is capable"? Do we enter into the silence of our meetings for worship with that implanted in our minds and hearts? Perhaps you have heard a disgruntled Friend say: "I didn't get much out of meeting today." And perhaps you have been tempted to ask: "Well, Friend, what did you bring?"— *Peter Donchian, 1986.*

"Draw nigh to God, and he will draw nigh to you. Cleanse your hands, ye sinners; and purify your hearts, ye double minded."— James 4:8

"Humble yourselves in the sight of the Lord, and He shall lift you up."— James 4:10.

I HAVE IN MIND something deeper than the simplification of our external programs, our absurdly crowded calendars of appointments through which so many pantingly and frantically grasp. These do become simplified in holy obedience, and the poise and peace we have been missing can really be found. But there is a deeper, an internal simplification of the whole of one's personality, stilled, tranquil, in childlike trust listening ever to Eternity's whisper, walking with a smile into the dark..

This amazing simplification comes when we "center down," when life is lived with singleness of eye, from a holy Center where the breath and stillness of Eternity are heavy upon us and we are wholly yielded to Him. Some of you know this holy, recreating Center of eternal peace and joy and live in it day and night. Some of you may see it over the margin and wistfully long to slip into that amazing Center where the soul is at home with God. Be very faithful to that wistful longing. It is the Eternal Goodness calling you to return Home, to feed upon green pastures and walk beside still waters and live in the peace of the Shepherd's presence. It is the life beyond fevered strain. We are called beyond strain, to peace and power and joy and love and thorough abandonment of self. We are called to put our hands trustingly in His hand and walk the holy way, in no anxiety assuredly resting in Him.— *Thomas R. Kelly, 1941.*

UNAIDED BY ANY ALLIANCE with the great or powerful; ridiculed and hated by the world, and everywhere pursued with contempt and cruelty, the principles of Friends silently spread through the kingdom winning the assent of men who were inferior to none in education, talents, and respectability. Amid the severest persecution, when deprived of every temporal good, torn from home and all its endearments, with every probability that they should seal the truth of their principles with the sacrifice of their lives, they faltered not. Though all around them looked dark and threatening, yet there was light and peace within; they not only met their sufferings with patience and fortitude, in the unresisting spirit of their Divine Master, but, through the goodness of God, were so filled with heavenly consolation, that they sang for joy even in the extremity of their suffering.

If the calamities in which Friends bore so large a share had no other good effect, they evidently tended to convince the nation of the folly of persecuting men for differences of opinion. More than thirty years of suffering had passed over, and not a single Quaker had been induced by it to abandon his profession. They were as prompt and diligent as ever in the open performance of their religious duties, and as ready patiently to submit to the penalties of unrighteous laws.— *Thomas Evans, (Introductory Remarks to the Life of George Fox).*

"For unto you it is given in the behalf of Christ, not only to believe on him, but also suffer for his sake."— Philipians 1:29.

IN THE EVENING my mind was unusually comfortable and easy; indeed, I felt something of a humble rejoicing, not very frequent with me; but I desire to be willing patiently to endure all the baptisms which are seen needful for me, not only on my own account, but also on account of the body at large; yet, she adds, "I dare say but little about the latter; I have so many things to strive with, so many wrong propensities that might get the better, if I were not thus proved and tried— self appears in so many different shapes, it would intrude itself upon almost every engagement without great care; this left hand of self would know, and take some credit for, what the right hand doeth, even after it has been done in sincerity of heart, as unto God, and not unto men. Oh, it is a precious thing to be lowly and simple-hearted! to let self be of no reputation, to be willing to be any thing or nothing, resigned fully either to do, or to suffer! I believe that divine help is never more conspicuous than in our weakness, that, under feelings of weakness, what we have to deliver, is more pure and free from the mixture.— *Elizabeth Robson.*

And whilst the sense of conscious sin,
My trembling soul with anguish shakes,
And hope thy pardoning love to win,
My fainting, sinking heart forsakes.
        —Amelia Opie.

I DO NOT KNOW whether or not I will be able to raise my voice when to do so may mean death, as it does in so many parts of the world today....Not by my strength alone. I cannot even dwell in the wide and difficult place to which I have been let without the light and strength which comes to me through the beloved community. And I have discovered, what I already knew, that Friends are only a part—albeit a dear part—of the beloved community.

We are called to break physical and societal yokes of poverty, powerlessness, racism, sexism, anti-semitism. We cannot—without the constant and continuing love of God and of each other. We are called to exercise power and yet resist the temptations of power in whatever reasonable guise it presents itself to us... We are called to remain open and vulnerable and caring, as the institutions of which we are a part process and dehumanize people in ways we cannot prevent... We are called to become instruments of change. Is it possible to do so without becoming agents of corruption? Maybe not. And never alone. But "We will try what love can do."....

My work on the court is the work to which I feel called at the present. How and where I may be called in the future remains to be seen. I am now exercising power at the very center of our system of government; I may one day be chained to the gate out front.

Early Friends, early Christians, did not ask if what they were led to do was politically feasible or if it was effective, cost or otherwise. We, too, have only to see with our eyes, and hear with our ears and understand to know the power that was theirs.—*Rosalie Wahl, Justice on the Supreme Court of Minnesota, 1980.*

WE QUAKERS have always argued that the war method is 1) "contrary to the mind of Christ," and that, therefore, neither an individual Christian nor a nation claiming to have Christian principles can participate in war; 2) that in the long run, the evil results of war far outweigh any good the war seems to have achieved; and 3) that the problems which lead to war, such as the economic exploitation of weak nations by the strong and military interference with the affairs of the weak by the strong, must eventually be solved by negotiation or other nonviolent means....

However, Quakers should, at this moment, have something very timely to say on this subject. There may be honest disagreement about when the right to life begins. But the question now is: when does the right to life end? Can it be that by the age of eighteen a human being has already outgrown his right to life?— *Dorothy Hutchinson, 1980.*

"That we henceforth be no more children, tossed to and fro, and carried about with every wind of doctrine, by the sleight of men, and cunning craftiness, whereby they lie in wait to deceive. But speaking the truth in love, may grow up into him in all things, which is the head, even Christ: from whom the whole body fitly joined together, and compacted by that which every joint supplieth, according to the effectual working in the measure of every part, maketh increase of the body unto the edifying of itself in love." Eph. 4:14-16.

IN THAT LOVE which in time past we have enjoyed together, do I heartily salute you, having in mind some few things to impart, as counsel and caution to us all, including myself therein.

We who apprehend ourselves called into this public station of preaching, ought closely to wait on our guide, to put us forth in the work. And, dear friends, I see great need for us carefully to mind our openings, and go on as we are led by the Spirit; for if we overrun our guide, we shall be confused, not knowing where, or how to conclude: but if we begin and go on with the Spirit, we shall conclude so, that all who are truly spiritual will sensibly feel that we are right: then will our ministry edify those who hear it.

Dear Friends, let us be singly and in sincerity devoted to the will of God, whether to preach or be silent; for if we are not sensible of such a resignation, we may set ourselves at work, when we should be quiet, and so bring an uneasiness upon our friends, and a burden upon ourselves...And, my dear Friends, every time you appear in the ministry, when it is over, examine yourselves narrowly, whether you have kept in your places and to your guide; and consider whether you have not used superfluous words, that render the matter disagreeable, or such tones or gestures as do not become the work we are about, always remembering that the true ministers preach not themselves, but Christ Jesus our Lord.— *Samuel Bownas (1676-1753).*

THE SUMMER I was seven, I felt God calling me to be a preacher, like my grandpa. The sense of being set aside for something holy grew in me. It took hold of my life and shaped in large measure the outer as well as the inner events.

My grandfather died a year later, and I kept all these things and pondered them in my heart. I began to prepare for my calling. I prayed. I felt God's presence as the companion of my days, and even more of my nights. I read the Bible regularly. I saved money from my allowances and bought myself a Bible of my own which I could underline and mark with cross references. It served me well into adulthood before it simply fell apart... At that time I read the Bible literally, as my grandfather had, and cherished his fundamentalist faith, although my own family's orientation was much more liberal.

My calling was not vaguely "to minister" but specifically to preach. Sometimes I went into our church when no one was around, climbed up in the pulpit and practiced projecting my voice to the back rows, with visions of rapt parishioners filling the pews. ...Girls could not be preachers, I was told in shocked tones....I never doubted my calling, for it was confirmed daily in my life as I prayed. I was, however, reluctant to be put down again. I became something of a loner, a serious, introspective child who wrote pious verses, and read the Bible for long periods....I did not confide my dream with anyone again until I was in high school.— *Elizabeth Watson, 1977.*

THOUGH OUR symbols of God are always incomplete, they are probably the best way to share our experience and make it real to others. Jesus, for instance, said that God was like a father. Many people who knew Jesus personally said that God was like Jesus. Both these views of God have brought comfort and illumination to many generations. Martin Luther, echoing the psalmist, said that God is like a mighty fortress. A Service Committee worker in a clothing depot in Vienna after World War II issued a serviceable winter coat to an elderly man. He thanked her and added, "God is like a warm coat." The poet, Rainer Maria Rilke, who has profoundly influenced my life, has many arresting symbols which delight and stimulate me, not the least of which is comparing God to a bouncing ball.

I have lived most of my life near a large body of water and early thought of God as being like an ocean—vast, constantly in motion, at times calm and supportive, at times wild and destructive. When I read George Fox's passage about the two oceans, it accorded with my own experience:

"I saw, also, that there was an ocean of darkness and death; but an infinite ocean of light and love, which flowed over the ocean of darkness. In that also I saw the infinite love of God..."

We need symbols to communicate our experience of God, but let us not confuse the description with the reality, or assume that everyone has the same angle of vision. Rather let us say, *this I know experimentally*, and then ask, *what canst thou say?—Elizabeth Watson, 1977.*

A HUMBLE reliance on the teachings of the Spirit, and a diligent use of the sacred Scriptures, were the means of leading our forefathers into all those distinguishing views and practices which are described in their writings if this be true, and we have abundant reason for believing it to be so, what ought to be our course? Shall we turn our backs on our high Christian views of the spirituality of true worship? Shall we return to ceremonial and figurative rites? Shall we make way in our meetings for a ministry which one man may prepare, and another appoint? Shall we cease from our testimony against all pecuniary corruption in the church? Shall we forget the sweetness and solemnity of true silence? Shall we surrender our Saviour's standard of the yea and nay, and no longer refuse an oath when expediency is supposed to demand it? Shall we, after all our peaceable professions, recur to the warfare of the world? Shall we forsake our simplicity in dress and language, and break down a hedge which so usefully protects many of our beloved young people from the vanities of the world? In short, shall we renounce that *unbending* adherence to the rule of right in which our forefathers were distinguished? If such, through the wiles of Satan, should be our course, how awful and affecting must be the consequence. The gracious purpose for which we were raised up to be a people will be frustrated through our want of faithfulness—*Joseph John Gurney, 1777-1847.*

FINALLY, I believe we must reawaken to the part of our faith which entails patience and the admission— as Paul put it— "our knowledge is partial." The simple fact that some situation of need or suffering has come to our attention does not mean that either we or someone we know must meet that need or alleviate that suffering. It could even be that some needs are not meant to be met, at least immediately. Some trials, some struggles, some sufferings are necessary occasions of growth for the persons living through them. Perhaps our experiences of inadequacy on occasions when we encounter these situations are essential to our growth.

I think the development of a commitment to "temporal simplicity" is something that will grow from a more complete comprehension of our Quaker faith, with a recognition of the character of our individual responsibilities for participation in the life of the Spirit. I also believe that this commitment is something Friends today must develop in order fully to embody our faith.

We can grow past the need to be all things to all people if we are willing to devote ourselves to being what God calls us to be. We will be better able to accept our own limitations and to "give ourselves time" when we understand our responsibility for nurturing and sustaining the gifts we were given to share with others. We can learn that saying "no" to undertaking just one more responsibility can be an affirmative act when we do so in order to say "yes" to the responsibilities to which we are already committed.— *Thomas H. Jeavons, 1980.*

AN IMPORTANT element in the Quaker doctrine of inward peace and its relation to what is somewhat misleadingly called "perfectionism" is indicated in the setting of Jesus' saying "Be ye perfect even as your father which is in heaven is perfect." Jesus begins by saying "Love your enemies" and ends by saying that this kind of perfection which is characteristic of God, who makes "his sun to rise both on the evil and on the good," is possible for men also (Matt.5:44-48).

To be perfect is to love your enemies for only by loving your enemies can you remove an inner source of conflict which prevents inner peace. He alone can secure inner peace who is at peace with the world around him even though the world around him may not be at peace with him.

Hatred, persecution, cursing (I quote Jesus' list) are expressions of inner disorder. Remove them and peace results; with it will come a sense of achieving that perfection which is characteristic of God who is kind to the evil (Luke 6:35). No man hates others without a sense of guilt, for in hating others he projects on them a secret unknown hatred for himself. Love removes this inner conflict which seeks satisfaction in outer conflict. The pacifist is sometimes called a perfectionist. This is true only in the limited sense that he possesses a means of removing that feeling of guilt in himself which generates conflict and hatred and is generated by them. Only when the pacifist attains inner peace does he truly live up to his name and become a peace-maker and only the peace-maker can attain inner peace.— *Howard H. Brinton, 1948.*

DOMESTIC LIFE presents many opportunities for the exercise of virtue, as well as the more exalted stations of honor and ambition. For, though its sphere is more humble, and its transactions are less splendid, yet the duties peculiarly incumbent on it constitute the basis of all public character. Perfection in private life is by far the more arduous attainment of the two; since it involves a higher degree of virtue, to acquire the cool and silent admiration of constant and close observers, than to catch the undistinguishing applause of the vulgar. Men, accustomed to the business of the world, may think it a mean occupation to be engaged in the duties of a family.

*   *   *

How many daily occasions there are for the exercise of patience, forbearance, benevolence, good humor, cheerfulness, candor, sincerity, compassion, self-denial! How many instances occur of satirical hints, of ill-natured witticisms, of fretfulness, impatience, strife, and envyings; besides those of disrespect, discontent, sloth, and very many other seeds of evil, the magnitude of which is perhaps small, but for the guilt of which we shall most assuredly be judged. When we consider that private life also has its trials, temptations, and troubles, it ought surely to make us vigilant, when around our own fire-side, lest we should quiet our apprehensions, and cease from our daily watchfulness.— *John Barclay, 1814.*

WHILE it has been productive scientifically to view man as a socialized animal, this leads to a dead end spiritually if we do not give equal weight to that which goes on inside a man. I will go further and say that man *will come to a spiritual dead end* if he does not allow time apart and in solitude for things to happen inside him. It is possible to drown children and adults in a constant flow of stimuli,forcing them to spend so much energy responding to the outside world that inward life and the creative imagination which flowers from it becomes stunted or atrophied....

In homes where silence is lived, the child finds it easy and comfortable to turn to it. In a large and noisy family (like my own) the period of hush that begins every meal sweeps like a healing wind over all the cross-currents that have built up in the previous hours and leaves the household clean and sweet. Times apart of special family worship, hard to come by in the daily routine, become hours to be remembered and valued for their very scarcity, and never fail to catch us up to another level of love and awareness. In these times we rediscover who and what we really are, as individuals and as a family, and can lay before God what we cannot easily lay before one another. It is an odd thing to say, but solitude can be shared. In a family where inward solitude is highly prized, individuals may slip easily into and out of each others' solitude. Some families must work harder than others to create the physical situation in which times of solitude become possible, but when silence is treasured, the quiet place is found. — *Elise Boulding, 1962.*

[Advice to Visitors to Women's Prisons:—]

MUCH depends on the spirit in which the visitor enters upon her work. It must be the spirit, not of judgment, but of mercy. She must not say in her heart, I am more holy than thou; but must rather keep in perpetual remembrance that "all have sinned, and come short of the glory of God"—that, therefore, great pity is due from us even to the greatest transgressors among our fellow-creatures.... The good principle in the hearts of many abandoned persons may be compared to the few remaining sparks of a nearly extinguished fire. By means of the utmost care and attention, united with the most gentle treatment, these may yet be fanned into a flame, but under the operation of a rough and violent hand, they will presently disappear, and may be lost for ever.

In our conduct towards these unfortunate females, kindness, gentleness, and true humility ought ever to be united with serenity and firmness. Nor will it be safe ever to descend...to familiarity; for there is a dignity in the Christian character, which demands, and will obtain, respect, and which is powerful in its influence, even over dissolute minds.....

...For experience proves that if those persons who visit them are harsh in judging and condemning them the effect is hurtful rather than beneficial. Neither is it by any means wise to converse with them on the subject of the crimes of which they are accused or convicted; for such conversation is injurious both to the criminals themselves and to others who hear them; and, it frequently leads them to add sin to sin, by uttering the grossest falsehoods.— *Elizabeth Fry (1780-1845).*

[Continued...]

THOSE who engage in the interesting task of visiting criminals must not be impatient if they find the work of reformation a very slow one. Such it will almost necessarily be in the generality of cases. Sensible of the natural corruption of our own hearts, let us learn patiently to bear with the hardened and the profligate, and let us be faithful and diligent in directing their attention to "the Lamb of God which taketh away the sins of the world: for it is only by faith in him that these poor wanderers can obtain the forgiveness of their past sins, or be enabled, for the future, to lead a life of true piety and virtue.— *Elizabeth Fry, (1780-1845).*

*   *   *

Testimony of a woman convict:

"But Mrs. Fry had a remarkable way with her— a sort of speaking that you could hardly help listening to, whether you would or no, for she was not only very good, but very clever. Just to avoid listening when she was speaking or reading, I learnt to count twelve backwards and forwards, so that my mind was quite taken up..

"Mrs. Fry had a way of speaking to one of us alone, and I was very anxious to shuffle this lecture....But when she was taking leave of us, she just called me on one side. She came close to me, and, looking at me in a very solemn sort of way, she laid her hands upon my shoulders, and her very fingers seemed to have a feeling of kindness toward me, and she gave me a pressure that told she felt for me. But it was no lecture she gave me— all she said was, "Let not thine eyes covet". Her words were low and awful."

QUAKERS have long since discarded the Quaker gray, the broad-brimmed hat, and the Quaker bonnet, which were once their distinguishing marks. Other Quaker ways have disappeared, too. If modern Friends use "thee" it is only within their immediate family. The prohibition against art, music, and theater is regarded as the sad mistake of another age. Quakers, a predominantly middle-class group, share the tastes and interests of most middle-class Americans.

And yet one Quaker can usually recognize another in a crowd. There is a penchant for a simple, direct style of dress, a habit of understatement, and a directness of approach which most Quakers share. In addition the birthright Friends, the descendants of the old Quaker families, bear a certain resemblance resulting from common ancestors. There is a Quaker look, just as there is a Yankee look, although it is difficult to describe.

Since the Quakers have remained a small group in society, the old Quaker families are generally interrelated. From Maine to California genealogy quickly becomes a topic of conversation whenever birthright Quakers meet. The years of isolation, of persecution, and of the championing of lost causes have developed among Quakers a family feeling rather unusual in the modern world. One Quaker is welcome in the home of another at almost any time and place. This fellowship is not reserved for the "old" Quakers, but extended to the convinced as well.— *Margaret Hope Bacon, 1969.*

NOW ALTHOUGH by our principles the use of anything which is merely superfluous is unlawful, this does not deny the enjoyment of luxury for those who are accustomed to it. Those who have abundant possessions, are accustomed to such things by education, may make better use of them without extravagance or waste than those who are unaccustomed to them or who do not have the capacity to utilize them.

Beyond doubt, whatever creation provides is for the use of man, and use in moderation is lawful. However, *per accidens*, some things may be lawful for some and not for others. For example, whoever is accustomed to eating meat or drinking wine, or clothing himself with the finest woolens, may continue to do so. If he can afford these by his estate in life and is accustomed to them by education, he may use them provided he does not do so immoderately or in excess. If he should attempt to eat or clothe himself as peasants do, he might prejudice the health of his body without advancing his soul. It would be unlawful, however, for a man who was accustomed to coarser food and rainment to exceed these if it was beyond his means and prejudiced his family and children. This would be so, even though he were to eat and be clothed in the same way as someone for whom it was lawful. The other person may have practiced as much denial, and been as mortified in coming down to that, as he was in exceeding his abilities and customary acts in aspiring to it.— *Robert Barclay, (1648-1690).*

THE SKY was dark at 3:45 a.m. near the little village of Clitheroe in central England, and it was drizzling rain. I was in a hurry to find the foot of Pendle Hill so that I might retrace the steps of George Fox and complete the ascent before sunrise.... There was a simple, handpainted sign indicating the direction to Pendle Hill. The lane, which ran through the farmer's pasture, narrowed to a well worn dirt footpath that rose sharply up the hill. The hillside was dotted by large rocks and numerous grayish-colored sheep...

I hurriedly ascended the footpath until it became quite steep... Perhaps George Fox's trip up the hill was a mere flight of fancy resulting from too much soul searching. The fact that the wet path was well worn and well marked meant that this was not going to be the unique experience that I had anticipated....

[Upon] my arrival at the top of the shrouded crest of the hill, I saw a loose stack of stones of various colors, sizes and textures. By custom, pilgrims...are asked to find a stone and place it with the larger group of stones. I, too, placed a stone with the stones of others who had come before me.

Within the quiet, peace-filled mist on top of the hill, I began to feel a sense of connectiveness with those who had traveled up the hill before me and with those who would in the future....

In the solitude of our hearts each of us, wherever we are, has the opportunity to experience the gift of feeling connected with one another... For me, this was my Pendle Hill experience. Thank you George Fox, for sharing your legacy.— *Donald C. Johnson, 1986.*

HAVE NOT many of us been already stript of all their outward substance?— not a bed being left them to lie on— not a stool to sit on— not a dish to eat from! Is there a prison in the nation, or a dungeon in a prison, which has not been a witness of our groaning? Have we not been tried by banishment, and proved by death itself? Death in New England, by the hand of the hangman! Death in Old England by the rough hand of rude and boisterous officers and soldiers, who have given divers of our friends those blows which in a few days have brought them to their graves!

I might add to these, burning in the forehead, cutting off ears, unmerciful beatings, whippings, and cruel scourgings. But did any or all of these deter us from the worship of God? Nay! hath not our cheerfully undergoing all these hardships sufficiently evinced to the world that our religion and consciences are dearer to us than our estates, our liberties, our limbs, or our lives? Why, then, will you repeat severities upon us, which have so often been tried before in vain? Can you take pleasure in putting others to pain, and delight yourselves in afflicting others...

Think not the worse of us for our faithfulness to our God! He that is true to God will be true to man also; but he that is false and treacherous to God, how is it likely he should be true to man?— *Thomas Ellwood, 1683.*

ON THAT NEVER-TO-BE-FORGOTTEN Sunday morning, I found myself one of a small company of silent worshippers, who were content to sit down together without words, that each one might feel after and draw near to the Divine Presence, unhindered at least, if not helped, by any human utterance. Utterance I knew was free, should the words be given; and before the meeting was over, a sentence or two were uttered in great simplicity by an old and apparently untaught man, rising in his place amongst the rest of us. I did not pay much attention to the words he spoke, and I have no recollection of their purport. My whole soul was filled with the unutterable peace of the undisturbed opportunity for communion with God— with the sense that at last I had found a place where I might, without the faintest suspicion of insincerity, join with others in simply seeking His presence. To sit down in silence could at the least pledge me to nothing; it might open to me (as it did that morning) the very gate of heaven. And since that day, now more than seventeen years ago, Friends' meetings have indeed been to me the greatest of outward helps to a fuller and fuller entrance into the spirit from which they have sprung; the place of the most soul-subduing, faith-restoring, strengthening and peaceful communion, in feeding upon the bread of life, that I have ever known. I cannot but believe that what has helped me so unspeakably might be helpful to multitudes in this day of shaking of all that can be shaken, and of restless inquiry after spiritual good.— *Caroline Stephen, 1890.*

IT IS FREQUENTLY said that to bear this world, we must become toughened, callous, hard. The sadness of the city-evils, the blighted lives we see, the injustices, the pain and tears! Without a protective covering of indifference, it seems rational to say we cannot endure the world. But the Eternal Presence, shining upon time, gives us, not a tough protection, but an exquisitely *tendered* spirit.   Overburdened men and women, blighted lives, slaveries in all their modern forms, nations and institutions in insane self-destruction and little children hoping for warmth and love and opportunity [are all laid upon us].   To our easier sympathy with physical pain there is added suffering because of the soul-blindness which we see everywhere to see hatred poison a life is suffering indeed....

Before, our chief suffering, the suffering about which we are disturbed, was *our own* suffering. The world's arrows were thought to be aimed at us. But with the great unselfing, the center of concern for suffering is shifted *outside* ourselves and distributed with breadth unbounded among all, friends and so-called enemies. For a few agonized moments we may seem to be given to stand *within* the heart of the World-Father and feel the infinite sufferings of love toward all the Father's children.   And pain inflicted on them becomes pain inflicted on ourselves. Were the experience not also an experience suffused with radiant peace and power and victory, as well as tragedy, it would be unbearable.— *Thomas Kelly, 1938.*

I WAS AT THE PLOW, meditating on the things of God, and suddenly I heard a voice saying to me, "Get thee out from thy kindred, and from thy father's house". And I had a promise given with it, whereupon I did exceedingly rejoice that I had heard the voice of that God which I had professed from a child, but had never known him....

And when I came at home I gave up my estate, cast out my money; but not being obedient in going forth, the wrath of God was upon me so that I was made a wonder to all, and none thought I would have lived. But after I was made willing, I began to make some preparation, as apparel and other necessaries, not knowing whither I should go. But shortly afterwards going a gate-ward with a friend from my own house, having on an old suit, without any money, having neither taken leave of wife or children, not thinking then of any journey, I was commanded to go into the west, not knowing whither I should go, nor what I was to do there. But when I had been there a little while, I had given me what I was to declare. And ever since I have remained not knowing today what I was to do tomorrow...[The promise was] that God would be with me, which promise I find made good ever day.— *James Naylor, from the examination at Appleby, 1652.*

Soon James Naylor appeared to some...as the ablest speaker in the new movement, and Friends became uneasy at his exaltations. City authorities sent Naylor to London, where he was convicted of blasphemy, and whipped, pilloried, branded, and had his tongue bored through and sent to prison.

THE QUALITY of his [Jesus'] life and the profound things he said drew me to him then, not the myths of his births and resurrection.   His life and teachings commanded my allegiance then, and still do......I am also a Christian because it is my heritage. I inherited the faith that nurtured my ancestors; its customs and holidays and doctrines were part of my life from my beginning. Its ways are dear to me and give meaning to my life. But had I been born in China, Japan, India, or Syria, my heritage might have been to look to Lao Tse, or the Buddha, or to Krishna, or to Mohammed as the great teacher and revealer of God. Who am I to say that they are wrong and Christianity is right?   Over and beyond us all is the Living God to whom there are many paths.

The truth of this came vividly to me in high school. I was sent by our church to a conference where the main speaker was a missionary just returned from India. Unknown to the conference planners she and her husband had just resigned their posts. They had come to know Mohandas Gandhi......and they felt the inconsistency of trying to convert Hindus to Christianity when Hinduism had produced this saintly, Christlike person. This was 1928, and the first time I had heard of Gandhi. Eagerly I read all that I could find about him.

Gandhi illuminates for me the life and death of Jesus. He, more than any person I know of, lived out all the implications of the teachings of Jesus in our own time. At that time, I made one of the basic commitments of my life: to non-violence. And I came to believe that God poured his message for the twentieth century into this little brown man. I still believe that.— *Elizabeth Watson, 1977.*

I THEN had my conversation much among people of no religion, being ashamed to be counted religious, or do anything that was called religious. In this restless state I let in every sort of notion that rose in that day, and for a time applied myself to examine them, and get out of them whatever good could be found; but still sorrow and trouble was the end of all. I was at length ready to conclude that though the Lord and His truth were certain, yet they are not now made known to any upon earth; and I determined no more to inquire or look after God.

So for some time I took no notice of any religion, but minded recreation, as it is called; and went after it into many excesses and vanities— as foolish mirth, carding, dancing, and singing. I frequented music assemblies, and made vain visits where there were jovial feastings. But in the midst of all this my heart was often sad and pained beyond expression. I was not hurried into those follies by being captivated by them, but from not having found in religion what I had sought and longed after. I would often say within myself, what are they all to me? I could easily leave all this; for it hath not my heart, it is not my delight, it hath not power over me. I had rather serve the Lord, if I could indeed feel and know that which would be acceptable to Him.

O Lord suffer me no more to fall in with any false way, but show me the Truth— *Mary Springett, 1650.*

WHAT THEN is our experience? Is it not of the possibilities of goodness? As we have learned more of how people interact with each other and of how they respond to the expectations of others, we now know that people tend to become what we expect them to be. Thus, if we regard people as fundamentally sinful, that is what they are likely to become. If we regard them as capable of love and goodness and trust, these are the capacities that they develop. We know as a Society that our belief in that of God in everyone has enabled us to find it and has led to spiritual growth— not only in the individual but in our meetings. So that what we believe about human nature is part of the complex process of the 'becoming' of human nature. How can we then believe in anything other than basic goodness?

What we believe about human nature also affects the way in which we treat each other and thus our beliefs have moral consequences for ourselves as well as others. The worst effects of belief in sin and damnation have come from the excuse it provides for punishment and repression. The belief that others are different and that they are hated by God has been the rationalisation for the persecution of heretics and witches and Jews.

Taken to the extreme, any belief that human beings are incapable of goodness destroys the motivation for moral actions and makes a mockery of our experience that there are many people who are good, loving, caring and responsible....Any way of looking at human nature must seek the unity between us. In our goodness and our sins we are all the children of God.— *Janet Scott, London, 1980.*

AS WE ACT in obedience to the Light Within, we may become mediators through whom God's love is known. We are called to share the task of God, to share the grief and the joy, the sorrow, the self-giving, and the reconciliation.

We are called upon to love the loveless and the unlovable, to reach out to the racists and the torturers, to all who hurt and damage, cripple and kill. They are God's unhappy children who need especial care. They have harmed themselves, but not irredeemably; and God, through us, and in many other ways, offers them healing love and divine pity and takes their hurts away.

We are called to that obedience which freely gives up self, possessions, life, beliefs, in following that vision, that greater love in which alone is life and peace. This does not mean that we lie down like doormats to be trampled on, or that we give up our freedom or our grasp of truth— it means that we join ourselves to the risk of creation, to the venture of authentic human being, that we "stand in the Light", reveal that measure of truth that is known to us...that we face the pain of the world, and match it with forgiveness.

To do God's work we do not have to be good people...Our hope and confidence is not in ourselves but in God whose grace is sufficient to complete the work and whose self-giving love reaches out to us however unworthy we are.

When we face our own unworthiness, when we share with others the pain of self-knowledge, the pain of the world's brokenness, we find that at the heart of the darkness, at the profoundest depths of the human anguish, God is already present, already strengthening and comforting, already bearing our cross.— *Janet Scott, 1980.*

MY MIND, through the power of truth, was in a good degree weaned from the desire of outward greatness, and I was learning to be content with real conveniences, that were not costly, so that a way of life free from much entanglement appeared best for me, though the income might be small. I had several offers of business that appeared profitable, but I did not see my way clear to accept of them, believing they would be attended with more outward care and cumber than was required of me to engage in. I saw that a humble man, with the blessing of the Lord, might live on a little, and that where the heart was set on greatness, success in business did not satisfy the craving; but that commonly with an increase of wealth the desire of wealth increased. There was a care on my mind so to pass my time that nothing might hinder me from the most steady attention to the voice of the true Shepherd.

My employer, though now a retailer of goods, was by trade a tailor... and I began to think about learning the trade, expecting that if I should settle I might by this trade and a little retailing of goods get a living in a plain way, without the load of a great business.... I believed the hand of Providence pointed out this business for me, and I was taught to be content with it, though I felt at times a disposition that would have sought for something greater; but through the revelation of Jesus Christ I had seen the happiness of humility, and there was an earnest desire in me to enter deeply into it; at times this desire arose to a degree of fervent supplication, wherein my soul was so environed with heavenly light and consolation that things were made easy to me which had been otherwise.— *John Woolman (1720-1772).*

OFTEN in the night and sometimes in the break of day I have returned home from my many meetings grievously condemned, distressed and ashamed, wishing I had not gone into such company and resolving to do so no more. But soon my resolutions failed me and away I went again and again. The Lord followed me close in mercy and often broke in powerfully upon me turning all my mirth into mourning; yet I still got over the holy witness, did despite to the spirit of grace and repaired again and again to the haunts of diversion.— Adored forever be the name of the Lord, he forsook me not, but followed me still closer and closer and sounded the alarm louder and louder in my ears.— The way was shown me but I would not walk in it. I knew my Lord's will but did it not; mine own I still delighted in.— My days I spent in vanity and rebellion; my nights frequently in horror and distress. Many a night I scarce durst enter my chamber or lay me down in bed...I prayed, I cried, I repented, I sinned.   God still interrupted my career, disturbed my casual satisfaction and blasted all my joys. In pursuing my course I knew I was pursuing my daily and almost unsupportable distress.

I knew myself a prisoner and yet I hugged my chains.

*   *   *

*(His dying words...*We shall be in the everlasting unity, which cannot be shaken by all the changes of time, nor interrupted in a never-ending eternity.   We cannot approve or disapprove by parts the works of Omnipotence rightly.   We must approve the whole and say, Thy will be done in all things...let self be of no reputation; trust in the Lord, and he will carry thee through all.— *Job Scott (1751-1793).*

THE QUAKERS do not believe, as do some other Christians, that man is born in a state of total depravity and remains in it until he is wholly changed by conversion which transforms him from a state of nature to a completed state of grace. Conversion is the beginning not the end of a process. When inward peace disappears *it is a sign that the next stage of growth is at hand* and peace can only be reached if that growth takes place. A divine call may come requiring an individual to speak in a meeting. If the call is resisted inward peace disappears.......

Inward peace is both an end and a means. As a means it becomes an evidence of divine approval while lack of it is an evidence that some divine requirement is not being fulfilled...Throughout the Quaker Journals we find frequent reference to the absence of inward peace as a sign that some "concern," possibly to undertake a journey "in the love of the gospel," possibly to engage in some effort for social reform, had been laid upon the individual. When that concern has been carried through there is reference to the return of peace.

It is not essential that the undertaking be successful for inward peace to result. It is only necessary that the individual feel that he has done all that he is able to do to carry out the requirement. God does not require more than is possible. He only demands that we live up to our capacity. As for consequences, how can a finite mind tell what they in the long course of time may be.— *Howard H. Brinton, 1948.*

HERE OR NEAR THIS ROCK GEORGE FOX
PREACHED TO ABOUT ONE THOUSAND SEEKERS
FOR THREE HOURS ON SUNDAY JUNE 13, 1652.
GREAT POWER INSPIRED HIS MESSAGE AND
THE MEETING PROVED OF FIRST IMPORTANCE
IN GATHERING THE SOCIETY OF FRIENDS
KNOWN AS QUAKERS. MANY MEN AND
WOMEN CONVINCED OF THE TRUTH ON THIS
FELL AND IN OTHER PARTS OF THE NORTHERN
COUNTIES WENT THROUGH THE LAND AND
OVER THE SEAS WITH THE LIVING WORD OF
THE LORD, ENDURING GREAT HARDSHIPS AND
WINNING MULTITUDES TO CHRIST.

— From a tablet on a great rock known as
"Fox's Pulpit", near Firbank Fell, England.

*   *   *

WHAT was the nature of that spiritual tide which rose
in the Lake Country of Northwest England three
centuries ago and flowed down the valleys to the rest of
England? What was the mystery of its contagion
whereby thousands were drawn into the main stream
and carried as apostles to many other lands?...

It is not enough to ascribe to George Fox and his
contemporary ministers alone the reason for that
spiritual movement, nor even to the thousands who
were caught in it— it was rather the master idea itself,
the way of life...Christ was not only real to them in a
historic sense, he had "come to teach his people
himself." Enthusiasm, no matter how fervent, could
not of itself initiate, and certainly could not sustain it.
God had broken into their gathered lives....— *Errol T.
Elliott, 1952.*

THOUGH the division between pastoral and non-pastoral Friends seems too great and often so sorrowful, the truth is that there is far more unity of aim as between the moderates on both sides...

The mistakes we made seventy-five years ago, when we started a system of pastoral leadership was not the mistake of providing better ministerial care. That was obviously needed. The meetings were dying for lack of intelligent concern for the spiritual welfare of the members...[and] that the first pastors brought immense relief, that they represented to the young people of two generations ago a victory over the dead hand of tradition which was terribly stultifying, and that the coming of pastors ended the exodus of Quaker young persons into other denominations.

Though the reasons for the pastoral system were good, a gigantic mistake was made. The mistake was that a fundamentally alien system was taken over, almost intact, from other Christian bodies. The result of this borrowing was that recognized Quaker ministers began to perform duties almost identical with those of conventional Protestant clergymen....The main point was that the Quaker pastor became the responsible head of a congregation, representing it officially on public occasions, conducting weddings and funerals, visiting the sick, and preaching constantly. The natural result was that, in many communities, the rank and file of the members ceased to feel any need of doing these things. They had the immense relief which comes from knowing that some other person is responsible. They, accordingly, could go about their regular business with easy consciences.— *D. Elton Trueblood, 1960. [Con't.]*

[...Continued]

THE TRUE pastoral leader, as Friends in our strongest periods have shown, is not a person of exalted status and certainly not the 'head' of the meeting. He is always at work encouraging this one, teaching that one, walking with another. He may speak on public occasions, but often his leadership is not obvious at all. He will not do anything if he can get another to do it, not because he is lazy, but because the doing will develop the other person, and it is development of others that is always his goal. He will speak if he needs to do so, but he knows that speaking is only one of many tasks which spiritual nourishment requires. He may teach more than he preaches, and he will not be afraid to be silent or to sit within the congregation rather than face it, if he believes this will facilitate the general sense of responsibility. He will have the best education which he can get, but he will not make capital of his degrees or expect that they be used by people who address him. He will resist endlessly being called "Reverend" and will not, in any way, show by dress any distinction between himself and others. He will work very hard, but primarily as a catalytic agent. He will be especially pleased if his work, though effective, is unnoticed.

Here is a noble and difficult ideal. What is important to see is that it is radically different from the ordinary Christian conception of the ministry, yet it is a ministry.— *D. Elton Trueblood, 1960.*

BEFORE he was eighteen years of age, William Penn had been sent to the Continent by his father, Admiral Penn, for the purpose not only of ordinary travel, but especially to have spread before him the allurements of a gay courtly life, in their most fascinating forms. By this means the father hoped to supplant and drive away the serious impressions his mind had received when an Oxford student, from the Quaker preaching of Thomas Loe.

William Penn was expelled from the University for refusing to wear the college cap and gown; for discussing among his fellow students the wickedness and absurdity of religious persecution; and more especially, for asserting the scriptural truth of Quaker doctrines. No gentle measures awaited his return home after his expulsion.   But it was in vain that the stern, authoritative admiral insisted on the abandonment of every new religious idea the son had taken up.

Personal flagellation and solitary confinement followed, till the father became aware that the religious convictions even of a youth of sixteen or seventeen were not so to be overcome. At length, when severity failed, continental travel was resolved on, and no arrangements were spared that could render it attractive. William Penn went abroad under the highest auspices, and with the companionship his father entirely approved of.

Two years later....he heard by accident that Thomas Loe, his old Oxford acquaintance, was in the city, and "intended to preach that night." He...wondered how the preacher's eloquence would stand the censures of his riper judgement...and [was] prompted to stay and listen.....

From that night on he was a Quaker in heart.— *Penns and Peningtons.*

THE FIRST STEP in the simple life is to turn to God. The way I do it is commonplace. Almost every morning I sit down for five, ten or fifteen minutes. Sometimes I neglect this practice for weeks at a time because I am not far along on the path of spiritual growth. Gradually these periods of neglect are disappearing and my morning worship or meditation is getting to be a settled habit.

I begin often with a Biblical phrase in my head, usually chosen from the Psalms:

O Lord, our Lord, how excellent is thy name in all the earth. Out of the depths have I cried unto thee.

The Lord is my shepherd, I shall not want.

I will look up unto the hills, from whence cometh my help. O God, our help in ages past, our hope for years to come.

At other times, I read a short selection from the Gospels or Epistles. Read at this rate, a book of the New Testament can last a long time; it is treasured as a devotional aid and not trotted through as a literary or historical excursion.

Lately I have been reading a paragraph or so from Brother Lawrence, Thomas Kelly, Joel Goldsmith or Francis of Assisi.

The Christian tradition is very dear to me. I find the glorious company of saints to be a friendly lot. Knowing that the psalms were recited [through the ages]... makes these old Hebrew poems come alive to me. It does not bother me that Christians are often hypocrites and sinners (am I not one too?)— *George Peck, 1973. [Con't.]*

FOR, SO FAR in my morning meditation, I am only in the willful human stage. Beyond that may lie merely a session of sweet silent thought or even worse, the rational consideration of some plan for the day. So that is that, and I turn to the usual activities, not with guilt but in dryness. "My God, why hast thou forsaken me?"

Sometimes, and with habit and practice ever more frequently, the willful human stage of meditation is replaced by a suffusion of divinity. My veins are filled with milk and honey. I am a particle of dust in a magnetic field. I hear the music of the spheres.... I understand Fox:

"And wait in the Light for Power to remove the earthly part...that with the Light your minds may be kept up to God, who is pure, and in it you may all have unity who in the Light of Life do walk."

Lately I have taken up again the habit of a nightly session of meditation or prayer, just before going to sleep.

Now I lay me down to sleep, I pray the Lord my soul to keep; If I die before I wake, I pray the Lord my soul to take.

My mother told me when I was four that there was a guardian angel at the head of the bed. I knew he was there though I never looked to see. Now sometimes I find him there again. He improves my dream life no end.— *George Peck, 1973.*

I OFTEN struggle for resignation, and a more complete acquiescence to the Divine will. I can say, with the Apostle Paul, "I keep under my body, and bring it into subjection;" but I do not feel capable of exerting the same influence over my mind. I believe this can only be effected by the operation of that Power who can "subdue all things unto himself." He watches over all the workmanship of his hands, and his providence is continually hovering over us for good. His power is the same over the perturbations of the soul as over the boisterous elements, and he can diffuse a calm over the mind as easily as over the tempestuous ocean. The prayer of faith will ascend to Him: He will pluck our feet out of the miry clay, and set them upon a rock whose foundations are fixed, and will stand firm against the rain, the floods, and the wind. I think we shall do well not to perplex ourselves with contemplating the various evils of life, or the mystery of iniquity. Secret things belong unto God, and he only can reveal them according to His good pleasure. Our concern is with those that are revealed; and we may trust that we shall be sufficiently enlightened to pursue the right way. Submission to the Divine will in all things is our duty, and will prove the source of our greatest happiness; for when our will revolts against the Divine will, nothing but misery can ensue.—*Margaret Woods, 1818, aged 70.*

VERY often in these meetings for worship, which held usually for nearly two hours, there were long periods of silence, for we never had singing to fill the gaps. I do not think anybody ever told me what the silence was for. It does not seem necessary to explain Quaker silence to children. They *feel* what it means. They do not know how to use very long periods of hush, but there is something in short, living throbbing times of silence which *finds* the submerged life and stirs it to nobler living and holier aspiration. I doubt if there is any method of worship which works with a subtler power or which brings into operation in the interior life a more effective moral and spiritual culture. Sometimes a real spiritual wave would sweep over the meeting in these silent hushes, which made me feel very solemn and which carried me— careless boy though I was— down into something which was deeper than my own thoughts, and gave me momentary sense of that Spirit who has been the life and light of men in all ages and in all lands. Nobody in this group had ever heard the word "mystical", and no one would have known what it meant if it had been applied to this form of worship, but in the best sense of the word this was a mystical religion, and all unconsciously I was being prepared to appreciate and at a later time to interpret the experience and the life of the mystics.— *Rufus Jones, 1926.*

I CAN REMEMBER my own disappointment when it opened out upon me that I was not going to find what I called a proof of God. I wanted something that was irrefutable; some chain of 'because' and 'therefore' leading up to a triumphant conclusion from which there could be no intellectual escape; and if I could not get that, nothing else seemed worth having; all was so shifting and unstable, so shadowy and unreal. I heard with impatience, amounting to anger, the saying of Pascal that 'the heart has reasons which reason does not understand'; it seemed simply an evasion to be told that God was most truly to be found in the deepest experiences of life. I have come to see, first, that I shall get no better evidence, and second, that that which I have is good. Intellectual considerations are in no degree whatever to be undervalued and in their place they are invaluable— but, at best, they only point the way, and in themselves they never take us to the end. In thus trusting ourselves to that which is best in us we shall not, as I have said before, find a solution of many of the problems which we so much want to solve, but as we set our faces in the way of following Christ, who has shown to men the mind and love of God as they had never known them before, life takes on a new quality. This we cannot describe to one who insists on professing that he knows nothing of it, any more than we could describe colours to one who has never seen them; but as we follow His voice in the dark, if for the time we cannot see Him in the light, His words come true, not as a piece of poetic rhetoric, but as an experience of our own, "He that followeth Me shall not walk in the darkness, but shall have the light of life."— *A. Neave Brayshaw, 1911.*

A NUMBER of things began to make me doubt whether I still wanted to be a professional minister, the calling toward which I had worked all my life. My devotion to Gandhi made me question the exclusive claims of Christianity. My concern for racial justice and my labor movement experience made me ask whether I might not serve my God better by working for the growth of community outside the church, which often seemed to drag its feet. And I was weighing the practical considerations of dovetailing a professional career in the ministry with my husband's career as a college professor. I had married George, a doctoral candidate in political science, at the end of my first year in Seminary. The men in the Seminary outnumbered the women by more than ten to one (and all those men had to get married to get a job, such being the tradition of the Protestant ministry)....

I considered myself adept at programming worship for others, and I was shaken by my first experience of unprogrammed worship. We began to attend Meeting regularly and both felt its rightness for us. As I turned to the creative process of God within me, it seemed clear that I was being called into the Religious Society of Friends and to a non-professional ministry embracing all my life. It seemed to me a much more creative, less limiting concept of ministry. Our membership in the Religious Society of Friends has underlain all our years together.— *Elizabeth Watson, 1977.*

I WAS OFTEN under great temptations; and I fasted much, and walked abroad in solitary places many days, and often took my Bible and went and sat in hollow trees and lonesome places till night came on; and frequently in the night walked mournfully about by myself, for I was a man of sorrows in the times of the first workings of the Lord in me.

*   *   *

My desires after the Lord grew stronger, and zeal in the pure knowledge of God and of Christ alone, without the help of any man, book, or writing. For though I read the Scriptures that spoke of Christ and of God, yet I knew him not but by revelation, as he who hath the key did open, and as the Father of life drew men to his Son by his spirit. And then the Lord did gently lead me along, and did let me see his love, which was endless and eternal, and surpasseth all the knowledge that men have in the natural state, or can get by history or books; and that love let me see myself as I was without him. And I was afraid of all company for I saw them perfectly where they were, through the love of God which let me see myself. I had not fellowship with any people, priests, or professors, nor any sort of separated people, but with Christ, who hath the key, and opened the door of light and life unto me. And I was afraid of all carnal talk and talkers, for I could see nothing but corruptions, and the life lay under the burden of corruptions. And when I myself was in the deep, under all shut up and had not hope nor faith..... Thus, in the deepest miseries, and in greatest sorrows and temptations, that many times beset me, the Lord in his mercy did keep me.— *George Fox, 1647.*

ELIZABETH COMSTOCK (1815-1891), the greatest part of whose Journal is concerned with the visiting of soldiers during the Civil War and work with the freedmen afterwards, recalls a few incidents connected with escaping slaves. At one time a Friend who was working with his pitchfork in the cattle yard, quickly hid an exhausted slave in a pile of straw just as his pursuers came to the gate.. They demanded to know what had become of their "nigger." A sudden deafness seemed to have seized the farmer. They came closer, shouting louder. The farmer looked up and, with his hand behind his ear, asked: "Lost a cow, did you say?" "No, a nigger!" "Did she have a white spot on her forehead, Alderney breed?" "No, you old fool!" they shouted and tried to make him understand that they intended to search his house and buildings for their lost property. At length the farmer replied that he did not think an honest man needed to be afraid of having his house searched, and when the pursuers finally left, having looked into every nook and cranny, including the clock case, the Friend remarked, "Pity you didn't take the word of an honest man. I told you he wasn't there." Near the gate they saw one of the farmer's sons and asked if he had seen the Negro. The youth, like most Friends' children in those parts, was not disposed to help a slave catcher and replied that he had seen such a man going up a hill about a mile away an hour ago. This sent the pursuit on its way. The fugitive stayed quietly with the Friends for several weeks before going on to Canada by the underground railway.— *Howard H. Brinton, 1972.*

IN THE united stillness of a truly "gathered meeting," says Caroline Stephen, "there is a power known only by experience." Every devout Quaker is familiar with the experience: Suddenly— and often the feeling takes us by surprise— one is not worshipping alone: the corporate body of assembled Friends becomes one unit; one has a sense of personal identity temporarily transcended; one feels nameless and yet one's real self emerges to blend completely with the immediate group, with timelessness and with God. It is a stirring feeling, the awareness of which sometimes makes us quake....

Are we in some way "programmed" to seek harmony, regularity, and rhythm in such group activities? Does the attainment of such a goal make us feel utterly fulfilled? Is there power in our midst when we worship together and the meeting is truly "gathered"? Does the harmony within, brought about by our discipline of waiting, spread around us to the point where the sum of our separate selves becomes greater than the whole?

The conventional images of saintly people in many religions depict them with auras— halos— around their heads. Is this the light that we ordinarily "hide under a bushel" and that we let come out when Friends around us in meeting bring their own lights out?...

And then there is the power of a gathered meeting. In [the] Penrose painting entitled *They Shall Not Be Afraid*, Friends of the late 17th century, worshiping in the meetinghouse of their new home in America, display no fear when the the threatening Indians erupt into their gathering.— *Fortunato Castillo, 1981.*

EXCEPTING Massachusetts and Connecticut, North America offered an asylum for the persecuted of every class, and for the people of every clime: we cannot therefore wonder that its unsectarian soil became the resort not only of English, but Irish and Scotch, and also emigrants from almost every nation in Europe.

In studying the history of the Society of Friends, the observant reader cannot, we think, fail to notice, that it was only in countries where darkness and popery had been much dispelled, that its spiritual and enlightened views found steady acceptance. Although our early Friends were engaged in Gospel labors in several of the Roman Catholic countries of Europe, we do not find that they were successful in the establishment of a single meeting.

The Reformation, therefore, was instrumental in preparing the way for the introduction of Quakerism into Christendom. But enfranchised as most of the settlers of the western world were, from the shackles of popery, and to a large extent from prelacy also, and consisting as they did of considerable numbers of pious individuals, who had been driven from their respective countries for the cause of religion, the colonies of America presented a sphere peculiarly adapted for the reception of those high and enlightened views of Christianity which the Society of Friends were called to uphold and to advocate among their fellow-men.—
James Bowden, London, 1850.

AND HERE we are confronted with the real "peculiarity" of Quakerism—its relation to mysticism....Mysticism in this sense is a well-know phenomenon, of which a multitude of examples may be found in all religions. It is, indeed, rather a personal peculiarity than a form of belief....Mysticism, as we know it, is essentially individual. It refuses to be formulated or summed up. In one sense it is common to all religious persuasions; in another, it equally eludes them all. Mystics, as I understand the matter, are those whose minds, to their own consciousness, are lighted from within; who feel themselves, that is, to be in immediate inward communication with the central Fountain of light and life. They have naturally a vivid sense both of the distinction and of the harmony between the inward and the outward—a sense so vivid that *it is impossible for them to believe it to be unshared by others.* A true mystic believes that all men have, as he himself is conscious of having, an inward life, into which, as into a secret chamber, he can retreat at will.

Let me not be understood to mean that the process of "keeping the mind" (in Quaker phrase) "retired to the Lord" is an easy one. On the contrary it may need strenuous effort. But the effort can be made at will, and even the mere effort thus to retire from the surface to the depths of life is sure to bring help and strengthening—is in itself a strengthening, steadying process. It is in degree only that the mystic's gift is exceptional. They may have the sight of an eagle, but they see by the same light as the bat.— *Caroline Stephen, 1890.*

MY MOTHER was a popular reconciler whenever there was trouble in the family or among relatives and acquaintances. Her technique, as far as I can judge after forty years, was very simple but notably effective. She would listen carefully to the complaints of one party, and having listened long enough to assure the much aggrieved speaker of her fullest sympathy, she would say kindly, but much worried, "I see all this very well, but it is really you who are at fault." And she would explain why this was the case. Then she would apply exactly the same treatment to the opposite party.

Usually it worked, maybe because after her explanations each side began wondering why this sympathetic listener had not accepted uncritically the self-righteous version of one's own point of view. He would ask himself, perhaps for the first time, whether nothing could be said for the other side. In this way his emotional state of mind would slowly be infused with greater reasonableness, and this gave the reconciler a chance of bringing about the conditions for the moral and psychological give and take in which the settlement of a personal quarrel consists. In this process it makes little difference whether material interests are involved or not. I do not think that my mother was ever much concerned with the objective rights and wrongs of a case, possibly because she was instinctively aware of the much deeper truth which is achieved by actual reconciliation. Nor was she a very religious person, in the ordinary sense of the word.— *Richard K. Ullmann, 1963.*

MANY a Christian peacemaker, frustrated in the use of personal approaches, has turned to these techniques without realizing that by using the tactics of pressure groups— lobbying and mass demonstrations— he has given up the assumption that peacemaking, unlike peace propaganda, is disinterested personal service. He no longer tries to meet the psychological and moral conditions of quarreling groups, but to push his own peace policies by hook and (sometimes) by crook. The reconciler's interest should be directed not toward policies but towards people. This is an important part of what we call "disinterestedness." If he loses it, he loses his spiritual power— the one power that can do without majorities, weapons, and other forms of material strength— because he has made his escape into mere politics where matter and matters count more than the spirit....

As a reconciler he works under a twofold discipline: to understand, and to be understood. Normally Friends stress only the need of understanding the other side. This seems all-important to them because most conflict situations arise from misunderstandings and an unwillingness to see the other side at all....

To quote [American Quaker] Paul Lacey and his friends: "Well-meaning people often look so hard for the obvious areas of agreement that they ignore the constructive uses of frank disagreement.... Time and again we found that our real unity grew not from agreement, but from the ability to see the other's point of view while maintaining our own with integrity— not from reducing the areas of conflict, but from distinguishing sharply the issues truly separating us."— *Richard K. Ullmann, 1963.*

WE TOOK the meetings in our way through Virginia; were in some degree baptized into a feeling sense of the conditions of the people, and our exercise in general was more painful in these old settlements than it had been amongst the back inhabitants; yet through the goodness of our Heavenly Father the well of living waters was at times opened to our encouragement, and the refreshments of the sincere-hearted....

Two things were remarkable to me in this journey: first, in regard to my entertainment. When I ate, drank, and lodged free-cost with people who lived in ease on the hard labor of their slaves I felt uneasy: and as my mind was inward to the Lord, I found this uneasiness return upon me, at times, through the whole visit. Where the masters bore a good share of the burden, and lived frugally, so that their servants were well provided for, and their labor moderate, I felt more easy; but where they lived in a costly way, and laid heavy burdens on their slaves, my exercise was often great, and I frequently had conversation with them in private concerning it. Secondly, this trade of importing slaves from their native country being much encouraged amongst them, and the white people and their children so generally living without much labor, was frequently the subject of my serious thoughts. I saw in these southern provinces so many vices and corruptions, increased by this trade and this way of life, that it appeared to me as a dark gloominess hanging over the land; and though now many willingly run into it, yet in future the consequence will be grievous to posterity. I express it as it hath appeared to me, not once, nor twice, but as a matter fixed on my mind.— *John Woolman, 1743.*

A FRIENDS' meeting for worship finds no room for debate or for answering (still less for contradicting) one another; if this is desirable, it will be left for another occasion. And if anything should seem to be spoken amiss, the spiritually minded worshipper will have the wit to get at the heart of the message, overlooking crudity and lack of skill in its presentation, and so far from giving way to irritation at what seems unprofitable, he will be deeply concerned for his own share in creating the right spiritual atmosphere in which the harm fades out and the good grows. Many a meeting has known this power, transforming what might have been hurtful into a means of grace.... The minister who, it is to be assumed, has wished to speak for the help of the congregation and not for the advertisement of himself, will be willing at least *to consider* the suggestions of those whose concern for the meeting's welfare is as deep as his own. The hard assertiveness which is determined to have its own word, resenting kindly counsel, even if such seems to be mistaken, is wholly out of place in a Friend's meeting, being alien to the spirit in which alone right ministry can be exercised. The true message, however plain spoken it may be, will win its way, not by truculence and discourtesy but by persuasiveness and love.— *A Neave Brayshaw, 1921.*

THE SPINNING WHEEL, such an important part of Gandhi's life,...[was] interpreted solely as an economic one...but Gandhi also regarded the art of spinning as a devotional exercise.   For in using the devices...it is necessary to introduce the fibers of cotton at the point where they are twisted into thread in a very consciously even way, otherwise the thread will be coarse and irregular in diameter. There is little opportunity when doing this hand spinning for wanderings and rovings of mind, for day dreaming. It is said that by examining a piece of Indian home-spun, one can assess the degree of spiritual centeredness of the craftsperson who produced it.......

The meditative silence practiced in Quakerism is one of the purest of such devotional techniques, provided that in our meetings we are seeking a shared *internal* silence, as well as a silence of physical externals. It is easy to forget that it is not the idea of the meditative silence practiced in Quakerism that those undertaking it will be engaging in private, mental movies, while merely maintaining an external hush in the physical realm.

In true silence all of these circling thoughts, inner conversations, and imaginings are laid aside....... Isaac Penington encourages us to still "the wanderings and rovings of mind."   Even the thinking of theological thoughts is to be laid aside, for there is a difference between thinking about theological concepts and actually experiencing the Divine Presence.   Inner silence is the quality of bringing ourselves wholly into the present moment, of bringing our spirits to the place where our bodies are, by stopping the circling thoughts which take our minds elsewhere. Inner silence is the quality of being thoroughly present here and now.— *Daniel A. Seeger, 1983.*

I HAD A DESIRE to go to another meeting of the Quakers, and bid my father's man inquire if there was any in the country thereabouts. He thereupon told me he had heard at Isaac Penington's that there was to be a meeting at High Wycombe on Thursday next. Thither therefore I went, though it was seven miles from me, and, that I might be rather thought to go out a-coursing than to a meeting, I let my greyhound run by my horse-side....I saw the people sitting together in an outer room, wherefore I stept in and sat down on the first void seat, the end of a bench just within the door, having my sword by my side and black clothes on, which drew some eyes upon me...and what [was spoken] was very suitable and of good service to me; for it reached home, as if it had been directed to me.

As soon as ever the meeting was ended and the people began to rise, I being next the door, stept out quickly and, hastening to my inn, took horse immediately homewards; and, so far as I remember, my having been gone was not taken notice of by my father.

This latter meeting was like the clinching of a nail, confirming and fastening in my mind those good principles which had sunk into me as the former...The general trouble and confusion of mind which had for some days lain heavy upon me and pressed me down, without a distinct discovery of the particular cause for which it came, began now to wear off; and some glimmerings of light began to break forth in me, which let me see my inward state and condition towards God...I found there were many plants growing in me which were not of the Heavenly Father's planting, and that all these, of whatever sort or kind they were or how specious soever thy might appear, must be plucked up.— *Thomas Ellwood, 1659.*

I FIND a high level of personal integrity among Friends. Perhaps my experiences have been unusual or I have been blind to certain realities. Regardless, I have this opinion. I have also found most Friends to be gentle people. Indeed there is no doubt in my mind but that the initial appeal of Quakerism for me was my perception of the personal characteristics of the Friends I met and came to know. Here, too, I will acknowledge the presence of exception....

I believe the concern for human welfare is the dominant characteristic of contemporary Friends. It is this characteristic which often robs us of our ability to achieve simplicity; prods us into a sense of guilt about our inability to be more responsive to social problems; and makes us so sensitive to the concerns of each individual within the group as to frustrate those who seek immediate and extensive attention to the concerns of those outside the group. It is this concern for human welfare in fact which leads some of us to such a sense of urgency and even desperation as to weaken our fibre as gentle people....

I believe if we are honest we must admit to some real doubt... as individuals, we have a sense of communion with God. Many of us do not have this sense of communion. We seek it, but fail to find it, and in response to this failure we focus primarily on other aspects of our identity as Friends...The difficulty here is that the value system is not divisible...Simplicity frees one of the clutter that interferes with communion with God.... Finally, it is this easy capacity to discriminate which removes much of the complexity of life and enables us to achieve simplicity in the midst of what seems like great confusion.— *Martin Cobin, 1970.*

THERE was I think more than one reason why the peculiar and primitive testimonies of plainness were given to, and upheld by the Society of Friends; and first, because they are congenial to the very nature of Christianity in its purest form, and agree better with its other testimonies.   And secondly, because if conscientiously maintained, they would serve to exhibit this constant acknowledgment to the world, "I am the Lord's!" And thirdly, because it would be an enclosure round about the tender plants of a rising generation; for by observing these peculiarities in language, manners, and appearance, there would not be that inclination to mix familiarly with others; and this has proved to our beloved youth a great preservation from the corruptions and vanities of the world.   In this point of view, the benefit to our Society has been incalculable; for though it is not these peculiarities of plainness that cause us to be fruitful, yet by them as an enclosure, the fruit may be kept from being devoured.   It is the good soil of the garden, well cultivated, that bringeth forth the fruit, but it is the fenced wall of God's providence round about, that keepeth it from being devoured by the creatures without.

And so far is this testimony from being a burden or a hardship...a choice blessing from his hand, and a blessing too, which if we as a people should begin to despise and lightly esteem, God will in his displeasure perhaps remove from us. Yea, and if the vine which he has planted, when he looked for grapes, should be found bringing forth only wild grapes, he will certainly remove this safe enclosure, and suffer the wild beast to tread it down; and he will also command the clouds that they should rain no rain upon it.— *John Wilbur, 1832.*

AND A GOOD degree of this experience is undoubtedly witnessed by individuals under different denominations; but the Society of Friends from the first, found it needful to adhere to greater purity of manners than other professors had done, in order to be more perfect followers of his example, as well as of his doctrine of the straight and narrow way which leads to life.......

And a small leak, if suffered to continue, will sink a ship, however good and richly laden, and as a small breach in the enclosure of the vineyard, however fruitful, will let in the devourer, so I believe if this testimony, (however small any may deem it) should be abandoned, it would greatly endanger our safety. Yea, and if the boundaries of demarcation between this people and other, as exhibited in our peculiar testimonies, were removed, or suffered to go down through the fear of controversy or of singularity; then should we be prepared to go aback, and mingle again with others, and that definite and honorable characteristic by which we have been known and distinguished from all others would be seen and known no more. Hence I consider it highly important to be ourselves faithful, and to train up, and instruct our families in these Christian testimonies, and other doctrines of Christ, by a constant exhibition of this good and comely order and example, as well as by clear plain argument, and open and full declaration of the hope within us.— *John Wilbur, 1832.*

RECOGNIZING that "walking in the Light" is sometimes a difficulty, we should see that the point of having a community of faith is that it provides an environment where we can support one another in our endeavors to be faithful. The commitment to mutual discipline as well as encouragement is based on the recognition that the Light is often more clearly discerned by many than by one. Thus keeping each other in the Light may require constructive, mutual criticism as well as self-criticism—just as it requires mutual support as well as individual initiative. Acceptance of criticism and admission of the need for support require trust and a willingness to be vulnerable, which points back to the importance of basing a Friendly notion of discipline on speaking truth in love.

To create in our meetings communities of faith where mutual trust and healthy interdependency can flourish is not easy. It demands, first of all, that we come to know each other well and really strive to be available to one another. It is not likely that we will come to trust in each other until we truly share in one another's lives. For most of us that would mean altering our priorities regarding our time and energy and how we relate to the meeting community....

For the Quaker vision of faith to flourish, we need to strive to create in our meeting communities an understanding of discipline as just one part of our commitment to love one another and serve the Truth....This discipline must be rooted in mutual respect and humility, encouraging growth in the Spirit and development of gifts for whatever service one is called to.— *Thomas H. Jeavons, 1981.*

HERE WE LEARN that the soul is immortal, and that nothing but immortality can satisfy its desires. This is proved by the experience of others and by our own experience from day to day. Solomon after all his riches, and honour, and labour, and toil, wound up in this, "Vanity of vanities, all is vanity and vexation of spirit." "Fear God, and keep his commandments; for this is the whole duty of man." But how are we to be led into this, and how are we to be instructed in the true fear of God? We never shall do it, but as we gather to the reprover in our own souls. There is nothing but this principle, this Immanuel, God in man, that can ever give us a true knowledge of God. There is no outward declaration, or external evidence, however great— not all the books, doctrines, and eternal evidence ever manifested upon the face of the earth, which can ever give us a knowledge of God, or make a true Christian. To be a true Christian, we must be a child of God. He and she only, who are in Christ, are Christians, and therefore, new creatures: and to be new creatures they must receive a new birth. We cannot see the kingdom of God, till we are born again of God; because nothing can be a son of God, but spirit— nothing can be a son of God, but that which is itself spirit. Therefore it is, that nothing but the soul— the immortal soul of man, can be a recipient for the spirit of God, and it is only that, which can lead us to worship God in spirit and in truth.— *Elias Hicks, Sermon, 1826.*

I NEVER received any religion from my ancestors. I was not a prophet, neither a prophet's son; neither was I trained up in the schools of literature, to make merchandise, more effectually, of the souls of the people. I was trained up to labour, and in the school of deep affliction I learned where peace was to be found. And I am willing to tell my fellow members where it can be found. It is not to be found in systems, it is not to be found in opinions, or principles, or sentiments, but in the operation of the spirit of God, producing principles which lead to a practical belief.

For instance, can any man become honest, except by a principle of honesty within him? Can he become merciful, except he be under the direction of the principle of mercy in himself? Can he love God the Father, and his neighbour as himself, except he be under the government of a principle of love?

And as these fruits grow, religion becomes an individual work, and is the immediate operation of the spirit of Christ upon our spirits, performing those miracles, giving those precepts, and preaching the gospel unto those who are poor in spirit. Thus we become members of that living body of which Christ is the head, and we know him to be all and in all.......

It is in us a teacher; it is known unto all. We must, therefore, come to the conclusion, when we follow the example of Christ by a daily and hourly obedience to the operation of the spirit, that God is not found merely at a great distance and beyond the grave, for he is manifest in our flesh.— *Thomas Wetherald, Sermon, 1826.*

AT TIMES the sense of Presence would well up in me. I seemed to feel the anguish of God at all the suffering in the world. Sometimes I had to turn away because I could not bear it.

The experience confirmed my intellectual awareness of God as a process, rather than an omnipotent deity outside our human struggles, holding life and death power over mortal. *This I know experimentally:* God is not *outside* the universe, but part of it, limited by the same laws of cause and effect, involved in our struggles, working beside us, and unable to save us from the chance disasters that befall us. As I experienced the anguish of God in my own grief, so in time I experienced the compassion of God. God suffers with us. We are not alone. This too, I know experimentally.

*   *   *

I have never regretted my decision to leave my training for the professional ministry to work directly for equal opportunities and civil rights by participating in specific campaigns, and more broadly by involvement in a diverse urban neighborhood at many levels. And the rightness of the decision was confirmed in another way. In joining the Religious Society of Friends, which from the beginning was non-sexist, I lost the chip on my shoulder, the need to battle my way in a predominantly male profession.... I am grateful to be a Friend, grateful for our heritage of valiant Quaker women who were free to use all their remarkable gifts and insights in many a good crusade.— *Elizabeth Watson, 1977.*

TO THE MULTITUDE of committees and good causes that press upon us we must often say no if we are to maintain true simplicity of life. Inner guidance from the Center of our lives will at all times restrain us even from good works that seem urgent.

Simplicity is closely akin to sincerity— a genuineness of life and speech in which there is no place for sham or artificiality. The care given by early Friends to avoid flattering titles and phrases and to aim for rectitude of speech undoubtedly has done much to turn attention to honesty in the spoken and the written word. Care is needed to avoid and discourage the insincerity and the extravagance that are prevalent in the social world. We need also to speak the simple truth, in love, when occasion requires it. Such an attitude does not exclude sincere cordiality and kindness.

A life of simplicity and sincerity may be full of activity but it must be a life centered in God. Of him who leads such a life it can be said, as it was of Brother Lawrence, "He was never hasty or loitering, but did each thing in its season with an even, uninterrupted composure and tranquillity of spirit. 'The time of business', he said, 'does not with me differ from the time of prayer, and in the noise and clatter of my kitchen, while several persons are at the same time calling for different things, I possess God in as great measure as if I were on my knees.'"— *Philadelphia Yearly Meeting, 1961.*

"HONESTY is the best policy." This is an old and a very true saying; but I know of no word in our language which has been more flattered, more cajoled, and more abused than this term. For all seem ready and willing to acknowledge the fact, but where is there a man or a woman willing to comply with its contents, and practically and operatively become truly honest men and women ?...We cannot profit by any thing without honesty. We hear a great many excellent and plain truths declared to us, but it is only the honest and upright in heart that will profit by them....and were we all concerned to be honest and truly upright, it would not only tend to bring about a conversion and reformation in every individual, but it would bring us into unity together, and, as it were compel us to love one another. There is nothing like justice to induce love between man and man. It would so regulate our whole lives, and it would so regulate all our conduct, that we never could, through any medium whatever, receive any thing from a fellow creature without an equal reward for it. It would keep our minds in a continual state of watchfulness. Its tendency would be to lead us to love our neighbours as ourselves, and therefore we could not take a bribe, we never could take anything as a reward for any labour or work which we do, that should exceed its true value. Here, not only would all our moral conduct be regulated toward one another, but it would produce a confidence in one another—a confidence that could not be shaken; we should depend on one another as on ourselves. It would put an end to all hirelings. Whether in matters of a moral nature, or of a religious character, none could receive any pay for that which was not worth what was received.—*Elias Hicks, Sermon, 1826.*

BUSINESS, in its proper sphere, is useful and beneficial, as well as absolutely necessary; but the abuse of it, or an excess in it, is pernicious in many points of view. I cannot approve, in very many respects, of the intense degree of application and attention which seems often to be required of those that are in business.

There is one danger to which the man of business is particularly exposed, and the more alarming, because it is concealed,—I mean the danger of gaining a worldly spirit, and of losing that tenderness of conscience, that love of religion, which is the ground of all virtuous conduct. The person who is engaged in worldly affairs, whether the sphere of his engagement be large or small, should be most anxiously attentive to his eternal interests, that they also may be kept in a flourishing, profitable condition: if this be not the case, the saying of W. Penn is true in regard to such a one— "He that loses by getting, had better lose than gain." He should also be very jealous of his scanty leisure, that he may not omit to employ some of it in his daily duties to his Maker, and to the constant cultivation of that holy frame of mind, which it is the slow though sure tendency of the spirit of the world silently to counteract. For, I own, I tremble at the very idea of any man's mainly pursuing his perishable interests, when perhaps in one short moment he is gone.— *John Barclay, 1815.*

I BELIEVE that the difficulty of distinguishing between the will, or the voice, or the light of God, and the wills and voices and lights of a lower kind from which it is to be distinguished, is not only not to be ignored, but that the very first step towards learning the lesson is to recognize that it is a lesson, and a hard one—nay, a lifelong discipline but just as the child trusts instinctively, absolutely, helplessly, before it has even begun to attempt to understand its parents, so, surely, we may and must trust God first and unreservedly, before we begin slowly and feebly, yet perseveringly, to acquaint ourselves with Him. And as the trust of the full-grown son or daughter is a nobler thing than the trust of the infant, so the experience of wisdom and prudence has doubtless a revelation of its own—a precious addition to that essential revelation which is made in the first place to babes, and to the wise only in so far as they too have childlike hearts. To have our senses exercised to discern between truth and falsehood, light and darkness, order and disorder, the will of God and the will of the flesh, is, I believe, the end and object of our training in this world. There is no royal road to it. Yet can we honestly say that it is impossible?

Therefore I believe that, before we can hope to enter into that intimate and blessed communion with God which transfigures all life, two great conditions must be fulfilled. We must have settled it in our hearts that everything, from the least to the greatest, is to be taken as His language—language which it is our main business here to learn to interpret—and we must be willing to face all pain as His discipline.— *Caroline Stephen, 1890.*

FROM TIME TO TIME efforts have been made to explain away George Fox's vision. Modern seekers, Quakers not excepted, sometimes have a mistrust of anything which suggests the supernatural. If we ourselves are not accustomed to seeing visions, we are tempted to reduce all our fellow-seekers to the same down-to-earth common denominator. But to understand something of George Fox's vision, even if one is not privileged to share it, one need only climb Pendle Hill on a clear day— best of all on a day in early spring, when the snows still linger on the distant heights and the wind blows over them with an exhilarating tang which sets the pulses racing. Scrambling up by the direct route, clutching the tough stems of the dense scrub of whinberry bushes as one's feet slip on the frozen slopes, one may well climb with "much ado" and spare some sympathy in passing for George Fox if he took that route in early summer wearing leather breeches. The way is too steep, too grim, for poetic musings. That is why the breath-taking view from the summit comes with such a sublime shock. Suddenly, almost without warning, the struggle is over, the world drops away, and the heavens declare the glory of God....The distant sea sparkles round the Lancashire coast...

Surely to many there have come such moments in life, when a new sense of direction has suddenly been given. Some may receive their marching orders in a time of worship with their fellow men; some in solitary communion with nature...others in the stirring example of a noble human life. That George Fox received his in a vision from the summit of Pendle Hill, there can be no doubt.— *Elfrida Vipont Foulds, 1953.*

THERE CAN be few Friends' meetings in the "1652 country" which do not number amongst their founders men and women who literally took their lives in their hands every time they attended a meeting for worship. In fields and barns and farmhouse kitchens they gathered, and from fields and barns and farmhouse kitchens they were taken, without warning and without pity, to be imprisoned for weeks and months without trial. There is still in existence a petition signed by a number of such Friends, some of whom had been imprisoned for fourteen weeks, and some longer, asking the justices for their right as Englishmen to be tried. They explained that they were "husbandmen and tradesmen upon whose Diligence and Daily labor the subsistence of our families [depends], the neglect whereof may...impoverish them and us and so bring an Unnecessary burden upon others...We Desire nothing from you but that we may live quietly and peaceably in our own houses, eat our own bread and follow our own Callings in the fear of God...and to meet together to serve and worship our God..." "But", they added, "if you will not Grant these things unto us, then shall we lie down in the peace of our God and patiently suffer under you."

That was the spirit which finally broke down the persecution. The men and women who left their footprints on the sands of Time, George Fox, Margaret Fell, Francis Howgill...and the rest, could not have done it alone. Behind them stood the ones who have left no memorial...men and women who snatched a scanty living from little hill farms, who kept small village shops, who tended sheep and who were prepared to face the loss of all....for a liberty which they themselves might never live to enjoy.— *Elfrida Vipont Foulds, 1953.*

A WAR, with all its cruel and destructive effects, having raged for several years between the British Colonies in North America and the mother country, Friends, as well as others, were exposed to many severe trials and sufferings; yet, in the colony of New York, Friends, who stood faithful to their principles, and did not meddle in the controversy, had, after a short period at first, considerable favor allowed them. The yearly meeting was held steadily, during the war, on Long Island, where the king's party had the rule; yet Friends from the Main, where the American army ruled, had free passage through both armies to attend it, and any other meetings they were desirous of attending, except in a few instances. This was a favor which the parties would not grant to their best friends, who were of a war-like disposition; which shows what great advantages would bedound to mankind, were they all of this pacific spirit. I passed myself through the lines of both armies six times during the war without molestation, both parties generally receiving me with openness and civility; and although I had to pass over a tract of country, between the two armies, sometimes more than thirty miles in extent, and which was much frequented by robbers, a set, in general, of cruel unprincipled banditti, issuing out from both parties, yet, excepting once, I met with no interruption even from them. But although Friends in general experienced many favors and deliverances, yet those scenes of war and confusion occasioned many trials and provings in various ways to the faithful.— *Elias Hicks, 1779.*

TO BEGIN THE WORSHIP, it is important that one arrive in time to join with others in settling into the silence. Many find it helpful to close their eyes as a way of avoiding distractions and of providing a proper atmosphere for inner activity. As one settles down, one usually experiences the manner in which the mind moves swiftly over a number of thoughts, memories, and intentions, all demanding attention. Some of these may at that time be of such importance that they should be given consideration. However, most such ideas after receiving courteous attention should be dismissed to make way for the more important work of the hour. The aim at the beginning is to "collect oneself", centering the self about God and our relation to the Divine.

As one moves into the silence, one recognizes that the Spirit of God is in the midst of the meeting. One may then wish to praise God— for God's greatness, God's love and concern for each person, God's wisdom and creativity in the past and in the present— for each of these and other qualities. They may be pondered and given silent expression...

The deepest point of worship is that of "wordless prayer," which might be thought of as spiritual openness...One enters into a state in which the spirit is simply waiting and watching, relaxed yet very alert and expectant. In the deep silence the worshiper may become aware in a marked way of the presence of the Inward Christ...— *Calvin Keene, 1981.*

Much of the work of the meeting lies in what in former times has been designated as meditation and contemplation...Millions of persons before us have sought for truth along the paths of religion. The worshiper does not start as though these spiritual guides do not exist. It is important that one discover and profit by what may be learned from these through meditating upon the great revelations and insights available in the writings of distant and recent past, particularly in the Bible, whose truths are deeper ones than those of science and philosophy. Other sources of spiritual insight may be called upon, but, as understood by Christianity and Quakerism, the New Testament is basic for us. Used as starting points for meditation, these Scriptures have the power to awaken and deepen insight and faith.

Finally, Friends meeting as group worship exists for and is dependent upon each person who attends. It is a fragile form of worship containing the potentiality of great strength and of weakness just because it depends so thoroughly upon each individual. Since the structure, trained leadership, and ritual of other Christian bodies is lacking, it follows that when attenders fail to carry the responsibility of worship in its most basic form spirit will be largely absent, distractions will be sensed, and spoken messages, if there are any, will tend to be shallow and superficial. It is in this regard that it is true that no form of religious expression makes so great a demand upon the worshiper as does the Friends meeting for worship...However, words are not essential for those worshiping in silence to experience the Presence in the midst and to be strengthened and uplifted to serve the Lord.— *Calvin Keene, 1981.*

SECOND, THIRD AND FOURTH DAYS...The evenings were partly spent in reading the scriptures, in which I greatly delight.   How excellent are those records! Although old, yet they seem ever new. The prophecy of Micah was a part of my present reading; what a dignified sense and clear view he had of the gospel state and worship; and how exceedingly it lessened the service and worship of the law in his view, in the clear sense given him of its full and complete abolishment, with all its shadowy rituals; when he was led to set forth its insufficiency, in this exalted language:

"Wherewith shall I come before the Lord, and bow myself before the high God? Shall I come before him with burnt offerings, with calves of a year old? Will the Lord be pleased with thousands of rams, or with ten thousands of rivers of oil? Shall I give my first-born for my transgression, the fruit of my body for the sin of my soul?"

No, none of these were sufficient to give access to the divine presence....

"He hath showed thee, O man, what is good; and what doth the Lord require of thee," not only by an outward, but by his inward, divine law, "but to do justly, and to love mercy, and to walk humbly with thy God."

This is the sum and substance of all true religion and worship, and needs not the continuance of any outward elementary washings or eatings or drinkings; but opens to the necessity of our drinking at that spiritual river, the streams whereof make glad the whole heritage of God.   For those that drink thereof will never thirst again, at least for the water of any other stream.— *Elias Hicks, 1814.*

[AN] INTERESTING EVENT was the liberation of ministers for religious service "in other parts." If the minister were a woman Friend, as often happened in our meeting, she came in with "a companion." They walked up the aisle and sat down with bowed heads. Slowly the bonnet strings were untied, the bonnet handed to the companion, and the ministering woman rose to say that for a long time the Lord had been calling her to a service in a distant Yearly Meeting; that she had put it off, not feeling that she could undertake so important a work, but that her mind could not get any peace; and now she had come to ask Friends to release her for this service. One after another the Friends would "concur in this concern," and the blessing of the Lord would be invoked upon the messenger who was going forth.

Some of these occasions were of a heavenly sort, and the voices of strong men choked in tears as a beloved brother or sister was equipped and set free. From this little meeting heralds went out to almost every part of the world, and the act of liberation was something never to be forgotten, and only to be surpassed by the deep rejoicing which stirred the same company when the journey was over "the minutes were returned."

*   *   *

I felt a certain awe because they always came with "a concern," which means that they had left their homes and had undertaken the long journey because they had received an unmistakable and irresistible call to go out and preach what was given them. This was no ordinary visit. Here was a man under our roof who had come because God sent him. I supposed that he had something inside which had told him to go and where to go. — *Rufus Jones, 1926.*

THE RETURN of spring does indeed afford much food for the contemplative mind, both of youth and age, though the thoughts of those very differently circumstanced classes may take an almost opposite direction. The former, exhilarated by the language of animal spirit and the universal smile of nature, look forward with sanguine, often too sanguine, expectations to the future; whilst those on whom these prospects have not only been opened but closed, and who have nearly seen the end of earthly perfection, are apt to look behind them.

Thus to me, and such as me, it is not an unpleasing though somewhat pensive employment, to number the lovely springs that have passed over our heads, and to turn over the chequered page of our own history, and that of the times in which we have lived, as I can readily do for more than half a century.

In tracing these records, although I find some blots, some blunders, and here and there a very zigzag and awkward line, yet I really have no desire to try the ground over again, even were I to begin with the advantages which the first experiment might be supposed to afford. For I find former experience, though of some value, is insufficient for preservation; it cannot supercede watchfulness, nor does it preclude warfare.— *Jonathan Hutchinson, 1818.*

"He causeth the grass to grow for the cattle, and herb for the service of man: that he may bring forth food out of the earth."— Psalm 104:14.

OUR POTENTIAL influence upon the shaping of history often seems so inconsequential as to leave us depressed. We have not given up, obviously, but we have moments of great frustration which at times drive us to actions which we would otherwise find uncomfortable. At such moments we are in a very real sense mentally ill. In such a condition there is a great need for us to be gentle, sympathetic, and forgiving with one another—just as we are with anyone caught in the grip of a painful disease.

Beyond gentleness, sympathy, and forgiveness, however, I believe there is also medicine available for those who can live in the manner of Friends. The medicinal benefits are derived from the realization that the struggle to influence history must have a justification in terms of the value system of those involved in the struggle. As soon as we realize this, we shift our focus from the military and political arena of history to the social and cultural arena, and we realize the significance which must be attached to the quality of our personal lives.

It is possible that we may sense greater progress and a greater capacity to influence events in the social and cultural arena, given the broad perspective of history over long periods of time. Even if this is not the case, however, there is an important consequence to the recognition of *why* we struggle: the awareness that we must not lose what we are struggling for in the process of struggle...we will not knowingly seek to obtain something by the use of methods which destroy what we are seeking.— *Martin Cobin, 1970.*

AS WE TRAVELLED we came near a very great hill, called Pendle Hill, and I was moved of the Lord to go up to the top of it; which I did with difficulty, it was so very steep and high. When I was come to the top, I saw the sea bordering upon Lancashire. From the top of this hill the Lord let me see in what places he had a great people to be gathered. As I went down, I found a spring of water in the side of the hill, with which I refreshed myself, having eaten or drunk but little for several days before...

The next First-day I came to Firbank chapel in Westmoreland, where Francis Howgill and John Audland had been preaching in the morning...While others were gone to dinner, I went to a brook, got a little water, and then came and sat down on the top of a rock hard by the chapel. In the afternoon the people gathered about me, with several of their preachers. It was judged there were above a thousand people; to whom I declared God's everlasting truth and Word of life freely and largely for about the space of three hours...

Now there were many old people who went into the chapel and looked out at the windows, thinking it a strange thing to see a man preach on a hill, and not in their church, as they called it; whereupon I was moved to open to the people that the steeple-house, and the ground whereon it stood were no more holy than that mountain; and that those temples, which they called the dreadful houses of God were not set up by the command of God and of Christ; nor their priests called, as Aaron's priesthood was; nor their tithes appointed by God, as those amongst the Jews were; but that Christ was come, who ended both the temple and its worship, and the priests and their tithes.— *George Fox, 1652.*

I COME IMMEDIATELY to the objections to this method of praying that are raised by our opponents. They say that if it is necessary to have such individual influences of the Spirit for outward acts of worship, they should be required before undertaking inward acts like waiting for, wanting, or loving God. But this is absurd. While the day of a man's visitation last there is never a time that God is not near him, and his Spirit is not wrestling with him to turn inward. If he will merely stand still, and forego his evil thoughts, the Lord will be near to help him. But outward acts of prayer require a greater influence and a more special motion of the Spirit, as has already been proved.

They say that it could also be claimed that one should only perform such moral duties as obeying parents or treating neighbors properly when moved by the Spirit. The answer is that there is a great difference between the general duties of man to man and the specific individual acts of worship toward God. One is spiritual and God has commanded it to be performed by his Spirit. The other is based on a mere natural principle of Self-love and must be done for that reason. Even beasts have natural affections for each other. This does not mean that these acts are unacceptable to God or without value for the soul, if they are done in the fear of God and with his blessing. In fact, if his children do everything under such circumstances, they will be accepted and blessed in whatever they do. — *Robert Barclay (1648-1690).*

THE PROBLEM we face today needs very little time for its statement. Our lives in a modern city grow too complex and overcrowded. Even the necessary obligations which we feel we must meet grow overnight, like Jack's beanstalk, and before we know it we are bowed down with burdens, crushed under committees, strained, breathless, and hurried, panting through a never-ending program of appointments. We are too busy to be good wives to our husbands, good homemakers, good companions of our children, good friends to our friends, and with no time at all to be friends to the friendless. But if we withdraw from public engagements and interests, in order to spend quiet hours with the family, the guilty calls of citizenship whisper disquieting claims in our ears. Our children's schools should receive our interest, the civic problems of our community need our attention, the wider issues of the nation and of the world are heavy upon us. Our professional status, our social obligations, our membership in this or that very important organization, put claims upon us. And in frantic fidelity we try to meet at least the necessary minimum of calls upon us. But we're weary and breathless. And we know and regret that our life is slipping away, with our having tasted so little of the peace and joy and serenity we are persuaded it should yield to a soul of wide caliber. The times for the deeps of the silences of the heart seem so few. And in guilty regret we must postpone till next week that deeper life of unshaken composure in the holy Presence, where we sincerely know our true home is, for *this* week is much too full.— *Thomas R. Kelly, 1941.*

THE PRACTICE and use of the plain language is consonant with the rules of grammar and the language of holy men of old; the Scriptures bear testimony; yet I was desirous to prove all things, to bring them to the standard of truth in my heart, and, if they stood the measure of that, to cleave to them. I began to use this language sometimes, and at other times not, when in my infancy; my near kinsfolk, I heard, said I was beside myself, therefore it was a cross to use it in their presence; but denying the cross brought sorrow and weakness along with it, and a fear, that if I went down the steps of Jacob's ladder, I should find it more difficult to recover the ground I had lost, than even to ascend to another step.

* * *

The change in my dress was a great cross, as I was always given to fashionable dresses, and at this time had sundry suits of apparel of this sort. I felt a solemn covering to come over my spirit early one morning, which drew me into deep silence and attention, when I felt it required of me to conform to the simple appearance of Christ's followers: His garment was all of a piece, so ought mine to be, of a piece with my speech, my life, and my conversation. This felt to be a severe stroke: no shelter was not left me, but I must appear as a fool to the world; my speech and then my garments would betray me, that I had been with Christ, and professed myself to be one of His disciples.— *John Conron, Ireland, 1772.*

SOMETIMES we think we can manage adequately without help on the so-called small things. We decide to leave only the big things to God. The difficulty with this is that we are not able to judge which things are "small" and which are "big."We are not as wise as God is, and one cannot compromise with God by using degrees of faith.

Nor does complete faith mean we can be irresponsible. We cannot sit idly by and expect God to do the work of the world without us. On the contrary, if one has faith in God's ability to guide us, communicate with us, and give us the imagination and energy to accomplish what we think is God's will, we can accomplish wonders.

It takes courage to trust in God. From long habit, we believe in our thoughts, our muscles, our energy. It takes a long time, sometimes, to understand that without God we would not have those things. In fact, we would not have life at all.

Miraculously, God can still work through our blocked minds, deficient vision, and dulled spiritual hearing. Once in a while, when we are experiencing a bit of humility and feeling less protective of our egos, wonderful things can happen. It is then that God lets us know the peaces of a worry-free moment. It is then that insoluble problems seem to work themselves out, without our attention. We must hold fast to the memory of these experiences of faith because they hold the promise of more faith and encourage us to surrender to God's Wisdom.— *Virginia W. Apsey, 1987.*

ALL THE EARLY FRIENDS were convinced not birthright members. They found their way to Quakerism by their own seeking. They were seekers become finders. They were convinced inwardly, not converted by propaganda. The Quaker Publishers of Truth, appealing to something already latent in them, whether a feeling of frustration and previous failure, or hunger for something sensed but not yet attained, invited them to share the discovery and the fellowship of the "despised people of God called Quakers." The group had its attractions— mutual love, radiant joy, and a companionship in seeking and finding. Even its fellowship of suffering under the prevailing conditions of public dislike and legal disability undoubtedly had its attraction. Yet attachment to the rather loose body was an act of personal commitment. Adherence was not a formal matter: it was the recognition by oneself and by others of an accomplished fact, namely the congeniality of the Quaker message to the inner experience and conviction. It was the outward sign or evidence of something within.

Ever since its earliest days Quakerism has been something appreciated by the adherent rather than deliberately advertised. For that reason it has not depended on definition and formulation....They are not blueprints of a course of development to be recommended. They are analysis of the deposits of experience. The Quaker mission has been to uncover potential Quakers. Both in the beginning and often in days since, it has seemed that accessions were already, in effect, Friends before they knew it. The function of the Friend to the non-Friend was to help discover what was already there, not to change or persuade but to disclose.— *Henry J. Cadbury, 1959.*

ONE OF THE SIGNS of spiritual growth is the simplification of life. This does not mean that daily routines cease, although inconsequential items do become less insistent. What counts is not so much concerned with outer complexities as with the inner conglomeration of desires, thoughts and aspirations that confuse and irritate the mind. When the center of consciousness becomes well established, this welter of mental distraction diminishes. The wayward themes seem to become harmonized; impulses relate themselves to a total pattern. It was very easy to open the self to meditation at the beginning of the day and at the end (if one could stay awake) but there are many hours between, when recollection needs to be sustained. "That which I will not that I do. " It is like learning to drive a car. You have to *remember* to do certain things at first, but gradually your reactions become automatic and you don't need to think about it any more. Just enjoy the scenery. Coinciding with this, when the Inner Light shines brightly nothing can intercept that steady beam. It is not necessary to adjust the vision. It just happens.

But to establish the practice of the presence of God so that it becomes as natural as breathing— that requires a rigorous apprenticeship....I resorted to some trivial and seemingly ridiculous ways of keeping myself reminded. For instance, I fastened a large safety pin to the front of my dress and I carried a button in my pocket that I felt every time I reached in to find a pencil or a handkerchief. These objects were preferable to Moslem prayer beads which, although they serve the same purpose, called for questioning, whereas no one suspected a safety pin or a button.— *Josephine Whitney Duveneck, 1978.*

THERE IS A WAY OF LIFE so hid with Christ in God that in the midst of the day's business one is inwardly lifting brief prayers...of praise, subdued whispers of adoration and of tender love to the Beyond that is within. No one need know about it. I only speak to you because it is a sacred trust, not mine but to be given to others. One can live in a well-nigh continuous state of unworded prayer, directed toward God, directed toward people and enterprises we have on our heart. There is no hurry about it all; it is a life unspeakable and full of glory, an inner world of splendor within which we, unworthy, may live. Some of you know it and live in it; others of you may wistfully long for it; it can be yours...

Our fellowship with God issues in world-concern. We cannot keep the love of God to ourselves. it spills over. It quickens us. It makes us see the world's needs anew. We love people and we grieve to see them blind when they might be seeing...

The deepest need of men is not food and clothing and shelter, important as they are. It is God. We have mistaken the nature of poverty, and thought it was economic poverty. No, it is poverty of soul, deprivation of God's recreating, loving peace...

Do we want to help people because we feel sorry for them, or because we genuinely love them? The world needs something deeper than pity; it needs love. (How trite that sounds, how real it is!) But in our love of people are we to be excitedly hurried, sweeping all men and tasks into our loving concern? No, that is God's function. But He, working within us, portions out His vast concern into bundles, and lays on each of us our portion. These become our tasks.— *Thomas Kelly, 1941.*

SCRUPLING to do writings relative to keeping slaves has been a means of sundry small trials to me, in which I have so evidently felt my own will set aside that I think it good to mention a few of them. Tradesmen and retailers of goods, who depend on their business for a living, are naturally inclined to keep the good-will of their customers; nor is it a pleasant thing for young men to be under any necessity to question the judgment or honesty of elderly men, and more especially of such as have a fair reputation. Deep-rooted customs, though wrong, are not easily altered; but it is the duty of all to be firm in that which they certainly know is right for them. A charitable, benevolent man, well acquainted with a negro, may, I believe, under some circumstances, keep him in his family as a servant, on no other motives than the negro's good; but man, as man, knows not what shall be after him, nor hath he an assurance that his children will attain that perfection in wisdom and goodness necessary rightly to exercise such power; hence it is clear to me, that I ought not to be the scribe where wills are drawn in which some children are made...masters over others during life.

About this time an ancient man of good esteem in the neighborhood came to my house to get his will written. He had young negroes, and I asked him privately how he purposed to dispose of them. He told me: I then said, "I cannot write thy will without breaking my own peace," and respectfully gave my reasons for it. He signified that he had a choice that I should have written it, but as I could not, consistently with my conscience, he did not desire it, and so he got it written by some other person. — *John Woolman (1720-1772).*

THE...POINT I want to make is the importance of developing a dialogue with those who do not share our approach to peace....If we take the "non-pacifist" seriously, then we must accept the validity of his premise that in international politics there are such things as threats, aggression, and problems of security. Once we accept such "realities", even if they are often realities based on perceptions rather than facts, then we might make progress in the process of taming and eventually abolishing war....

Let us be realists and see things as they are. But let us be optimistic realists and not pessimistic realists. The pessimist has not gone beyond the vision of a never ceasing struggle among the world's powers, which periodically try to resolve their quarrels by a trial of armed strength. The optimist believes not only that the instinct of self-preservation is forcing men to look for less destructive means with which to settle their disputes, but that it will lead them to the discovery that cooperation is potentially more effective than competition in furthering human enterprise and that wars are not the inevitable destiny of the human race. — *Wolf Mendl, 1981.*

("The journey continues...I am not shaken in my pacifist convictions in spite of all the exposure to the other side—and it can be very seductive. But I believe that one of the great weaknesses of so many pacifists is that they do not take enough trouble to learn to know and understand those with whom they disagree. In this respect I want to be a bridge-builder, but I also want to nudge the world on a little bit toward the abandonment of war as a method of settling disputes.")

LET THY ACCOUNTS be kept with care,
See that there be no errors there,
Do not defer till thou are ill
The due completion of thy will.

Be strictly honest in thy dealings,
Discouraging all greedy feelings,
And do not speculation choose
Or thou wilt very likely lose.

We trust that thou wilt do thy best
That games of chance may be suppressed,
Nor would the meeting feel annoyed
If Billiard Tables were destroyed.

Seek after friends of modest worth
Rather than great ones of the earth,
And (if allowed to by thy wife)
Aim ever at the simple life.

Let living plain and thinking high
Be the good rule thou livest by,
And, if thou shouldst prepare a feast,
Ask not the greatest but the least.

So, when thy earthly course is run,
And all thy work below is done,
By living thus thou yet may'st end
A "tolerably consistent Friend."

> —*James I'Anson, Journal of Friends Historical*
> *Society, 1956.*

SEVERAL YEARS AGO I had the experience of feeling called to go speak in love and friendship to an old friend who had shunned me. I was very nervous. He might reject my friendship. I might make a fool of myself. But as I walked to his house, I felt that I was carried by something bigger than myself. Afterwards, I felt elated. I had answered the call. Clearly God had been with me, directing and supporting....

One of my greatest fears is of assertively expressing opinions and having them rejected. I don't know exactly why, and I try not to give in to it, but the fear remains. On this occasion...I felt that I was part of something bigger than myself, that my ego was not involved, and I shared my perceptions with ease. It was a great relief to have found a voice for my spiritual calling.

Later, however, the old feelings of fear caught up with me. As I recalled having spoken openly of my beliefs, I went through a period of feeling very vulnerable and shyer than usual. I wanted to go hide and lick my wounds.

I was discouraged, as if my fearful reaction disqualified me as a servant of God, even if I had been faithful. But then I realized that the Spirit calls us and empowers us as we are. Even Jesus was human as well as divine. It's all right to be afraid, to fall back and nurture ourselves for a while, to admit our weaknesses, and then to wait, knowing that in spite of fear, we do get called, and that we can answer the call with courage.

We are all different, and so are our particular fears and vulnerabilities. But I believe that being open to the Spirit has an element of fear for all of us. We don't know what we'll be called to do. It might be hard for us.—
Patience Schenck, 1988.

THERE IS NOTHING comparable to the sweetness of the truth! all the pleasures and possessions of this world are but as a bubble— the blessed truth as it is in Christ Jesus our Lord.

Those who live under the power and guidance of truth will be distinguished from others by a light about them, which will be even as the halo represented round about the head of Jesus.

There are those in all the walks of life, who look to God for his help and counsel. Anything we can do is but as filthy rags. Bear it in mind, my friends. Nothing but the grace of God can cover us in such an hour as this. I have long sought God's counsel and help. Keep humble. Don't do anything to please the pride of the eye. Keep to duty. Don't think it will expose you: it will not. It will bring peace. The blessing of God rest upon you all. Give glory to God in the highest. Oh! that I could proclaim to all the world the sweetness I feel, and the power of the ever-blessed truth, which is more to me now than ten thousand worlds.

My case is a very doubtful one, but life is uncertain at all times. The great object of life is to prepare for death.

Do not give me anything to benumb my faculties. I want my mind clear. I want to lift up my heart to him, who alone can help.— *George Howland, New Bedford, Mass., 1852.*

RELIGION means living and walking with God; experiencing the power and triumph of knowing Him— in short, living in the sense of the imminence of God.

St. Francis came nearer than has any other man to reliving the life of Jesus. His was a personality that radiated gentleness, power, and joy. His nature awoke such reverberations of loyalty that his followers formed orders of men and women which were to emulate his life. Some of these were patterned upon withdrawal from the world, but most of his followers he sent back to their native villages and communities to live with their families lives of service and frugality. These were Franciscans of the Heart—folk whose cells were within themselves and who lived God-given lives in the midst of everyday problems while earning their living and that of their families. We need such a "third" order" today, and there is such an order among us made up of people who have a quiet spot of peace in their own beings. For all such, life has become evaluated for they have at last looked upon the face of the Almighty. For them the world is neither to be hated nor shunned. They neither seek nor abhor fame. A dedicated life can be lived in the midst of poverty or plenty. Environment doesn't really matter.

A man should be so clothed in God that no one can reach Him without touching His coat. It is an area of our will, and not merely an intellectual vivisection of problems, that we are talking about here. We need to know the depth of love and suffering, to keep the cross shining in our interior cell until we know its meaning. We will then have a totalitarian commitment to God. The most fundamental thing anyone can do is to bring a man into the presence of God, and leave him there.— *Thomas Kelly, 1966.*

TO THE CHRISTIAN there is one and only one absolute, the kind of love in which we truly care for individuals. This, of course, includes caring for the victim of the aggressor as for the aggressor. Our responsibility is to the murderer and also to those whom he is about to murder. Though love provides the major premise of our Christian syllogism, it never provides the minor premise. The minor premise is arrived at only by reason and common sense and experience. Love may certainly mean different things in different situations. That is why no man can rightly dogmatize, or universalize his own judgement, on moral issues. There is, in every situation, a real right, but people who live in the finite predicament can never know, absolutely, what that real right is. All that we can do is to try, and to be tender in our judgment of others whose decisions are not identical with our own....

Quakers may not be able to "answer" complex human problems, but their entire heritage prepares them to "respond" to such problems. Examples of such response in Quaker history are already numerous, ranging from the establishment of work camps in areas of tension to the support of interracial housing projects and the schools for young diplomats. There are probably many new developments which Quakers should sponsor, but which are waiting for the emergence of a dedicated imagination. What is needed is not a static position, but new wine in new wineskins. The testimony which the time requires is a "Testimony of responsibility."— *D. Elton Trueblood, 1966.*

THE HUMBLE, meek, merciful, just, pious, and devout souls are everywhere of one religion; and when death has taken off the mask they will know one another, though the divers liveries they wear here makes them strangers. This world is a form; our bodies are forms; and no visible acts of devotion can be without forms. But yet the less form in religion the better, since God is a Spirit; for the more mental our worship, the more adequate to the nature of God; the more silent, the more suitable to the language of a Spirit.— *1693*

Words are for others, not for ourselves, nor for God, who hears not as bodies do, but as spirits should.— *William Penn.*

True godliness [doesn't] turn men out of the world, but enables them to live better in it, and excites their endeavours to mend it: not hide their candle under a bushel, but set it upon a table in a candlestick...

Whoever they are that would come to Christ, and be right Christians, must readily abandon every delight that would steal away the affections of the mind, and exercise it from the divine principle of life, and freely write a bill of divorce for every beloved vanity; and all, under the Sun of Righteousness, is so.— *William Penn, 1682.*

IN THE...MEETING I was concerned to show the dangerous and hurtful tendency of our submitting to be led and governed by the customs and manners of others, without a strict and careful examination thereof; and bringing them to the test of the light in our own conscience. For although the frequency of a thing, and a habitual conformity to that which is not right, often blunts the edge of conviction, and reconciles us to that which is contrary to truth, and derogatory to our true interest; yet the custom of sinning will not lessen its guilt.

For in the awful day of final decision, all our fig-leaf coverings will be torn off, and things will then appear as they really are; and we shall all stand in need of that substantial covering, represented by the coats of skins, which the Lord made for our first parents, and gave them in lieu of their fig-leaves; that is, something of their own inventing, that so that nakedness might no longer be exposed.

My mind was also opened to set forth the design and end of the shadowy or law dispensation; and that by its consistency..., it was a just...representation of the gospel state and dispensation. Many of its precepts were not good, nor consistent with the justice and mercy of the all-beneficent and gracious Jehovah; but were only so, as they stood in relation to the very low, degraded and wicked state of mankind at that time; and were therefore justly suited to Israel's state, and the states and conditions of the surrounding nations concerned therein, as saith Ezekiel: "Wherefore I gave them also statutes that were not good, and judgments whereby they should not live."— *Elias Hicks, Journal, 1813.*

IN A MORE PEACEFUL time than ours, Charles Lamb, the eighteenth-century essayist, stumbled upon a partial antidote to his experience of the "assault against silence". He writes: "...when the spirit is sore fretted, even tired to sickness of the janglings and nonsense-noises of the world, what a balm and a solace it to go and seat yourself for a quiet half-hour upon some undisputed corner of a bench, among the gentle Quakers!" This tranquil effect seemed to him to be produced by the fact that, "although frequently the meeting is broken up without a word having been spoken...the mind has been fed. you go away with a sermon not made with hands...you have bathed in silence".

This personal discovery of the healing power of silence by Charles Lamb, who for all his admiration of Quaker worship never became a Friend, was well known to the first Friends. Their sense that it was unnatural to people was largely coloured by the contemporary practices of church services. These were occasions for great verbalizing in lengthy sermons, prayers and character. This is not to say that early Quakers avoided polemics and emotion themselves. There is, however, considerable evidence that, arising from their actual experience of the practice of being still and quiet they found a way to the restoration of their mental and physical resources. This they achieved in the first place at the level of ordinary life, though it must be emphasized that they were quite unable to restrict their interpretation of its meaning to this level.— *George H. Gorman, London, 1973.*

ONCE THE BIG RIP that separates from God is mended, life is different. Things which perhaps were not seen in need of mending before are now seen as needing it, and there is a change both in personal behavior and in what is urged upon others. We see this, for instance, in the development of the "peace testimony." The sense of belonging to a community of revelation led very quickly into the experience of being members in a "Covenant of peace...."

At the particular moment of George Fox's experience the "covenant of peace" expressed itself through an act of withdrawal from the conflict that was tearing England apart, rather than a search for reconciliation. Withdrawal is very important; we cannot mend what we are continuing to rip apart. The mending itself may come later, but withdrawal from further tearing is an important step towards the ultimate mending. Peace is certainly one of the most persistent of the Quaker testimonies. If the Christ within represents an internalization of the teaching and example of Jesus, loving one's enemies is certainly part of it. While loving one's enemies does not necessarily mean liking them or even approving of them, it always means treating them as fellow human beings and not denying their humanity, as war always does. There is nothing in the life of Christ which says one cannot have opponents and even persecutors, but one cannot really have enemies, people whose lives and welfare have a negative value for you.— *Kenneth E. Boulding, 1986.*

I AM AT PRESENT like a ship out to sea without a pilot. I feel my heart and mind so overburdened. I want some one to lean upon. My mind is in so dark a state that I see everything through a black medium. I can comprehend nothing. I doubt upon everything. Without passions of any kind, how different I should be! I would not give them up, but I should like to have them under subjection; but it appears to me (as I feel) impossible to govern them; my mind is not strong enough; as I at times think they do no hurt to others. But am I sure they will hurt no one? I believe, by not governing myself in little things, I may by degrees become a despicable character, and a curse to society; therefore, my doing wrong is of consequence to others, as well as to myself. I feel by experience, much entering into the world hurts me; worldly company, I think, materially injures; it excites a false stimulus, such as a love of pomp, pride, vanity, jealousy, and ambition; it leads to think about dress, and such trifles, and when out of it, we fly to novels and scandal, or something of that kind, for entertainment. I have of late been given up a good deal to worldly passions; by what I have felt I can easily imagine how soon I should be quite led away.— *Elisabeth Gurney, aged 16 years.*

"He that waverth is like a wave of the sea, driven with the wind and tossed."— James 2:6.

I AM CONVINCED, too, that our worship is affected by the quality of the relationships between the worshippers. Here I think we tend to look the other way sometimes and to pretend that this is not the case. Every family, every pair of friends, every community, must from time to time experience strains when people get across each other, often for very trivial reasons.... Groups experience equally trivial upsets, though sometimes the disturbances are deeper. Offence is taken at something done or said by another, and the offence is just as irritating if one party is entirely oblivious that they have done something offensive. It may be our unconscious assumptions, our deeply seated mannerisms, which get between us most awkwardly. Families, lovers, find their own ways of making up when disputes and pain have been caused, but it may be harder for members of a group, and particularly for a religious one, to find ways of becoming reconciled. Every meeting which I have known well has experienced, at one time or another, various stresses, resulting in greater or lesser pain, from the two Friends who would avoid speaking to each other, whenever possible, to those who become so alienated that they worshipped in another meeting, or refrained from public worship altogether. Why are we sometimes less than honest about these things? I sense that we dislike such 'family' disagreements because they threaten our own self-contentment... Our "Book of Discipline" is not bereft of help here, and perhaps we need to be less hesitant in turning for help to those Friends who are professionally engaged in one sort of "helping" work or another, as teacher or social workers...— *Christopher Holdsworth, London, 1985.*

BUT AT THE FIRST convincement, when Friends could not put off their hats to people nor say "you" to a particular, but "thee" and "thou"; and could not bow nor use the world's salutations, nor fashions, nor custom, many Friends, being tradesmen of several sorts lost their custom at the first; for the people would not trade with them nor trust them, and for a time Friends that were tradesmen could hardly get enough money to buy bread. But afterwards people came to see Friends' honesty and truthfulness and "yea" and "nay" at a word in their dealing, and their lives and conversations did preach and reach to the witness of God in all people, and they knew and saw for conscience sake towards God, they would not cozen and cheat them, and at last that they might send any child and be as well used as themselves, at any of their ships.

So then things altered so that all the enquiry was, where was a draper or shopkeeper or tailor or shoemaker or any other tradesman that was a Quaker; insomuch that Friends had double the trade, beyond any of their neighbours. And if there was any trading they had it, insomuch that then the cry of all the professors and others was "If we let these people alone they will take the trading of the nation out of our hands."— *George Fox, 1653.*

DURING the past 40 years I have changed considerably in how I talk about God. Forty years ago I was a college freshman who talked about God in theistic, personal terms, such as Heavenly Father. Thirty years ago I was a young Ph.D., a beginning college teacher, who talked about God in pantheistic, transpersonal terms, such as Divine light. Now I talk about God in both personal and transpersonal terms....

Whether I talk about God in personal symbols or in transpersonal symbols, I believe I am talking about God as a unifying divine reality. I experience this unifying power as that which pervades all persons, all life, all nature. This divine reality makes each person sacred without destroying the uniqueness and creative freedom of that person. I experience this unifying power of love and truth among Friends in worship and feel it overflowing into the larger society in social concerns.

At the conclusion of a meeting for worship I sometimes feel deep unity and harmony with those present. This feeling is rooted in the shared experience of a closer relationship to the divine, even though personal and transpersonal symbols of God were used...in spoken messages. God is spoken of sometimes personally as Father and sometimes transpersonally as Light, as Friends have done since the time of George Fox. The different messages often combine into what I feel is a communal truth about God greater than any individual truth. Such messages touch my heart and give me assurance of the unifying power of the love of God. As I live in the power of this unifying love perhaps my life will better communicate what God means to me than talking about God with a hundred inadequate verbal symbols.— *Wallace Cayard, 1987.*

"WHAT is God's will for me?"

"Who me?"

Such is likely to be the first reaction to the idea of God's will. God is too big and I am too small. If any one presumes to bridge that chasm and to claim he is acting out God's will, we shy away from him. It smacks of fanaticism. Paul's formulation "not I, but Christ in me" seems more humble, because Paul was close to Jesus.... Few people, I think, are struck by the bolt from the blue....

To me the process of turning to God is a gradual one, accompanied by a gradual growth in spiritual power. In all our lives we are making choices—both conscious and unconscious. Many of these choices are reduced for convenience into habits, and we must re-examine the latter from time to time to see if they are still answering the purposes for which they were formed.... I am convinced that our lives are formed by the choices we make and not determined by outside forces. The dictum of the Commencement speaker rings true: "Beware of your goals, for you are likely to achieve them. Much of the dryness and frustration of middle age seem to result from the achievement of goals which were limited in the first place and for which adequate replacements have not been found.

When we turn to God in worship, are our goals consonant with what we know of the Light?....The best starting point is to examine our present patterns of behavior, for these express our true beliefs, no matter what we may aspire to or pretend to or claim. Such self-examination is neither easy nor rapid. A healthy person comes up with the answer, "I'm okay, but where do I go from here?"— *George Peck, 1973.*

A LIFE OF INDULGENCE is not the way to arrive at Christian perfection. There are many things that appear trifles, which greatly tend to enervate the soul, and hinder its progress in the path to virtue and glory. The habit of indulging in things which our judgments cannot thoroughly approve, grows stronger and stronger by every act of self-gratification, and we are led on by degrees to an excess of luxury which must greatly weaken our hands in the spiritual warfare.

I was led to these reflections by the consideration how lying late in bed of a morning creeps on by degrees. It appears a very trifling thing, and we can hardly believe that half an hour's indulgence that way amounts to a crime; in itself it may not, and a general rule it would be impossible to fix; but I believe each individual is apt to determine one in his own mind, and the crime lies in extending our indulgence beyond that standard which our judgments have fixed. In every other action of life, the same reasoning takes place. If we do not endeavor to do that which is right in every particular circumstance, though trifling, we shall be in great danger of letting the same negligence take place, in matters more essential.

In the hour of cool meditation, how frequently do we hear the soft whisper of conscience not only condemning the evil, and leading us to repentance, but pointing out to us the way by which we may arrive at happiness and glory. — *Margaret Woods, 1771.*

THE MORE FUNDAMENTAL testimony of strict veracity and honesty had an impact far beyond the limits of the Society of Friends. Friends are credited with introducing the convention of the fixed price in retailing and the reduction of bargaining. Friends evidently felt that bargaining could not be done without lying, saying you were going to do something when actually you were prepared to do something else. Quaker shopkeepers and merchants, therefore, adopted the custom of the fixed price, leaving it up to the buyer as to whether to buy at that price. This not only saved a great deal of time and energy that otherwise might have been spent on haggling, but it made something to do with the rise of the market economy....

There is a certain basic similarity between the ethic which underlies science and the ethic of the Society of Friends...a high value on curiosity, on testing, on veracity— that is, not telling lies— and a very high value on abstaining from threat and reliance on evidence as a means of persuasion. The emphasis in the Society of Friends on direct personal experience, rather than reliance on authority, in a sense combines the emphasis on curiosity— what is the world really like? What is the real truth?— with the emphasis on testing that we find in science. The insistence on veracity is extremely important. We can never be quite sure that what we think we know is the truth, but we usually know when we are telling lies. Deliberate falsification of experimental results is the unforgivable sin in science. The abstention from threat as a means of persuasion is closely related to the covenant of peace.— *Kenneth E. Boulding, 1986.*

THEY FAIL to read clearly the signs of the times who do not see that the hour is coming when, under the searching eye of philosophy and the terrible analysis of science, the letter and the outward evidence will not altogether avail us; when the surest dependence must be upon the Light of Christ within, disclosing the law and the prophets in our own souls, and confirming the truth of outward Scripture by inward experience; when smooth stones from the brook of present revelation shall prove mightier than the weapons of Saul; when the doctrine of the Holy Spirit, as proclaimed by George Fox and lived by John Woolman, shall be recognized as the only efficient solvent of doubts raised by an age of restless inquiry. — *John Greenleaf Whittier, 1870.*

John Greenleaf Whittier passed his early years working on the farm at Haverhill, Massachusetts, where he was born, earning the money for school fees by making slippers. Taking up work as a newspaper editor, he had thoughts of entering political life, but felt the call to devote himself to the cause of the abolition of slavery, though his strenuous advocacy of it involved unpopularity and sometimes great personal risk. In later life, when giving counsel to a fifteen-year-old lad, he said: "My lad, if thou wouldst win success, join thyself to some unpopular but noble cause." His deep love of humanity found expression in his poems. The strength of his appeal to the religious instinct of men, far beyond the boundaries of his own religious Society, is shown by the place which is held by his poetry in modern hymn-books.

LIKE SO MANY OTHERS I have found that my life is too full of external stimuli, of mere busyness. So I don't spend much time with the radio, television and the daily paper. A car without a radio is a place for contemplation. When friends object that I don't know what is going on and am not concerned with the life of our society, I answer that they are deluded. History does not happen by the day. Once I read every copy of a leading newspaper from January to September, 1870, with the intention of discovering the nature of the historical forces of that period. What I did discover was a host of superficialities, fleeting illusions, and enormous blind spots as to what was really going on....

...The most important choice concerning the use of time in our lives is the choice of occupation...Most of our days are spent at work, and it is primarily in this area that we make our contribution to the lives of our fellow men....

What seems important to me is not what a person does, but how he does it.

Mostly we make these important decisions as to occupations early in life,and later on we find out that our work does not fully express our desire to be of service to our fellow men. So we moonlight. We have kept out some time in our life for pastoral visits, draft counseling, serving on town committees...

By this time of day, is there any time left?... Our days are really full— of worship, work, recreation, mulling things over, playing with the family, and singing. And more and more I am learning to let this happen naturally...and [not] plan out every day down to the last tyrannical minute.— *George Peck, 1973.*

AS I LAY in bed one night, light from above seemed to beam upon me and point out in a very explicit manner the duty of submitting to decided Quakerism, more particularly to the humbling sacrifice of "plainness of speech, behaviour and apparel". The visitation was strong, but my will was stronger; I would not, I did not comply; putting off what appeared to me almost unbearable to a more "convenient season". I was then rather more than twenty-one years old...Many persons might say that, taking into view the danger of imagination in such measures, I did well in resisting this call. After a space of nearly thirty years, full of a variety of experience, I am not of this judgment; for I believe that nothing is more profitable than the ready obedience of faith, and nothing more dangerous than the contrary. In my own case the effect of irresolution was a painful state of spiritual weakness; and when at last I made the sacrifice, it was but lamely done, and under circumstances of still greater humiliation to the pride and vanity of my own heart than it would have been at first. In the meantime I enjoyed some very precious religious privileges....The first was a visit to our Meeting from our Friend Ann Jones (then Ann Burgess). I was powerfully affected and subdued under her ministry, almost, if not quite constrained to surrender at discretion by the love of Christ. The second was an attendance at the Yearly Meeting, to which, in spite of my youth and lapelled coat, I was appointed representative.... The Yearly Meeting was to me, in this as in other years, an occasion of inexpressible solemnity — and I hope of edification. — *Joseph John Gurney, 1812.*

SOON AFTER my return home I was engaged to a dinner party at the house of one of our first county gentlemen. Three weeks before the time was I engaged, and three weeks was my young mind in agitation from the apprehension, of which I could not dispossess myself, that I must enter his drawing room with my hat on. From this sacrifice, strange and unaccountable as it may appear, I could not escape. In a Friend's attire, and with my hat on, I entered the drawing room at the dreaded moment, shook hands with the mistress of the house, went back into the hall, deposited my hat, spent a rather comfortable evening, and returned home in some degree of peace. I had afterwards the same thing to do at the Bishop's; the result was, that I found myself the decided Quaker, was perfectly understood to have assumed that character, and to dinner parties, except in the family circle, was asked no more.

The wearing of the hat in the house is not my practice. I have no wish to repeat what then happened; but I dare not regret a circumstance which was...made the means of fully deciding my course....Here I would observe that when scruples on points of a religious and practical nature are well founded they abide the test of time and experience. This has been completely the case with me, as it relates to plainness. Never have I regretted the change which I then made; never have I doubted that in that direction precisely lay my appointed course of religious duty. I might have taken a more dazzling course in the world, or even in the "religious world"; but I believe that, in proportion to my willingness to be circumscribed within these somewhat humiliating boundaries, has been, in fact, the scope both for usefulness and happiness.— *Joseph John Gurney, 1812.*

I FIND THAT I have little to say about techniques of ministry; instead, I am led to speak, as I often have before, about the ground out of which all ministry flows. It is good to remember that all ministry is one, and should flow from the same source. This is true of what we call ministry in a meeting for worship just as it should be true of *everything* which happens in a meeting— for worship— for business, for in that meeting we are ministering through our decisions either to ourselves or to the world beyond us....

So can we, on our comfortable padded benches, stay in that centered place, knowing that the more of us who can stay faithfully grounded in God, the easier it will be for others to find it— and to stay in it also. In this state we can spend hours in a business meeting without tiring or losing our patience, resting in this sea of divine Light and love which washes through all people present....

Sometimes we are led to speak, to minister out of this ground we have been describing. And let us remember that in Quaker theory— and I hope in Quaker practice— all speaking in a business meeting arises out of this ground, and can therefore be called ministry. We know that the true inward motion to speak often lies far beneath our first instinct to respond to an issue. So it is well to wait, to go deeper.

Yet Truth is quick, and the longer we have been experienced in waiting, the more quickly we can learn to recognize the true motion even in an instant, so that we can respond to the Spirit's timing and not our own.— *William Taber, 1988.*

WE HAVE NO RIGHT to ask or expect an exemption from the chastisement which the Divine Providence is inflicting upon the nation. Steadily and faithfully maintaining our testimony against war, we owe it to the cause of truth, to show that exalted heroes and generous self-sacrifice are not incompatible with our pacific principles. Our mission is, at this time, to mitigate the suffering of our countrymen, to visit and aid the sick and the wounded, to relieve the necessities of the widow and the orphan, and to practice economy for the sake of charity. Let the Quaker bonnet be seen by the side of the black hood of the Catholic Sister of Charity in the hospital ward. Let the same heroic devotion to duty which our brethren in Great Britain manifested in the Irish famine and pestilence be reproduced on this side of the water, in mitigating the horrors of war and its attendant calamities. What hinders us from holding up the hands of Dorothea Dix in her holy work of mercy in Washington? Our society is rich, and those to whom much is given much will be required in this hour of proving and trial.— *John Greenleaf Whittier, 1862.*

* * *

The levelled gun, the battle-brand,
    We may not take;
But Calmly loyal, we can stand
And suffer with our suffering kind
    For conscience' sake.

And we may tread the sick-bed floors
    Where strong men pine,
And, down the groaning corridors,
Pour freely from our liberal stores
    The oil and the Wine.—J.G. Whittier.

LEARNING, indeed, is the key to mending the world. We have to learn to sew before we can mend. We have to learn how to live at peace or we will destroy ourselves. This is not easy, but it can be done. The Vikings turned into the modern Norwegians. Brutal feudal barons turned into courtiers. Gunslinging cowboys turned into rodeo stars. People gave up wearing swords. Duelling, an ancient custom, disappeared almost overnight in the nineteenth century. We now have what I call the "great triangle" of stable peace from Australia and Japan, across North America to Western Europe. We have eighteen countries that have no plans whatever to go to war with each other. The institution of stable peace is the only really effective means of national security. It has been growing around the world ever since it started, probably in Scandinavia after the Napoleonic Wars. We have learned up to a point how to diminish poverty, improve health, broaden education, and diminish burdensome, dull and demeaning jobs. We have enormously expanded the cultural repertoire of the human race. With all this, however, we have clearly not done enough. We still have a great deal to learn....

In this large and almost inconceivably complex world it may seem almost ludicrous to suppose that a group as small as the Society of Friends— only one out of about 25,000 human beings is a Quaker— could make any contribution to this overwhelmingly important problem....The Society of Friends, at least in some of its branches, has a disproportionate number of members of the scholarly community. Is it too much to hope that some of us might make a commitment...to the search for new ideas and concepts towards human betterment?— *Kenneth Boulding, 1986.*

ELIZA HARRIS of "Uncle Tom's Cabin" notoriety...was sheltered under our roof and fed at our table for several days....She said she was a slave from Kentucky....Her master got into some pecuniary difficulty, and she found that she and her only child were to be separated....She watched her opportunity, and when darkness had settled down and the family had retired to sleep, she started with her child in her arms and walked straight toward the Ohio river. She knew that it was frozen over at that season, but when she reached its banks at daylight, she found that the ice had broken up and was slowly drifting in large cakes....In the evening she discovered pursuers [were] near and, with desperate courage she determined to cross the river, or perish in the attempt....Clasping her babe to her bosom with her left arm, she sprang on to the first cake of ice, then from that to another and another. Sometimes the cake she was on would sink beneath her weight, then she would slide her child on to the next cake, pull herself on with her hands, and so continue her hazardous journey. She became wet to the waist with ice water and her hands were benumbed with cold, but as she made her way from one cake of ice to another, she felt that surely the Lord was preserving and upholding her, and that nothing would harm her...

In the summer of 1854 I was on a visit to Canada, accompanied by my wife and daughter....At the close of a meeting which we attended, at one of the colored churches, a woman came up to my wife, seized her hand, and exclaimed: "How are you, Aunt Katie? God bless you!"...My wife did not recognize her, but she soon called herself to our remembrance by referring to the time she was at our house in the days of her distress.—
Levi Coffin (1798-1877).

IN MY LATE religious journey over the peninsula of the Eastern Shore, I did indeed observe—as I have done whenever I have travelled, or been present in a country where slavery was practiced— that it not only tended to produce outward poverty by preventing improvements, and deterioration of the lands, but that it produced a still more disastrous penury in the minds of the slaveholders, by divesting them of those mental qualities upon which we are all dependent for comfort, and the want of which cannot be compensated by even the revenues of the word....I have long been of the persuasion that much of the good that might have been done, has been obstructed by the attempts which have been made to abolish slavery, having originated and been prosecuted upon political, instead of religious motives and convictions....

They have seen, in so prominent an aspect, the wrongs and sufferings of the slave, that the still greater calamities of the master have been scarcely noticed....

As a consequence of this mode of proceeding, the slaveholder has considered himself injuriously assailed,— his mind has become exasperated, and he has placed himself upon the defensive, or become an assailant in his turn; and the result has been, that, like all other political contentions, the conflict has been degraded into a combat of persons, instead of a contest between the principles of right and wrong.—*Edward Stabler (1769-1831).*

WHAT THEN is worship? It consists in obedience to the operation of that divine illimitable principle, which is designed to guide out of every evil and into all truth. This is the kind of spiritual religion which is enjoined on every one of us, and is to be performed by actions, and reduced to daily practice, whether we sit in the house or walk by the way....But let us remember my friends, that it is not only when we are thus assembled that we ought to labour to come to this continued Sabbath, in which we are brought to a state of willingness to do everything for the glory of God, and in which we can testify with Christ himself, "my meat and my drink is to do the will of him that sent me, and to finish his work....."

And this is an operative principle; it does not depend on the opinions of others— of our forefathers, the scriptures of truth, or any other external cause. There is no principle prepared by others, which can ever nourish up the soul to eternal life. Not all the costly food that can be eaten by others, will ever nourish our bodies; we must be partakers ourselves. We cannot see with another's eyes, or hear with another's ears; neither can we understand with the heart of another. If we ever come to see, hear, or understand, and to be converted, it must be with our own faculties, and not with those of another. If we are ever converted, we must experience the dealings of God with us. Here is a religion which is immediately adapted to each individual.— *Thomas Wetherald, sermon in Philadelphia, 1826.*

IF THERE is something of great moment going on behind the screen of outward events and this great impulse of redemptive love is forever besieging us, why are we not more open to its guidance? There is an old story of a small boy who was puzzling over Holman Hunt's great painting that shows the figure of Jesus knocking at the door of a house— a weed-clogged door that is only able to be opened from the inside. The child asked his father why the people didn't open the door, and then with a cry of discovery he gave his own answer. "I think I know why they don't open the door. They're all down in the basement and they don't hear him."

This basement where the gentle knocking is inaudible is so expressive of the human condition as we know it today, that it seems for many to take shattering experiences to rouse them to what is already going on. Phillips Brooks, who had no gift for keeping discipline, was literally run out of his first job at the Boston Latin School....Thomas Kelly had a crushing blow to his academic ambitions dealt to him in the autumn of 1937 and he went through a time of brokenness and despair....

For some it is the running away from home of a precious adolescent child, or the loss of a secure post, or a breakdown in mental or physical health, or the loss of a wife or a husband or a child through death that breaks through the hard hull of self-assurance. W. H. Auden has a line which says, "It is where we are wounded that God speaks to us." Auden does not say that God sends these wounds. But he seems to be saying that for some of us it is only in the depths of suffering that we seem open enough to listen to what, upon the occasion of this suffering, God has to say to us.— *Douglas V. Steere, 1966.*

I WAS...led to call upon my Friends to persevere in this noble and righteous concern , that nothing might be left undone on our part, in restoring strict justice and right to this deeply oppressed part of our fellow creatures; not only on their account and for their relief, but on our own account also.

For, I believe, we are in a very peculiar manner called upon, agreeable to our profession, of being led and guided by an unerring principle of perfect righteousness, to exalt the standard of truth and righteousness in the earth: and believing, as I do, that it is not in the power and wisdom of man to effect this, by all the coercive laws which can be enacted, nor by all the force of the arm of flesh. For nothing can destroy and put an end to sin and wickedness, but a principle in man of perfect righteousness and justice;... to have no fellowship or communion, either immediately or remotely, directly or indirectly, with any acts of injustice or oppression. Hence, I believe, that if we as a people were faithful and obedient to this first principle of our profession, we should be led thereby to abstain from all kinds of commerce or dealings in the produce of our country or elsewhere, which we had cause to believe originated out of, or through the medium of, the labour of slaves, wrung from them and sold by their tyrannical masters. And I am well assured that nothing short of such an exalted testimony to truth and righteousness will ever put a full end to oppression and injustice; and, I believe, He who called our worthy predecessors to exalt the testimony of truth in the earth...is looking for this testimony of strict justice and righteousness at our hands.— *Elias Hicks, 1817.*

THE THING which had the most to do, however, with my deliverance from fear was my childlike discovery that God was with me and that *I belonged to him.* I say "discovery," but it was a discovery slowly made and in the main gathered from the atmosphere of our home. God, as I have said, was as real to everybody in our family as was our house or our farm. I soon realized that Aunt Peace *knew* him and that grandmother had lived more than eighty years in intimate relation with him. I caught their simple faith and soon had one of my own. I gradually came to feel assured that whatever might be there in the dark of my bedroom, God anyhow was certainly there, stronger than everything else combined. I learned to whisper to him as soon as I got into bed—I never learned to pray kneeling by the bedside. I never saw anybody do that until I went away to boarding school. I "committed" everything to him. I told him that I couldn't take care of myself and asked him to guard and keep the little boy who needed him. And then, I believed that he would do it. I knew Aunt Peace never doubted and I tried to follow her plan of life. There were times in my childhood when the God I loved was more real than the things I feared and I am convinced that all children would be genuinely religious if they had someone to lead them rightly to God, to whom they belong.......

When I was ten came one of the crises of my life. It was a great misfortune, which turned out to be a blessing, as is usually the case, if one has the eyes to see it. It was the injury to my foot which nearly cost me my leg and seriously threatened my life. Through all the pain and suffering I discovered what a mother's love was.— *Rufus Jones, 1926.*

"JORDAN is a hard road to travel."...Only a day or two ago I lost my temper because somebody who was not a saint, but only an average church-member, was perverse and ill-dispositioned; and I disputed the bill of an Irishman who thought it right to make spoil of a Protestant Egyptian, and I dare say he went away with no satisfactory evidence of my saintship....

The longer I live, I see the evil in myself in a clearer light, and more that is good in others; and if I do not grow better, I am constrained to be more charitable. I shudder sometimes at my fierce rebuke of evil-doers, when I consider my own weakness and sins of omission as well as commission....

[My friends complain] at one time I am all warmth and feeling, at another cold, distant and absent. Certainly those who know me best have learned that my temperament and not my heart is at fault. I know that my habits of self-abstraction and reserve have become fixed upon me, and when I obtain the mastery over them I am very likely to go too far in the other direction. Alas, how often have my best feelings been misinterpreted, my kindness and love failed of their object and left me nothing but error and self-distrust.— *John Greenleaf Whittier, (1807-1892)*

THE PURPOSE of business meetings is to make decisions about the life of the Meeting jointly under the guidance of the Holy Spirit. In the Holy Spirit there is no hostility, no disunity, no tedium, and no preoccupation with irrelevancies....

Let us listen more carefully to each other— certainly without interrupting each other. I suspect that some of us tend to formulate our own thoughts while others are speaking. We would do better to listen more deeply, considering the exact message made explicit; the emotional content in the context of the speaker's life and commitments; the sources, rational and emotional, of our own acceptance or rejection of the message; and the source in divine love of the message and of our response to it.

To do this kind of listening is hard work, and we need a brief silence after each person speaks to hear the echo of the message in our own soul and to judge if a response is needed. Such a brief silence is also a guard against interruption....

When meetings go badly, they should be stopped to give way to a silence, not just to let heads cool but to allow prayer for guidance and greater clarity.

Proposals for action, statements, letters speaking for the Meeting, and reports should be worked out and approved in committee before they are brought to the meeting. We simply are not prepared to deal adequately with raw ideas without a great deal of time wasted and aggravation of feelings. Half-dead committees should be reactivated if only for that purpose....Members should be encouraged to express their concerns for details [in statements, concerns, letters] to that committee rather than burdening the business meeting.— *Pieter Byhouwer, 1971.*

QUERIES for Meeting for Business:

1. Are your meetings for business held in a spirit of love, understanding, and forebearance? Do you seek the right course of action with a patient search for unity and a willingness to accept the authority of truth?

2. Do you come to meeting eager to search for God's will rather than to try to win acceptance for a previously formed opinion of your own?

3. Are you prepared to assist by silent, prayerful consideration, speaking only if you feel you have a helpful contribution to make?

4. Do you give each member credit for purity of motive, notwithstanding differences of opinion?

5. Is your love for your neighbor so strong that you are as eager to understand as to be understood?

6. When the Clerk is searching for the sense of the meeting, do you overcome diffidence and express your view without undue delay? Do you maintain silence while the minute is being composed?

7. Do you avoid bringing to meeting matters that should first be considered by a committee? Do you allow unimportant matters to be disposed of quickly?

8. When a decision is being reached with which you disagree, do you accept your responsibility to speak at that time rather than later?

9. Do you refrain from pressing your own views unduly, if the judgment of the meeting obviously inclines to some other view?

10. When the meeting has come to a decision, do you accept it as "our" decision, rather than "theirs"?— *San Francisco Meeting, 1961.*

"ALL LIVE IN PEACE, in love, and in the power of the Lord God, and keep your meetings, every one of you, waiting upon Him in his power, that in it ye may have unity with God the Father and with the Son, and one with another. And let wisdom guide you in patience, and do not strive with any in meetings, but dwell in the power of the Lord God, that can bear and suffer all things; and make no strife among Friends, but live in that which makes for peace, and love and life...

...That nothing may be done in strife to occasion words; for you are called to peace and holiness, in which the kingdom stands, and to serve one another in love.

Above all things, live in that which stops strife, contention and jangling, even in the love of God, by which ye come to serve one another in love which thinks no evil, envies not, nor is easily provoked.... And let not prejudice boil in any of your hearts, but let it be cast out by the power of God, in which is the true unity and the everlasting kingdom. Thus may ye all witness a being made heirs of the same kingdom of peace, and sitting down in the same, knowing your own portions and increasing in the heavenly riches...

Do not strive about outward things, but dwell in the love of God, for that will unite you together, and make you kind and gentle towards one another, seeking one another's good and welfare; and to be helpful one to another, and see that nothing be lacking among you, then all will be well. Let temperance, patience, kindness and brotherly love be exercised among you, so that you may abound in virtue and the true humility. Live in peace, and show forth the nature of Christianity, that you may all live as a family... — *George Fox, 1676.*

HE THAT COMMANDED that we should love our Enemies, hath left us no Right to fight and destroy, but to convert them. And yet we are of Use, and helpful in any Kingdom or Government: for the Principle of our Religion prohibits Idleness, and excites to Industry; as it is written, *They shall beat their Swords into Ploughshares, and their Spears into Pruning-hooks:*...we, by so great an Example (the Lord Jesus Christ), do freely pay our Taxes to Caesar, who of Right, hath the Direction and Application of them, to the various Ends of Government, to Peace or to War, as it pleaseth him, or as Need may be, according to the Constitution or Laws of his Kingdom......

The Kingdoms of this world shall all become the Kingdoms of our "God and his Christ:...But until this be finished by Degrees, as it is now begun and proceeds, the Kingdom of Christ on Earth is, and shall be, as at the first, a holy Nation, a Royal Priesthood, a peculiar people, zealous, not to fight and destroy, or to meddle with the Kingdoms or Rule of the World, but of good Works; against whom there is no Law, founded upon Righteousness and Truth: But until this be accomplished, Nation will lift up Sword against Nation, and they will learn and exercise Wars: but as to us, we through the Mercy and Goodness of God, are of those in whom this Prophecy is begun to be fulfilled, and we can learn War no more.*(1747)*

*   *   *

I being innocent, if I was killed...my soul might be happy; but if I killed him, he dying in his wickedness, would, consequently be unhappy; and if I was killed, he might live to repent; so that if he killed me, I should have much the better, both in respect to myself and to him.— *Thomas Chalkley, 1754.*

SO FAR...I have emphasized the negative side of the Quaker peace testimony; in other words, what Quakers have refused to do rather than what they do. In every war throughout Quaker history, Quakers have done relief work during and after the war. To describe all of this would take a large volume......

Religious pacifism as a positive way of life rather than as a negative attitude toward fighting can be considered to be a direct derivative from worship. True worship which pierces through the surface where multiplicity lies, finds in the depths, beyond words and even thoughts, what George Fox called "the hidden unity in the Eternal Being." Here the worshiper feels as a present experience rather than as abstract theory his kinship with his fellow men in God. The early Friends seldom used the phrase "joined to the Lord" without adding its complementary expression "and to one another." Out of this unity comes a sensitizing of the soul, a feeling of oneness with all men which rules out conflict......

*   *   *

The Quaker belief in peace is not just a negative refusal of war, but also an endeavor to appeal to "that of God" in other men regardless of nationality, race, or social status. This appeal may not at first appear successful, but it is the only appeal which can be successful in the long run. — *Howard K. Brinton, 1972.*

WE ARE a small conservatively inclined group of "Wilburite" type of Quakers. I want to say first and foremost that we believe that Christ is the "only begotten Son of God, the only Foundation", and that it is only through His Name that we must be saved....

We use what is known as "plain speech", but this is a minute part of what constitutes our understanding of simplicity. Simplicity should affect all aspects of our lives and our relationships to other people. As I see simplicity there are more reasons than one for its place in our lives. A truly simple existence should be of service to us in maintaining an open channel of communication between us and the shining of the Inner Light. We desire a freedom from that which might distract our attention from the still small voice, that which would exercise a binding control over us, and that which would hinder our full loyalty to the one and only Almighty. We also believe in a simple life as a means of witness, a witness to the fact that the goals as determined by the world are not our goals. In this sense we believe plainness is a means of communication and we desire to communicate that which is honest, sound and upright....

We are "Quietist" only in the sense that we do not dare go beyond the measure of truth, the measure of the Spirit, or the level of experience that has been given from above. We dare not generate our own experience and joy, nor kindle the sparks of our own kindling...we are not willing to go beyond what is given us and therefore we are not wanting to speak before we are spoken to, but we are human and make mistakes....My occupation is making horse-drawn buggies, and carts.— *Stuart Banister, Indiana, 1984.*

FROM THE TIME that I went to live with my brother William in London, I regularly attended Friends' Meetings; Not that I was acquainted with their peculiar views; indeed, there seemed to be a *prohibition* of aught but simple *evidence* and *obedience.* The experience of others did not seem to reach my case; all was to be given up, that all things might be new; and such were the sacrifices required, from time to time, as none can know or understand, save those who have been led in a similar way.

About this time, in consequence of my decided resolution to attend the meetings of Friends, my dear father, (no doubt in faithfulness to his own religious views, and from the desire to rescue a poor child from apprehended error) requested me not to return to the paternal roof, unless I could be satisfied to conform to the religious education which he had conscientiously given me.   This, with a tender, heart-piercing remonstrance from my dear, dear mother, was far more deeply felt than I can describe; and marvelous in my view, even to this day, was the settled, firm belief that I must follow on, to know the soul's salvation for myself; truly in a way that I knew not!— *Mary Capper, aged 32.*

"All the paths of the Lord are mercy and truth, unto such as keep his covenant and his testimonies. The troubles of my heart are enlarged: O bring thou me out of my distresses."— Psalm 25:10,17.

MUST I FOREVER give up the dear, pleasing hope of being received into the house and affections of my once kind, indulgent parents? Oh? my sister, will you, can you despise me? I have no firm consolation but in the belief that I am guided by a superior Power. I have exerted every faculty of my mind; I have resolutely mortified my body, endeavoring to bring it into subjection, free from the influence of passion and deceiving sense; and I have a secret intimation that the kingdom of heaven is within us; that in the silence of the creature, is the power of God made known.

O! my Rebecca; if you would examine the uniform desire of my life, the earnestness of my supplications, and my present wish of being humble, pure, wholly dependent upon God my Maker, without any confidence in men; if you would thus consider me, without prejudice, I think you would not, could not reject me! Of my own willings, or self-abilities, I deserve little; but, in my heart and understanding, I submit to a perfect Teacher; and in his light, is my life and my hope. Think not, my Rebecca, that I have contracted ideas which circumscribe salvation to any particular sect. God forbid! my heart is contrariwise enlarged in universal charity. Let each be satisfied in his own mind, and the censures or applauses of multitudes can only be a secondary consideration of no weight.— *Mary Capper, aged 32.*

EVERYWHERE Friends went, they certainly acknowledged and accepted others' way of becoming just and kind.... Besides having great faith in what they found, these early Friends described their faith and its foundation. This, in my opinion, has raised much difference, unhappiness, and unkindness amongst us ever since. While many have kept to the faith itself and tried to talk about it, others have taken greater stock by the words describing faith and its underpinnings, arguing over the words' correctness. Some groups of Friends wish—almost demand—that we all approve certain strings of words or think in only certain ways.

The words are not the discipline. The words INDICATE the discipline. "These things we do not lay upon you as a rule or form to walk by, but that all, with the measure of light which is pure and holy, may be guided...for the letter killeth, but the Spirit giveth life." In a way, of course, we can get rid of or change all the words because the Almighty creates as well without them. But Friends and others have seen—right now as we rewrite books of discipline and attract new seekers and members-that we need the guide of language.

We need it to remind us gently and firmly of our commitment and our hopes. It reminds us that our economy and traditions are not our religion. It reminds us how accepting we can be; and that God, Christ, the universe, humanity, our friends, and even ourselves can and will welcome us back even after we go out in a huff and blow everything away. It reminds us that we can empower or pay no one to perform what is our own responsibility; living our religion and keeping up our society. It tells us that we can suffer torture, shame and abuse, be poor, and yet live on.—*John L.P. Maynard, 15th St. Meeting.*

OUR PARENT GROUP is Ohio Conservative Yearly Meeting. We meet on the basis of silence, not having special paid ministers, and in general stay clear of political activity. We try in our meetings for worship, as in the rest of our lives, to know and to do what Christ would have us do.

Neither the knowing nor the doing is always easy. We make mistakes and we put our own desires ahead of God's. But we know that He never forgets us, that He always wants us to do His will, and that He never asks more than a person can manage *because He gives the grace and strength to do right as they are needed.*

"Plainness" is, or should be, more than "thee and thou". Part of plainness is simplicity. Our family dresses in a plain manner, and our house is furnished that way to some extent. We don't have window curtains, for example, or lots of pictures, etc., on the wall. Plainness also involves speech, not just special words, but speaking so as to mean what we say. That means avoiding both sarcasm— saying the opposite of what one means, and also excessive politeness or "beating around the bush." We use numbers for the days of the week and the months, continuing a tradition started by early Friends.

Our lifestyle and dress set us apart from others. As we are set apart, we should be reminded that we are called to serve God and to conduct ourselves in a way that honors Him. We hold that obedience to God's will, even in little daily matters, is very important. It is through obedience in little matters that one comes to be obedient in more far-reaching decisions. Also, what may seem little and insignificant to one person... may be an important link in God's plan for someone else.— *Susan Smith, Virginia, 1984.*

IF WE, who have all lived completely different lives, are to keep up the Society of Friends, we shall have to continue to seek what we have in common. Thereby going beyond words, we have varied beliefs. As an example, my friend says he believes nothing, distrusting the words of belief. He feels he has great faith, due to what has transpired in his life. He asserts that he wants to know what goes on inside others and says, "I don't care what Peter says or Paul says. I care what you say. Don't tell me what you say, tell me what you do!" Does this sound familiar? Could it be an old Quaker message, scorching, personal, caring?

What do we do after we have worshipped and prayed? "If someone arrested thee for being a Friend, what would the evidence be to convict thee?" Perhaps it would be a couple of cups of after-meeting refreshment, a few cancelled checks made out to the meeting, a protest demonstration, a subscription to a Friends' magazine, or maybe several commitments and re-commitments to Christ. This is certainly not exactly a living...or compelling faith.

The only tradition and discipline of Friends' beginnings may have been Christianity, inquisitiveness, human decency, and the wish to disclose to others what one had understood. I suppose monthly meetings, advices and queries came about to make sure that mayhem did not reign, and to deter Friends from straying...in ways that would make communication and mutual caring impossible.

If we had that spirit and temperament now it might be wonderful! If we remembered that all aspects of our lives are under divine guidance, what would that mean? After all, we have all repeatedly chosen to be Friends: what have we chosen?— *John L. P. Maynard, 15th St Meeting.*

EVEN THOUGH we may be at times aware of strains between us, I am sure that it is better to try to worship together, than to withdraw from it, provided, of course, that we go willing for reconciliation, and ready to respond to any leadings which may come to help bring it about. If, on the other hand, we go to worship in a state of tension with another Friend without being willing to find a way of reconciliation with that person, then it seems possible that the blockage will become more deeply imbedded, pushed further into ourselves and so, sadly, more difficult to remove.

Such times of strain are only one of the circumstances in which we may feel so great an emptiness, pain or trouble, that we doubt whether we have any business going to meeting. I am convinced by my own experience, that these are just the moments when we should go. It was precisely when I felt at lowest ebb, when I knew that I had, so to say, no gift to take to the altar, that I found meeting had something to give me. The economy involved here is not very extraordinary....Those who have apparently little to give in meeting, do, it seems to me, give themselves to God, and to those with whom they worship, and just their very presence may release ministry in another during meeting of direct help for their need, or a helpful word, or look afterwards, so that their emptiness begins to be filled. All of us sometimes face the prospect of meeting feeling like [this], but can be surprised if we make the journey. But what we never try, we shall never know.— *Christopher Holdsworth, 1985.*

UNTIL THIS YEAR, 1756, I continued to retail goods, besides following my trade as a tailor; about which time I grew uneasy on account of my business growing too cumbersome. I had begun with selling trimmings for garments, and from thence proceeded to sell cloths and linens; and at length, having got a considerable shop of goods, my trade increased every year, and the way to large business appeared open, but I felt a stop in my mind.

Through the mercies of the Almighty, I had, in a good degree, learned to be content with a plain way of living. I had but a small family; and, on serious consideration, believed truth did not require me to engage much in cumbering affairs. It had been my general practice to buy and sell things really useful. Things that served chiefly to please the vain mind in people, I was not easy to trade in; seldom did it; and whenever I did I found it weaken me as a Christian.

The increase of business became my burden; for though my natural inclination was toward merchandise, yet I believed truth required me to live more free from outward cumbers; and there was now a strife in my mind between the two. In this exercise my prayers were put up to the Lord, who graciously heard me, and gave me a heart resigned to his holy will. Then I lessened my outward business, and, as I had opportunity, told my customers of my intentions, that they might consider what shop to turn to; and in a while I wholly laid down merchandise, and followed my trade as a tailor by myself, having no apprentice.... In merchandise it is the custom where I lived to sell chiefly on credit, and poor people often get in debt...I found it good for me to advise poor people to take such goods as were most useful, and not costly.— *John Woolman, 1756.*

THIS, INDEED, is a great achievement of reconciliation on the level of personal relationship: We stop judging each other by our own rules of the game, we accept the fact that there are different games being played according to different rules. Without adopting the other's code, we no longer question his honesty when he follows it honestly; indeed, we respect him for it. We begin to grasp that many concepts on the other side are not due to hypocrisy, ill-will, and hostility, but to the existence of a different code. We must live in the hope that the mutual respect discovered on the personal level may survive after the interlocutors return to their own environment and may help to increase...understanding between groups and nations.......

Soon after the last war a German girl who suffered from the conflict between two nations she had learned to love, broke out into the words: "The worst thing is that one can understand both sides." Perhaps we should consider this worst thing a blessing, a real achievement on her part. But it is an understanding that brings little happiness.   Where is the reconciler to go from there to help both sides to an understanding of each other?...And how to coax... surrenders [of] some of their own just rights? It may well happen to the reconciler that in his frequent contacts he knows himself loved by many on each side.   Hence, with every spoken or unspoken rejection of his friends on either side, he feels himself rejected together with them.   It is at such moments that he knows how little his human efforts count. Only faith, faith in the cross, can sustain him in his service of reconciliation, beyond any consideration of success and failure.— *Richard K. Ullmann, 1963.*

WHILE THE ACHIEVEMENT of justice is certainly a worthy aim, I believe there is a loftier aim to which we as a religious people should be committed. I think we should be seeking a society that is not only more fair, but also one that is more loving, and we can nurture greater love in our society only when we change people's hearts as well as their minds. Justice will be on firm foundations only when it is rooted in true caring and not merely in some philosophical or utilitarian notion.

Our fellow citizens' capacity for love limits or enhances our society's capacity for justice and our world's capacity for peace. In an ironic and even paradoxical manner the nurture of people's capacity for love must both precede and follow upon our endeavors for greater justice.

Since we are living in a time when even a just society seems a distant and receding ideal, the hope for building a loving society can surely seem like a foolish dream. I believe, though, that in that foolish dream we can discern God's deepest aspirations for us. Can it be that only by striving for the realization of such a foolish dream will we be able to move with certainty toward the less distant ideal?....... Justice is in many ways merely the approximation of love, different in that it does not provide for giving and caring without measure and does not function without a concern for reciprocity. If we work merely for justice, and fail, we may be left only injustice. If our vision is more inspired...in working for a loving society we can be laying the foundation of justices even while failing to realize the vision of our dreams. Our larger calling requires the changing of hearts as well as the changing of minds.— *Thomas Jeavons, 1981.*

REMEMBERING the Lord our gracious God, in his ways and merciful dealings with me from my youth; how he found me among his lost and strayed sheep on the barren mountains of fruitless professions, and how he drew me to an inward experience of his power and sanctifying work in my heart, and to know his teachings and spiritual ministry; thereby to enable me by degrees experimentally to minister to others, and oblige me to live accordingly; as also to suffer patiently, with resignation of liberty and life, for Christ's sake, when called thereunto, and being supported by his power, and cheerfully carried through many great trials and deep sufferings for his name's sake, and having had many eminent deliverances and preservation, even from my young years.

I say considering these things, I have been the more concerned for my friends and brethren, who for conscience sake deeply suffered by imprisonment and spoil of goods; and in the tender bowels of Christ Jesus have truly sympathized with the faithful in their sufferings and afflictions, and in his love been many times stirred up to plead their innocent cause before authority, as well as to solicit with great industry on their behalf; wherein the hand of the Lord has been often with me.— *George Whitehead, 1692.*

*　　*　　*

[All Friends] should study to be quiet and mind their own business, in God's holy fear, and none to be meddling or exercising themselves in things too high for them.— *George Whitehead, Letter, 1692.*

"Many are the afflictions of the righteous: but the Lord delivereth out of them all."— Psalm 34:19.

WE ARE MEN of double personalities. We have slumbering demons within us. We all have also a dimly formed Christ within us. We've been too ready to say that the demonic man within us is the natural and real man, and that the Christ-man within us is the unnatural and the unreal self. But the case is that our surface potentialities are for selfishness and greed, for tooth and claw. But deep within, in the whispers of the heart, is the surging call of the Eternal Christ, hidden within us all. By an inner isthmus we are connected with the mainland of the Eternal Love. Surface living has brought on the world's tragedy. Deeper living leads us to the Eternal Christ, hidden in us all. Absolute loyalty to this inner Christ is the only hope of a new humanity. In the clamor and din of the day, the press of Eternity's warm love still whispers in each of us, as our deepest selves, as our truest selves. Attend to the Eternal that He may recreate you and sow you deep into the furrows of the word's suffering....

There is nothing automatic about suffering, so that suffering infallibly produces great souls. We have passed out of the prewar days when we believed in the escalator theory of progress...when we thought that every day in every way we were growing better and better and we thought that the Kingdom of God on earth was just around the corner, if we...cooperated and didn't halt the process...now in the light of world war we are forced to abandon that easy view and go infinitely deeper....No, there is nothing about suffering such that it automatically purges the dross from human nature and brings heroic souls upon the scene...No, only those who go into the travail of today *bearing a seed within them*...can return in joy.— *Thomas Kelly, 1941.*

AS A VERY SMALL BOY, I sat in meeting with my mother. I remember exactly where we sat, on a seat very near the south door which opened out onto the porch. I think I was supposed to sleep during the meeting hour, but I was afraid to do this. I knew that the meeting house was locked up from one meeting day to the next and I was afraid that if I were to go to sleep I might not know when meeting was over and the house would be locked up with me still in it. Maybe that explains why I never had much trouble keeping awake in meeting.

At a later age, I sat with my father in meeting on the men's side of the house. I could, also, locate this seat today, if it were still there. Then, at a still later time, I was to sit with one of my older brothers farther back in the room where the young people sat.

The closing of the shutters between the men's and the women's part of the room in preparation for the business part of Monthly Meeting was an intriguing operation. As I became older, I often was obligated to help with this procedure if I were sitting near enough to the partition...

Among my treasured memories are those of sitting in meeting on a lovely First Day morning in the summer with the windows open and the soft, fragrant breezes gently blowing through while I listened to the birds singing in the woods back of the building. I called them woodthrushes. I do not know if they were or not, but their music was heavenly. I needed no other music to help me worship. At that time both sides of the meeting house were pretty well filled up every meeting day. I can remember the names of almost all the occupants of those seats and where they sat.— *J. Howard Binns, 1985.*

THERE WERE HEATING stoves in the meeting house in those days, one in the women's side and one in the men's side of the building. My father "kept the meeting house", in other words he served as janitor. On very cold winter mornings he would have to go early to get the fires started and the stoves hot enough to make the building somewhat comfortable by meeting time. The women of the meeting had cushions to put their feet on during meeting. The floor was not carpeted and those floors could get extremely cold. Each woman had her own cushion and what an interesting variety of colors and kinds they were. Most of them were covered with scraps of some kind of carpet....If I were there to help my father with his janitoring it was my duty to see that all of these cushions were piled around the stove to get warm. Not too close to the stove, but near enough for them to get nice and warm...As each lady came in to meeting, she carefully picked out her cushion, carried it to her seat, and placed it on the floor....The men were not so fastidious. They wore shoes or boots with heavy soles and while their feet may have been just as cold they would not have been helped much by a warm cushion, or at least they could take the cold. I do remember many times when the older men would sit for a short time near the stove to get partially warmed before taking their seats in the gallery.

Those were good meetings. When I think how far many of those Friends came in all kinds of weather by horse drawn conveyance, and then sat through the meeting in temperatures which may have been bearable but certainly not enjoyable, I am sure that they were able to gain spiritual strength and renewal from their experience.— *J. Howard Binns, 1985.*

WHEN I WAS ABOUT eleven years of age, a maid servant who tended on me and the rest of the children, would read Smith's and Preston's sermons First-day, between the sermons. I heard her diligently read, and liking not to use the Lord's Prayer only, I got a prayerbook and read prayers, morning and night, according to the days and occasions.

About this time my mind was serious about religion, and one day after we came from public worship, this forementioned maid servant read one of Preston's sermons on the text, "Pray continually." Much was said of the excellency of prayer— that it distinguished a saint from the world; for that in many things the world and hypocrites could imitate a saint, but in prayer they could not. This wrought much in my mind, and it seemed plain to me that I knew not *right prayer*, for what I used as a prayer, an ungodly man might do by reading it out of a book, and that could not be the prayer which distinguished a saint from a wicked one.

As soon as she had done reading and all gone out of the chamber, I shut the door, and in great distress flung myself on the bed and cried out aloud, "Lord, what is prayer?" At this time I had never heard any nor of any that prayed otherwise than by reading or by composing and reading a prayer, which they called a form of prayer.— *Mary Proude, England, 1635.*

"Likewise the Spirit also helpeth our infirmities: for we know not what we should pray for as we ought: but the Spirit itself maketh intercession for us with groanings which cannot be uttered."— Rom. 8:26.

IT CAME INTO my mind to write a prayer of my own composing, to use in the mornings. So I wrote a prayer, though I then could scarcely join my letters, I had so little a time learned to write. It was something of this nature: that as the Lord commanded the Israelites to offer up a morning sacrifice, so I offered up the sacrifice of prayer, and desired to be preserved during that day. The use of this for a time gave me some ease, and I soon left off using my books, and as the feelings arose in me, I wrote prayers according to my several occasions. The time when this circumstance took place, was when the spirit of Puritanism began to be manifested in the Churches. The reading of the common prayers of the Church of England Prayer-book, both in public and private worship, was one of the practices to which these Puritans— as they were in ridicule called— objected.

The next prayer I wrote was for an assurance of pardon for my sins. I had heard one preach, how God had pardoned David his sins of His free grace; and as I came from our place of worship, I felt how desirable a thing to be *assured* of the pardon of one's sins; so I wrote a pretty large prayer concerning it.

I felt a fear of being puffed up with praise, as several persons had praised me for the greatness of my memory; so I wrote a prayer of thanks for the gift of memory and expressed my desires to use it to the Lord.— *Mary Proude, 1635.*

THESE THREE PRAYERS I used with some ease of mind for a time, but not long; for I began again to question whether I prayed right or not. I knew not then that any did pray extempore, but it sprang up in my mind that to use words according to the sense I was in of my wants, was true prayer, which I attempted to do, but could not; sometimes kneeling down a long time, but had not a word to say.

This wrought great trouble in me, and I had none to reveal myself to, or advise with, but bore a great burden about it on my mind; till one day as I was sitting at work in the parlor, a gentleman who was against the superstitions of the times came in, and looking sorrowful, said "It was a sad day." This was soon after Prynne, Bastwick, and Burton were sentenced to have their ears cut and to be imprisoned. It sunk deep into my spirit, and strong cries were within me for them, and for the innocent people in the nation. It wrought so strongly in me, that I could not sit at my work, but left it and went into a private room, and shutting the door, kneeled down and poured out my soul to the Lord in a very vehement manner, and was wonderfully melted and eased. I then felt peace and acceptance with the Lord, and was sure that this was prayer in spirit and in truth, which I never was acquainted with before, either in myself or anyone else.— *Mary Proude, 1637.*

"Rejoice evermore. Pray without ceasing. Quench not the Spirit."— 1 Thess. 5:16,17,19.

WHENEVER A GREAT SPIRIT plumbs the depths of human experience, she or he does indeed summon us to something which, if not awful and unnatural, is at least beyond the commonplace. Whether they speak about becoming Enlightened, as Buddhists do, or entering the *moksha*, as Hindus do, or finding the Kingdom of God within us, as Christians do, they indicate to us that we have within us something very great, something of God, something farseeing and all-transcending, something which, if we ever receive the grace to get in touch with it, enables us to be born again of the Spirit and to live in a new and different way.

This new way of living is not the property of any particular religious faith. One line in the film [Gandhi], has him proclaiming: "I am a Hindu, I am a Muslim, I am a Christian, I am a Jew, I am a Sikh." And indeed, when an individual or a company finds this new level of life— George Fox and the Valiant Sixty, St. Francis of Assisi, Dorothy Day, Martin Luther King, Mohandas Gandhi, Thich Nhat Hanh, Mother Theresa, or Ham Sok Hon— we immediately recognize in them something which is neither of the East nor the West, neither ancient nor modern, but something which is simply the Truth, the plain Truth. And the works of social change and of service which are born out of this great Truth are at once so awesome and so sweet, so firm and so clear, that they fill us with joy and hope and wonder.— *Daniel A. Seeger, 1983.*

"TO COME NEAR to God is to change" is a cryptic Christian statement of a great truth. And the most open and vulnerable way at man's disposal to "come near to God" is prayer....If my prayer is real, my surface self, my ego...must decrease and he must increase in me. I dare not stay as I am and come near to such a love as his. I could not bear it. The many hucksters in me— the mean, demanding deceivers— are put to confusion by such a love.......

There is nothing that God cannot heal, and his forgiveness is given before we even approach him...

Forgiveness is a condition in which the sin of the past is not altered, nor its inevitable consequences changed. Rather in forgiveness a fresh act is added to those of the past which restores the broken relationship and opens the way for him who forgives and him who is forgiven to meet and communicate deeply with each other in the present and in the future. Thus, forgiveness heals the past, though the scars remain and the consequences go on. These keep the sinner humble. But now the past can no longer throttle....

There is, however, a condition for receiving God's gift of forgiveness. Man must be willing to accept it. Absurd as this may seem, there are few who will believe in and accept the forgiveness of God so completely as to let him bury their sin in his forgiving mercy; or who, having once accepted his forgiveness, will leave their sin with him forever. They are always re-opening the vault where they have deposited their sin, and are forever asking to have it back in order to fondle it, to reconstruct, to query, to worry over it, to wear it inwardly. Thus their sin ties them to the past, and finally dooms their lives in both the present and the future.— *Douglas Steere, 1962.*

ON A FIRST-DAY I went into the steeple-house at Bootle; and when the priest had done, I began to speak. But the people were exceedingly rude, and struck and beat me in the yard...

In the afternoon I went again. The priest had got to help him another priest, that came from London, and was highly accounted of....

The London priest was preaching. He gathered up all the Scriptures he could think of that spoke of false prophets, and antichrists, and deceivers, and threw them upon us; but when he had done I recollected all those Scriptures, and brought them back upon himself. Then the people fell upon me in a rude manner; but the constable charged them to keep the peace, and so made them quiet again. Then the priest began to rage, and said I must not speak there. I told him he had his hour-glass [timer], by which he had preached...and time was free for me, as well as for him, for he was but a stranger there himself.

So I opened the Scriptures to them, and let them see that those Scriptures that spoke of the false prophets, and antichrists, and deceivers, described them and their generation; and belonged to them who were found walking in their steps, and bringing forth their fruits; and not unto us, who were not guilty of such things. I manifested to them that they were out of the steps of the true prophets and apostles; and showed them clearly, by the fruits and marks, that it was they of whom those Scriptures spoke, and not we. And I declared the Truth, and the Word of life to the people; and directed them to Christ their teacher.— *George Fox, 1653.*

MY HEART FROM CHILDHOOD was pointed towards the Lord, whom I feared and longed after from my tender years. I felt I could not be satisfied with, nor indeed seek after the things of this perishing world, but abideth forever. There was something still within me which leavened and balanced my spirit continually, but I knew it not distinctly so as to turn to it, and give up to it entirely and understandingly.

In this temper of mind I earnestly sought after the Lord, applying myself to hear sermons and to read the best books I could meet with, but especially the Scriptures, which were very sweet and savory to me...but was much afraid of receiving men's interpretations upon them myself; but waited much, and prayed much that...I might receive the true understanding of them...

And indeed I did sensibly receive of His love, of His mercy, and of His grace, and at seasons when I was most filled with the sense of my own unworthiness, and had least expectation of manifestations of them.— *1658.*

*   *   *

Are there not different states, different degrees, different growths, different places?..What wisdom and spirit is that, which doth not acknowledge this, but would make all equal?..Therefore, watch every one to feel and know his own place and service in the body, and to be sensible of the gifts, places, and services of others.

*   *   *

Our life is love, and peace, and tenderness; and bearing one with another, and forgiving one another, and not laying accusations one against another; but praying one for another, and helping one another up with a tender hand.— *Isaac Penington, 1667.*

"YOU WERE DARKNESS once, but now you are light in the Lord. Be like children of light, for the effects of light are seen in complete goodness and right living and truth. Try to discover what the Lord wants of you....So be very careful about the sort of lives you lead, like intelligent and not like senseless people. This may be a wicked age, but your lives should redeem it."

(Eph 5:8-10, 15, 16)

I find this a remarkable passage. I suppose as a Quaker I have an affinity for the light imagery, but there is more to it than that. I am particularly struck by the last verse, "This may be a wicked age, but your lives should redeem it."

Surely this is a weighty charge! How can our lives redeem our "wicked age"? How should they? In trying to answer these questions I begin with the assumption that we need to take this passage at face value.

It does not say that our good works, or our testimonies, or our beliefs, or our doctrines should redeem our times. It says our lives should redeem our times....Look[ing] at the word being translated "lives," the Greek term..."kairos"...more often is translated as "occasion" or "opportunity." In other words, it is our occasions or opportunities to live in the manner just described which can serve to redeem our times.

This redemption will come about, then, not so much through what we do as through how and why we do it; and it comes about not so much through how we articulate our faith as through how we embody it....The redemption of our times may come about in the way we exist, the way we are, in the times or moments or occasions the Lord gives us.— *Thomas Jeavons, 1982.*

ALL OF US come with various experiences from which we need to be released, things which we have done, or left undone, which we sense as soiling, weakening, but often on our own we can not summon up the strength, or open our wills wide enough, so that we can be released. Yet when we gather in worship we can draw strength from one another, and through each other and the sense of the presence of God working among the group, be enabled to let go, to be cleansed in the pool of silence. So, we need to be at meeting to help one another towards that healing place, and as we help one another, we may find our own burden being lifted.

Yet, I wonder whether the most significant thing which holds us back from going to meeting, and which affects the quality of worship once we are there, is not our lack of a spiritual discipline during the week? Thomas Green put the matter succinctly and clearly: "We have put upon Sunday meeting a burden which it can not stand". What he had in mind was those very weekday rituals or patterns which used to mark the lives of Friends, and in which I, like so many others of my generation was surrounded, silence at meals, family reading, private meditation and prayer. These regular times of redirection which provided release and nourishment for each individual so that he came to meeting with a store from his inward journeyings, have now well-nigh disappeared. Now, we are like Mother Hubbards who arrive at meeting to find our store is almost bare...I am convinced that the vitality and practical effectiveness of our Society, as of any church, is directly related to the degree to which each of us manages to find time to explore our inner space during the week. — *Christopher Holdsworth, 1985.*

IN THE MORE SIGNIFICANT periods of their history, [Quakers] have been a source of social disturbance, not simply going along with their times, but challenging certain established ways, asking for more than their times could give. Perhaps they were "right too soon," believing it was never too soon to be right! Naive though they may have been at times, they have generally been a creative disturbance. Time was with them—their supposed heresy of yesterday being tolerated today and approved tomorrow.

They were not always right. One can hardly read their history without a measure of sympathy with some who opposed them, for they were not a people of unerring judgment. To say the least, they were sometimes "difficult," but the rightness of their principles and objectives has been generally attested by history.

Their course through history has been uneven. They have had periods of confrontation with what they believed were wrong ideas and practices, especially in their first half-century. In later periods they lapsed into a self-defensive retreat....

When the fires of the first movement burned low there were always embers glowing in the lives of many of them, ready to kindle a new beginning and make Quakerism a significant movement. At no period was it a spent force, for the original experience was too real, too much needed for it to be lost in a forgotten history.

For an understanding of the present we must see more than our own decade and discern the inner side of the past century. Movements and rebirths are never sharply dated, they move by no schedule, they are extra-calendar in their nature, yet they can be seen within time periods.—*Errol T. Elliott, 1972*

WILLIAM DEWSBURY (1621-1688) was one of the sweetest and wisest of the early Quakers. He spent a great part of his life in prison, chiefly at Warwick. His undaunted faith and reconciling spirit contributed greatly to the Quaker movement.

Then I could no longer fight with a carnal weapon against a carnal man, and returned to my outward calling, and my will was brought in subjection for the lord to do with me what his will was— if he condemned me, he might: and, if he saved me, it was his free love— and in this condemned estate I lay crying in the depth of misery. And the cry of my condemned soul was great, and could not be satisfied, but breathed and thirsted after Christ, to save me freely....— *1655.*

From some expressions of William Dewsbury near a week before his departure out of this life:

For this I can say, I never since played the coward, but joyfully entered prisons as palaces, telling mine enemies to hold me there as long as they could: and in the prisonhouse I sung praises to my God, and esteemed the bolts and locks put upon me as jewels, and in the Name of the Eternal God I always got the victory, for they could keep me there no longer than the determined time of my God.

If any one has received any good or benefit through this vessel, called William Dewsbury, give God the glory; I'll have none, I'll have none, I'll have none.— *William Dewsbury, 1688*

IN ORDER TO APPREHEND the divine in others, we must recognise it in ourselves. But it is somehow easier, at least for me, to accept that others are the daughters and sons of God than that I am. When others are unkind, foolish or downright bad we can make excuses for them— they were worried, ill-informed, had an unhappy childhood, were under strain, etc. Where we ourselves are concerned, however, we are all too aware of the trivial thoughts, the dubious motives, the laziness, vanity, greed and so on. How can we believe in that of God in ourselves? What shred of evidence have we?

Well, to start with, we have other people. We may be aware of their flaws, but the more profoundly we know them, the more we see miraculous qualities. When they might have been expected to curse, they speak with charity; when they might have been expected to give up, they are steadfast; when they might have been expected to hate, they love. Against every deterministic pressure, they demonstrate their freedom. I see in these people a wisdom that is deep, penetrating and compassionate. I see a strength manifested in vivid aliveness, a type of energy and power in which the physical and spiritual are inseparable and which is demonstrated in the capacity to give comfort— a word that, of course, implies strength. I see love in the sense of an overflowing and all embracing warmth that admits no barriers. And I see that these human qualities, which those who manifest them most would often see least in themselves, are universal. This is true of you and me. Those others can see it in us, as we can see it in them.— *Adam Curle, 1981.*

THERE ARE TIMES when we come to plateaus and when we do not seem to be able to get beyond them. Sometimes we have poured out all that we have into a family, a husband, a career, or into a series of ventures and have seemed now to come to the end of this life state. It is strange business how certain things have to die before others can be born.

I remember the late Elin Wagner, the only woman writer...to be a member of the Swedish National Academy, telling me how one time when she reached a point in her fifties, having already written a shelf of books, she had come to the end of her tether. She had written herself out, and she determined that she would not write another page until something within her opened up.... She told the Lord that unless he spoke to her and opened this new vein in her she would remain silent. She went about her ordinary household and garden chores in her little home,...saw something of her friends, but did no writing. Then, after several months, one fine morning she was overwhelmed by a sense of God's presence and by something that seemed to say to her, "How could you expect to have me speak to you when you have kept me gagged for so long!" A whole new wave of release came to her and a tumble of creativity emerged. Strangely enough, up to that time she had tried fiercely to keep from revealing in her books any of her own private life, some of which had been highly painful. When this new burst came, it swept away all of that restraint. Now if she had anything in her private experience that might encourage or comfort others, it was free and available for use. Plateaus need not be permanent or final if we are open for a disclosure of God's further landscape.— *Douglas V. Steere, 1966.*

MAN CERTAINLY has the talents and resources adequate to reduce drastically the frustrations which generate violence. Of course, constructive programs and reforms will never completely eliminate tensions and frustrations. Hence we must devise and employ effective alternatives to violence for handling conflicts which arise. Strictly speaking, every action except a violent one is nonviolent. It is necessary, therefore, to indicate what types of nonviolent means one advocates.

A very effective nonviolent approach was that of John Woolman, Quaker leader in Colonial America, who did more than any other individual to awaken his fellow Quakers to the evils of slavery. His method was primarily one of face-to-face persuasion. His character was so infused with humility and love that he aroused very little resentment as he drove home his message. In any age and situation those who oppose evil can derive considerable insight from an understanding of Woolman's personality as reflected in his *Journal*. Whatever other nonviolent methods one might employ, to exercise the sort of influence Woolman did through personal character and forceful persuasion would strengthen one's total impact tremendously. Yet his methods alone would not be adequate in the far more complex world of the late twentieth century.......

Gandhi...concentrate[d] on the purity of the means and considere[d] the realization of truth and enhancement of personality more important than the attainment of specific ends. Martin Luther King emphasized the coherence of means and ends: the means represent the end in process...the end is preexistent in the means. Hence an evil means cannot produce a good end.— *Phillips P. Moulton, 1971.*

I HAVE BEEN READING and have just finished the
journal of the life and religious labors of Mary
Alexander. I have not read very many of the journals of
deceased Friends, but from those which I have read,
there has been impressed upon me many an instructive
lesson. It is in such accounts that we gain that treasure
of experience, which without books or writings, would
be only attainable by the aged. We see from these
narratives, at one comprehensive view, the importance,
the value the object, and the end of human life. The
Travelers whose pilgrimages are described, seem to
traverse their course again under our inspection: we
follow them through their turnings and windings—
through their difficulties, discouragements, and
dangers— through the heights of rejoicing, and depths
of desolation, to which in youth, in age, in poverty, in
riches, under all conditions and circumstances, they
have been subject. From these accounts, we learn the
many liabilities which surround us, and we may (unless
through wilful blindness), unequivocally discover where
the true rest and peace is to be found, and in what
consists the only security, strength, and sure standing.
O! how loudly do the lives and deaths of these worthies
preach to us; they being dead do indeed yet speak,
exhorting and entreating that we who still survive may
lay hold and keep hold of those things in which alone
they could derive any comfort in the end.— *John Barclay,*
1817.

PLAYING MEETING

"TWAS a rainy morning. My children four—
Ernest and Belle, Louise and May,
And two little Dixons over the way,
Had been noisy in play an hour or more,
When all at once such a quiet lay
On the room, that I guessed it was "meeting day".

So I noiselessly drew to the door ajar,
And sat and listened; they could not see
My form, but the group was plain to me:
Ernest, with face drawn gravely down,
His little head lost in his father's crown,
Had the highest seat in the gallery.

And Alice Dixon, whose placid face
In its sober moods was pictured rest,
With a kerchief folded on her breast,
Sat next to him in the preacher's place;
And the younger ones on stools below,
Louise and Belle, and May and Joe.

A solemn silence filled the room;
I know not then, I know not now
If it could be so, but it seemed somehow
That the Spirit of Goodness did descend,
The same that we feel in its holy sway
In the grown-up meetings not formed for play.

(Continued next page)

(....Continued)

THEN ALICE, the preacher, rose to speak;
Belle giggled a little, but all the rest
Sat perfectly quiet as if possessed—
And she said in a voice that was clear and sweet—
"Dear Friends, I know we are young and small,
But I think the good Lord loves us all."

And then she went on further to show
How when they got cross at their work or play,
Or were naughty, He turned his face away,
And she prayed "to be good," and her prayer I know
Was very simple in thought and word,
But a sweeter one I have never heard.

Then the hands were shook and the meeting broke,
And the children laughed to be free again;
But I thought perhaps not all in vain
Was that meeting held or that sermon spoke,
For playing good may induce the state,
And simple things confound the great.

—*Author unknown, Ohio Conservative Friends Review*

OUR SOCIAL COMMITMENT, undertaken with God as it may be, lies in the realm of human history, and that means in the realm of human freedom. Here God is indeed our partner, but we truly do not know what limits are set to our freedom, and cannot speak meaningfully of such limits. We can only see how terribly far mutual destruction has proceeded in the past and there is little hope there....

That does not mean that faith is not real. It means that faith is now, and our hope is now. God does not wait for us at the end of time, nor in a future world of peace. God is with us. And it is with God that our faith lives. With God, not with success, nor confidence of success. For if faith is real at all, it remains when all possibilities have been stripped away; though it knows no limits that can not be broken, nonetheless, it trusts, and bereft of every kind of effecting power, its love endures. With God alone is there such faith.

But where is God to be found? There are times when God seems a distant and elusive vision. If meditation and prayer brings a moment's peace, our neighbor's emptiness soon chases it away. For while heaven's comfort is withheld from those around us, how can we both love and care for them in all their need and still regard the reality of our special spiritual privilege? In loving our neighbor we have already taken our place beside him, and in that place the heavens seem closed. But even there in the silence, the work of faith and faith itself begins.... When our acceptance of each other becomes commitment, when love means responding... the spirit gives birth to community.

That is the real opposite of the anti-human powers dominating the world today.— *W. Russell Johnson, 1969.*

A QUAKER! we glory in the name. Unworthy as we are of the appellation, we can feel a pride in its application to ourself. A Quaker! he can boast of no chivalric ancestors, no war-like heroes in the simple annals of his family. But he can boast of their moral power— of their triumph over self— of their heroic firmness in the dark days of New-England persecution. No blood has flowed to the demon of intolerance on the peaceful altars of his sect. In the hour of bigotry and persecution, when the scaffold of death was erected on the grave of liberty, the Quakers alone stood forth— not in arms— not in worldly power, but in calm and unbending opposition to tyranny. And they died in their firmness— perished on the ignominious scaffold— the pioneers in the cause of religious liberty.

*   *   *

IF we are not free, generous, tolerant, if we are not up to or above the level of the age in good works, in culture and love of beauty, order and fitness, if we are not ready recipients of the truths of science and philosophy,— in a word, if we are not full-grown men and Christians, the fault is not in Quakerism, but in ourselves...

*   *   *

I have never joined in the popular clamor against those who are so unfortunate as to doubt or disbelieve the divine origin of the Gospel: I have on all occasions, and at some cost, vindicated their rights of speech and fair hearing; and have, at the risk of misapprehension and obloquy, rebuked the intolerance of and bitter spirit of some of their assailants, who had undertaken to be God's avengers in the matter.— *John Greenleaf Whittier, c.1845.*

IN THE TIME of trading I had an opportunity of seeing that the too liberal use of spirituous liquors and the custom of wearing too costly apparel led some people into great inconveniences; and that these two things appear to be often connected with each other. By not attending to that use of things which is consistent with universal righteousness, there is an increase of labor which extends beyond what our Heavenly Father intends for us. And by great labor, and often by much sweating, there is even among such as are not drunkards a craving of liquors to revive the spirits; that partly by the luxurious drinking of some, and partly by the drinking of others (led to it through immoderate labor), very great quantities of rum are every year expended in our colonies; the greater part of which we should have no need of, did we steadily attend to pure wisdom.

When men take pleasure in feeling their minds elevated with strong drink, and so indulge their appetite as to disorder their understandings, neglect their duty as members of a family or civil society, and cast off all regard to religion, their case is much to be pitied. And where those whose lives are for the most part regular, and whose examples have a strong influence on the minds of others, adhere to some customs which powerfully draw to the use of more strong liquor than pure wisdom allows, it hinders the spreading of the spirit of meekness, and strengthens the hands of the more excessive drinkers....

Every degree of luxury hath some connection with evil....I have found by experience, that in such circumstances the mind is not so calm, nor so fitly disposed for Divine Meditation, as when all such extremes are avoided.— *John Woolman, 1755.*

I SAT IN THE SILENCE of a Quaker meeting recently. It had been several years since I last sat in the silence, and I came with anticipation. Quiet settled over the room as each of us turned within, listening to ourselves and preparing to listen to one another. Yet, it never really became silent. As the meeting settled, I became aware of the sound of breathing throughout the room, each person with an individual quality of sound and tempo. Then came the little noises of children unable to sit still any longer and of adults shifting position. One Friend went to sleep and for awhile her regular breathing dominated the room. A small airplane flew overhead. A lawnmower started up. Even the sunlight, reflecting off windshields and moving across the wall as the hour went by, made a sort of "noise."

We sat in silence, but it was not silent. Yet, we were silent, and not so much silent as listening.

I cannot speak for everyone, but I found that the sounds around me did not disturb the silence within. I heard the sleeping Friend and the rustling of the children, I marked the passage of the sun, but within I listened for other voices.

I value the people who encourage silence, and I value the places that make listening easy, but I know that silence is not so much a particular time or place as a state of mind. It has to do with turning oneself in the right direction, with tuning in to the right channel. Sounds are not a hindrance to silence. The wilderness canoeist can find silence while drifting across a remote lake, and the city apartment dweller can find it above the traffic. — *Dwight Ericsson, 1988.*

CYRUS PRINGLE was one of the many Quakers who battled with their consciences at the time of the Civil War. He left behind him a diary of this inner struggle...

31st. Here we are in prison in our own land for no crimes, no offense to God nor man; nay, more: we are here for obeying the commands of the Son of God and the influences of his Holy Spirit. I must look for patience in this dark day. I am troubled too much and excited, and perplexed....

Camp Near Culpepper. 25th— A council was soon held to decide what to do with us...[that] insisted as it was their duty to supply a gun to every man and forward him, that the guns should be put upon us, and we be made to carry them. Accordingly the equipment was buckled about us, and...in this way we were urged forward through the streets of Alexandria....

We came over a long stretch of desolated and deserted country, through battlefields of previous summers, and through many camps now lively with the work of the present campaign. Seeing, for the first time, a country made dreary by the war-blight, a country once adorned with green pastures and meadows and fields of waving grain, and happy with a thousand homes, now laid with the ground, one realizes as he can in no other way something of the ruin that lies in the trail of a war. But upon these fields of Virginia, once so fair, there rests a two-fold blight, first of slavery, now that of war. When one contrasts the fact of this country with...New England, he sees stamped upon it in characters so marked, none but a blind man can fail to read, the great irrefutable arguments against slavery and against war.- *Cyrus Pringle, 1863.*

IN THE FAMILY the unlimited liability is never relinquished. Who knows what this amazing school for charity known as the family will ask of me next? Who knows what hidden secret is sheathed in those islands of mystery known as children? Who knows what the life partner may disclose in the way of new and undreamed of levels of creativity which it is hers or his to develop, and what adjustments may be called for in order to make this possible?

When a father complained to the great Hasidic spirit of eighteenth century Judaism, Baal-Shem Tov, "My son is estranged from God—what shall I do?" he replied, "Love him more." When a married partner complains that she is not really understood by her husband, that he seems estranged from her, would the answer be any different? Someone has suggested that all the troubles come from not saying what we mean and not doing what we say. How swiftly the family discloses the gaps between what we mean and what we say, and what we say and what we do, and how often is forgiveness and a fresh start necessary? How restored a parent often is by having the child in the family quicken again the awe-filled, wonder-tipped child in his own heart out of which all that is best in him comes. And what gaiety and fun and special secrets and family projects grow out of this relationship?

The notion of each being liable without limits to help the others come through to what they are meant to be is an assignment beyond any we may have reckoned with when we were in the callow state of considering what a Christian family asked of its members. But is there any "this far and no further" that dare to be put on the family's liability for each other?— *Douglas V. Steere, 1966.*

THE TRUE GOD is a Spirit, and is infinite, eternal and everlasting, the Creator of all things, the life and being of all things, the power by which all things stand.

All creatures have a being in him: and by him and without him no creature is, or doth move upon the face of the earth. This is He whom we worship, and fear, and obey, and nothing can prevent the purpose of his mind but his counsel stands forever.

He is the righteous judge of all things, and before him must all mankind come to judgment, and the living and the dead by him must be judged: he is a rewarder of every one according to their deeds, whether they be good or whether they be evil. His greatness, power, majesty and dominion are over all and beyond all, ruling above all in the power of his own will, and who may say, what doest thou?

His eye seeth all, and his presence filleth all, and no creature can be hid from his sight; he is near at hand and afar off; he searchest man's heart and trieth the reins, and shows unto man his own thoughts. He justifieth the righteous and condemneth the wicked. He is light itself, and in him is no darkness at all.

This is the true God whom we worship.— *1657.*

*　　*　　*

The divine mystery of the infinite God is revealed and discovered in the hearts of the sons of men whom He hath chosen; and He hath given us to enjoy and possess in us a measure of the same love and life, of the same mercy and power, and of the same divine nature...— *Edward Burrough, London, 1660.*

AND now dear friends and brethren, in all your words, in your business and employments, have a care of breaking your word and promises to any people; but that you may consider before-hand, whether you may be able to perform and fulfil both your words and promises, that your yea be yea, and nay, nay, in all things; with Christ hath set up instead of an oath, yea above an oath and swearing, in His new covenant and testament.

So let none make any promise, or speak yea, yea, or nay, nay rashly, which they cannot perform: for such kind of inconsiderate and rash speaking is not in the everlasting covenant of life, light, and grace; take heed, lest ye be numbered among the truce-breakers as the Apostle speaks of, 2 Tim.iii, "which have a form of godliness, but deny the power thereof, from such turn away," said the apostle. And therefore they that deny the power of godliness will not be faithful to God nor man; and such cannot exercise a good conscience to God, in obedience to Him, nor to man, to perform that which is just, righteous, and honest.

And David said: "Who shall abide in thy tabernacle: and who shall dwell in thy holy will? He that walketh uprightly, and worketh righteousness, and speaketh the truth in his heart."— *George Fox, 1682.*

"But let your communication be Yea, yea, Nay, nay, for whatsoever is more than these cometh of evil."

— Matt. 5:37.

ELIZABETH [COMSTOCK] was a committed unionist while still holding to the Quaker peace testimony—a position not easily held by all Friends. She would not yield to the idea that war was the right answer in the conflict of views over slavery.......

Testimonials by military officers on the nature and value of the ministry of Elizabeth Comstock in military hospitals offer abundant proof of her warm reception. From a Brigadier General came a "pass" stating that "Mrs. Elizabeth L. Comstock, of the Society of Friends, is engaged in visiting the hospitals of the army for the purpose of administering religious consolation and instructions to the sick and the wounded. Her character and the value of her services to the soldiers, entitle her to every courtesy and aid in her labors." Another official wrote, "I accompanied these good "Angels of Mercy" in one of their visits to the hospitals here [Cincinnati] and never witnessed closer attention than that bestowed upon Mrs. Comstock in her address to the soldiers...."

In military hospitals she went from cot to cot where young soldiers, ill and wounded welcomed her as a motherly person. A wounded boy, in the delirium of fever, mistaking her for his far-distant mother, said, "Mother, I knew you would come." She talked to him about One who said "as one whom his mother comforteth, so will I comfort you." As death relaxed his body she noticed a ring he had clutched in his hand. By this she was able to identify him to his mother hundreds of miles distant. Sometimes when Elizabeth was mistaken for the mother of an ill or wounded boy she simply played the part of a mother, kissed and comforted him.— *Errol T. Elliott, 1972.*

AND OH, HOW SWEET and pleasant it is to the truly spiritual eye to see several sorts of believers, several forms of Christians in the school of Christ, every one learning their own lesson, performing their own peculiar service, and knowing, owning, and loving one another in their several places and different performances to their Master, to whom they are to give an account, and not to quarrel with one another about their different practices (Rom. 14.4). For this is the true ground of love and unity, not that such a man walks and does just as I do, but because I feel the same Spirit and life in him, and that he walks in his rank, in his own order, in his proper way and place of subjection to that; and this is far more pleasing to me than if he walked just in that track wherein I walk. Nay...I cannot so much as desire that he should do so, until he be particularly led thereto, by the same Spirit which led me. And he that knows what it is to receive any truths from the Spirit, and to be led into practices by the Spirit, and how prone the fleshly part is to make haste, and how dangerous that haste is, will not be forward to press his knowledge or practices upon others, but rather wait patiently till the Lord fit them for the receiving thereof...

The great error of the ages of the apostacy hath been to set up an outward order and uniformity, and to make men's consciences bend thereto, either by arguments of wisdom, or by force; but the property of the true church government is, to leave the conscience to its full liberty in the Lord, to preserve it single and entire for the Lord to exercise, and to seek unity in the light and in the Spirit, walking sweetly and harmoniously together in the midst of different practices.—*Isaac Penington, 1659.*

EXACTLY WHAT is the prize we seek? Doesn't it have something to do with supporting people in their efforts to live in peace with themselves, their loved ones and their communities? I feel that what the world needs now is more peace-able people— ready, willing, and able to communicate not merely the contentions of peace but the spirit of peace, not merely by what we do, but also what we choose *not* to do and allow to happen when we come into the presence of God in others.

Many have had good experiences standing up and speaking out against something we feel is wrong. Given the nature of our world it seems clear that we can expect additional opportunities to do so.......

I am convinced that our efforts to bring peace and well-being to the "body politic" must be undertaken in [a] holistic spirit and style. As a religious peace movement, we are not called to "make war on war" but to disempower war by glorifying the universality of goodness and presuming for ourselves the right to live at peace with all of life. I see little hope of arresting the self-destructive effects of the war system upon our society and the world except as some significant progress is made in restoring peoples' confidence that life works for us and that our best hopes for peace and security lie in availing ourselves of the power of good around and within us. By focusing attention on all that is wholesome in our experience and environment, we commute the self-isolation effects and immobilizing sentence of fear. And the more we grow attuned to discerning and availing ourselves of all we have going for us, the more confident we become in that Spirit which infuses all life and leads us from one good thing to another.— *Ross Flanagan, 1981*

I HAVE DECIDED to entrust the ultimate demise of the war system to God, the self-corrective nature of life and that same U.S. public which rejected civil defense shelters, when their nonsense became self-evident. I am choosing, instead, to lend my creative life energy to human empowerment and those communities of people who are presuming for themselves the right to develop their own conception and experience of "The Peaceable Kingdom."

Contrary to the many foreboding signs of social instability going on about us these days, something profoundly good and revolutionary is taking place in our country, to which our religious peace movement has an opportunity to make a significant contribution. I find myself being forced to acknowledge that peace cannot and will not be established simply because of the effort which we put into peacemaking.   Peace springs from our trust in God and our commitment to seek, find and share the very best that life has to offer us. As the Scriptures remind us in Leviticus 26:2,4 and 6:

You shall keep my sabbaths, and reverence my sanctuary: I am the Lord. Then I will give you rain in due season, and the land shall yield her increase and the trees of the field shall yield their fruit. And I will give you peace in the land, and you shall lie down, and none shall make you afraid.

For this dawning truth I am especially grateful.— *Ross Flanagan, 1981.*

DEAR FRIENDS, BRETHREN AND SISTERS:

...And now it is good for us all to go on and continue hand in hand in the unity and fellowship...in humility and lowliness of mind, each esteeming others better than ourselves; and this is well-pleasing to God.

And let us all take heed of touching anything like the ceremonies of the Jews; for that was displeasing unto Christ, for he came to bear witness against them, and testified against their outside practices, who told him of their long robes and of their broad phylacteries,...So that we may see how ill he liked their outward ceremonies. So let us keep to the rule and leading of the eternal Spirit, that God hath given us to be our teacher; and let that put on and off as is meet and serviceable for everyone's state and condition. And let us take heed of limiting in such practices; for we are under the Gospel leading and guiding and teaching, which is a free spirit,....not bound or limited.

Legal ceremonies are far from gospel freedom: let us beware of being guilty or having a hand in ordering or contriving that which is contrary to Gospel-freedom....

It's a dangerous thing to lead young Friends much into the observation of outward things, which may be easily done; for they can soon get into an outward garb, to be all alike outwardly, but this will not make them true Christians: it's the Spirit that gives life; I would be loath to have a hand in these things. The Lord preserve us, that we do no hurt to God's work; but let him work whose work it is. We have lived quietly and peaceably thus far, and it's not for God's service to make breaches.— *Margaret Fell Fox, last epistle to Friends, 1698.*

I DO NOT feel that ours is the only lawful manner of worship; I do not even think it at all clear that it would be for all people and at all times the most helpful. But I do believe it to be the purest conceivable. I am jealous for its preservation from any admixture of Adventitious "aids to devotion." I believe that its absolute freedom and flexibility, its unrivalled simplicity and gravity, make it a vessel of honor prepared in an especial manner for the conveyance of the pure water of life to many in these days who are hindered from satisfying their souls' thirst by questionable additions to the essence of Divine worship.

I know that, in Friends' meetings as elsewhere, one must be prepared to meet with much human weakness and imperfection; many things may be heard in them which are trying to the flesh—yes, and perhaps to the spirit also. Certainly many things may be heard which are open to criticism from an intellectual and literary point of view. Let no one go to Friends' meetings with the expectation of finding everything to his taste. But criticism fades away abashed in the presence of what is felt to be a real, however faltering, endeavour to open actual communication with the Father of spirits, and with each other as in His presence and His name.

People have said to me again and again, if you want to be silent, why cannot you be silent at home?....But the worthier answer is that, whether our utterance be prearranged or spontaneous, we meet in order to kindle in each other the flame of true worship, and also to show forth our allegiance to the Master, in whom we are so united as to feel our need for each other's sympathy in drawing near to Him.— *Caroline Stephen, 1890.*

A GREAT LIGHT and spiritual power blazed out in England, beginning about 1650, which shook thousands out of their complacent formalism, which kindled men and women with radiant fires of divine glory and holy joy. It sent them out into the market places and the churches, ablaze with the message of the greatness and the nearness of God, His ready guidance and His enfolding love. The blazing light illuminated the darkness, the shams, the silly externalities of conventional religion. It threw into sharp relief the social injustices, the underpaying of servants, the thoughtless luxuries, the sword as an instrument of social or "Christian " justice.

You and I exist today as paled-out remnants of the movement which sprang out of that discovery and that light. Those fires of 1650 and 1660 flicker low. We are for the most part respectable, complacent, comfortable, with a respectable past, proud of our birthright membership in the Society of Friends which guarantees us entrance, if not into heaven, at least into very earthly society....All too many of us, Quakers, near-Quakers, non-Quakers, have become as mildly and conventionally religious as were the tepid church members of three centuries ago....

But the blazing discovery which Quakers made, long ago, is rediscovered again and again by individuals, and sometimes by groups. The embers flare up, the light becomes glorious. There is no reason why it cannot break out again, today, with blazing power....It is in the hope that you and I, today, may rediscover this flaming center of religion that those words are written— not in an historical interest in a charming past.— *Thomas Kelly, 1939.*

KEEP OUT of the vain fashions of the world; let not your eyes, and minds, and spirit run after every fashion in apparel; for that will lead you from the solid life unto unity with that spirit that leads to follow the fashions of the nations. But mind that which is sober and modest, and keep your plain fashions, that therein you may judge the world, whose minds and eyes are in what they shall put on, and what they shall eat.

But keep all in modesty, and plainness, and fervency, and sincerity, and be circumspect; for they that follow those things that the world's spirit invents daily, cannot be solid. Therefore all keep down that spirit of the world that runs into so many fashions, to please the lust of the eye, the lust of the flesh, and the pride of life.

And let your minds be above the costly and vain fashions of attire, but mind the hidden man of the heart, which is a meek and a quiet spirit, which is of great price with the Lord. And keep to justice and truth in all dealings and tradings, at a word, and to the form of sound words, in the power of the Lord and in equity, in yea and nay in all your dealings, that your lives and conversations may be in heaven, and above the earth; that they may preach to all that you have to deal with; so you may be as a city set on a hill, that cannot be hid, and as lights of the world, answering the equal principle in all; that God in all may be glorified.— *George Fox, 1667.*

"And be not conformed to this world, but be ye transformed by the renewing of your mind."— Rom. 12:2.

SOON AFTER we located at Newport, I found that we were on a line of the Underground Railroad. Fugitives often passed through that place, and generally stopped among the colored people...who were the descendants of slaves who had been liberated by Friends many years before and sent to free States at the expense of North Carolina Yearly Meeting....These people were often pursued and captured, the colored people not being very skillful in concealing them, or shrewd in making arrangements to forward them to Canada....I inquired of some of the Friends in our village why they did not take them in and secrete them, when they were pursued....I found that they were afraid of the penalty of the law. I told them that I read in the Bible when I was a boy that it was right to take in the stranger and administer to those in distress, and that I thought it was always safe to do right. The Bible, in bidding us to feed the hungry and clothe the naked, said nothing about color....I was willing to receive and aid as many fugitives as were disposed to come to my house. I knew that my wife's feelings and sympathies regarding this matter were the same as mine, and that she was willing to do her part. It soon became known to the colored people in our neighborhood and others, that our house was a depot where the hunted and harassed fugitive journeying northward, on the Underground Railroad....

In the winter of 1826-27, fugitives began to come to our house, and as it became more widely known on different routes that the slaves fleeing from bondage would find a welcome and shelter at our house, and be forwarded safely on...the number increased.— *Levi Coffin, reputed President of the Underground Railroad, 1876.*

I SOON BECAME extensively known to the friends of the slaves, at different points on the Ohio River, where fugitives generally crossed, and to those northward of us on the various routes leading to Canada. Depots were established on the different lines of the Underground Railroad,...a perfect understanding was maintained between those who kept them. Three principal lines from the South converged at my house; one from Cincinnati, one from Madison, and one from Jeffersonville, Indiana...Seldom a week passed without our receiving passengers by this mysterious road. We found it necessary to be always prepared to receive such company and properly care for them. We knew not what night or what hour of the night we would be roused from slumber by a gentle rap at the door. That was the signal announcing the arrival of a train of the Underground Railroad, for the locomotive did not whistle, nor make any unnecessary noise. I have often been awakened by this signal, and sprang out of bed in the dark and opened the door. Outside in the cold or rain, there would be a two-horse wagon loaded with fugitives, perhaps the greater part of them women and children...the conductor...having driven the horses perhaps, twenty-five or thirty miles in the rain....Frequently, wagon-loads of passengers from the different lines have met at our house, having no previous knowledge of each other. The companies varied in number, from two or three fugitives to seventeen.

The care of so many necessitated much work and anxiety on our part,..but we bore it cheerfully....My wife [would] rise from sleep, and provide food and comfortable lodging for the fugitives...this work was kept up during...a period of more than twenty years.—
Levi Coffin, 1878.

ONE THING the world needs now is people who can tolerate ambiguity, people who are challenged, not threatened by the state of the world. I want to suggest a few things such maturity might require.

First, do not seek security in things, nor yet in status. The care of possessions, and position, is time-consuming and energy-consuming, and they can be taken from you by a thief in the night, by a fire in the night, by a change in political fortunes, by any numbers of disasters. Whatever security you have lies in yourself:

Henceforth I ask not good fortune. I myself am good fortune.

If you understand yourself, both your strengths and limitations, if you like the person you are, if you acquire coping skills through experience, if you are not too encumbered, and if you know— inwardly— that disaster cannot ultimately overcome you, then you have gone a long way to maturity. You will be part of the solution, not part of the problem.

Second, don't rest in intellectual security, for your philosophy and the knowledge on which it rests are likely to become obsolete....Wisdom is not amassing facts....

Third, the only real security in the end is the love we have given and the love we have received. All else can be taken from us. So pour out your love and friendship and do not hoard it...And don't delay or hesitate in standing up to be counted with the oppressed.

Finally, cultivate the light touch. Develop a sense of humor. Learn to light up a room with joy when you enter. Accept the challenge of our chaotic and dangerous word with a sense of adventure, of gratitude that *our* time is now.— *Elizabeth Watson, 1980.*

DEAR FRIENDS, mind the Light of God in your consciences, which will show you all deceit. God is not the author of confusion, but of peace. All jarrings, all schism, all rents, are out of the Spirit, for God hath tempered the body together, that there should be no schism in the body, but all worship Him with one consent.

*   *   *

And beware of discouraging any in the work of God. The laborers are few that are faithful for God. Take heed of hurting the gift which God hath given to profit withal, whereby ye have received life through death and a measure of peace by destruction of evil. Pray that peace may be multiplied, and the ministration of life, to the raising of the dead, that the *seed of the woman may bruise the serpent's head*, discover all deceit, and rend all veils and coverings, that the pure may come to life, which deceit hath trampled upon.. And all take heed to your spirits; that which is hasty, discerns not the good Seed. Take heed of being corrupted by flatteries; they that know their God, shall be strong. And therefore all mind your gift, mind your measure; mind your calling and your work. Some speak to the conscience; some plough and break the clods; some weed out, and some sow; some wait, that fowls devour not the seed. But wait all for the gathering of the simple hearted ones; for *they that turn many to righteousness, shall shine forever.* — *George Fox, 1651.*

"In him was life; and the life was the light of men. And the light shineth in darkness; and the darkness comprehended it not." — John 1:4,5.

WE MAY SEE ourselves crippled and halting, and from a strong bias to things pleasant and easy find an impossibility to advance forward; but things impossible with men are possible with God; and our wills being made subject to his, all temptations are surmountable.

This work of subjecting the will is compared to the mineral in the furnace, which through fervent heat, is reduced from its first principle: "He refines them as silver is refined; he shall sit as a refiner and purifier of silver." By these comparisons we are instructed in the necessity of the melting operation of the hand of God upon us, to prepare our hearts truly to adore him, and manifest that adoration by inwardly turning away from that spirit, in all its workings, which is not of him.

And now, as thou art again restored, after thy sore affliction and doubts of recovery, forget not Him who hath helped thee....I am sensible of that variety of company to which one in thy business must be exposed; I have painfully felt the force of conversation...from men deeply rooted in an earthly mind, and can sympathize with others in such conflicts, because much weakness still attends me.

I find that to be a fool as to worldly wisdom, and to commit my cause to God, not fearing to offend men, who take offence at the simplicity of truth, is the only way to remain unmoved at the sentiments of others..

The fear of man brings a snare. By halting in our duty, and giving back in the time of trial, our hands grow weaker, our spirits get mingled with the people, our ears grow dull as to hearing the language of the true Shepherd, so that when we look at the way of the righteous, it seems as though it was not for us to follow them.— *John Woolman, letter, 1754.*

I WILL BEGIN here also with the beginning of time, the morning. So as you wake, retire your mind into a pure silence, from all thoughts and ideas of worldly things, and in that frame wait upon God, to feel his good presence, to lift up your hearts to him; and commit your whole self into his blessed care and protection. Then rise, if well, immediately.

Being dressed, read a chapter or more in the Scriptures, and afterward dispose yourselves of the business of the day, ever remembering that God is present, the overseer of all your thoughts, words and actions...

And if you have intervals from your lawful occasions, delight to step home— within yourselves, I mean— and commune with your own hearts and be still....This will bear you up against all temptations, and carry you sweetly and evenly through your day's business, supporting you under disappointments and moderating your satisfaction in success and prosperity. The evening come, read again the Holy Scripture, and have your times of retirement before you close your eyes, as in the morning. So the Lord may be the Alpha and Omega of your lives.— William Penn, 1693.

*　*　*

God often touches our best comforts, and calls for that which we most love, and are least willing to part with. Not that he always takes it utterly away, but to prove the soul's integrity, to caution us from excesses, and that we may remember God, the author of those blessings we possess, and live loose to them. I speak my experience; the way to keep our enjoyments is to resign them; and though that be hard, it is sweet to see them returned, as Isaac was to his father Abraham, with more love and blessing than before.— *William Penn, 1682.*

BOTH GANDHI AND MARTIN LUTHER KING believed that we are meant to love our fellows. Insofar as a method encourages animosity and hatred, it is wrong. Whereas violence generally seeks the good of only one contending party, nonviolent direct action, guided by love, seeks the personal fulfillment of all concerned. Love is viewed not as a limitation, but as a dynamic force to overcome the fears and hatreds of the opponents and thus aid in solving the issues at stake. It is practical in the sense that whereas one cannot be sure of the effects of specific acts, he can know that love is good and must eventually produce good fruit. "Love suffereth long, and is kind; love...seeketh not its own, is not provoked...beareth all things, believeth all things, hopeth all things, endureth all things. Love never faileth (IICor.13:4ff).

A further conviction relevant to this issue is that one makes a decision on ethical grounds, such as to reject violence, added insight, power, and creativity are gained for the employment of appropriate methods. When Gandhi was asked what nonviolent plan he had to prevent World War II, he replied:"I have no ready-made concrete plan. For me too this is a new field. Only I have no choice as to the means. It must always be purely nonviolent, whether I am closeted with the members of the working committee or with the viceroy. Therefore what I am doing is itself part of the concrete plan. More will be revealed to me from day to day, as all my plans always have been." This is akin to the Christian faith that after a radical moral decision is made, further light is granted and the decision ultimately validated.— *Phillips P. Moulton, 1971.*

IN THE CONDITION I have mentioned, of weary seeking and not finding, I married my dear husband Isaac Penington. My love was drawn to him because I found he saw the deceit of all mere notions about religion; he lay as one that refused to be comforted until he came to His temple, who is truth and no lie. All things that had only the *appearance* of religion, were very manifest to him, so that he was sick and weary of show, and in this my heart united with him, and a desire was in me to be serviceable to him. I gave up much to be a companion to him.

I resolved never to go back into those formal things I had left, having found death and darkness in them; but would rather be without a religion, until the Lord manifestly taught me one. Many times when alone, did I reason thus:— Why should I not know the way of Divine life? For if the Lord would give me all in this world, it would not satisfy me. Nay, I could cry out, I care not for a portion in this life; give it to those who care for it: I am miserable with it. It is acceptance with God, of which I once had a sense, that I desire, and that alone can satisfy me.

Whilst I was in this state, I heard of a new people called Quakers, but I resolved not to inquire after them, nor their principles. I heard nothing of their ways except that they used thee and thou to every one; and I saw a book written about plain language by George Fox.—
Mary Penington, 1650.

DURING the mental struggles above alluded to, Mary Penington does not appear to have sought or maintained any intimate acquaintance with the Friends, or to have made a practice of attending their meetings; but it is most probable she had been reading some of their writings, after she had given up all her worldly reasoning against the pointing of her own enlightened conscience.

She adds, "I then received strength to attend the meetings of this despised people, which I intended never to meddle with. I found they were truly of the Lord, and my heart owned and honored them. I then longed to be one of them, and minded not the cost nor pain; but judged it would be well worth my utmost cost and pains to witness in myself such a change as I saw in them— such power over the evil of human nature. In taking up the cross, I received strength against many things that I once thought it not possible to deny myself. But oh! the joy that filled my soul at the first meeting held in our habitation at Chalfont. To this day I have a fresh remembrance of it, and of the sense the Lord gave me of His presence and ability to worship Him in that spirit which was undoubtedly His own.

Oh! long had I desired to worship Him in the full assurance of acceptance, and to lift up my hands and heart without doubting, which I experienced that day.— *Mary Penington, 1658.*

IN CASES WHERE our activism is carried out through coalitions or agencies organized in an ecumenical spirit, where the work draws together people of many faiths and backgrounds, it can happen that we often deliberately dilute the faith content of the atmosphere so as not to seem dogmatic or sectarian. Our correct understanding that the God of our universe is the loving shepherd of many flocks, and that none has an exclusive monopoly on the truth, rather than leading to an enriching sharing of insight, somehow causes us to remove all faith issues whatsoever from the agenda.......

Our capacity for faith, for spiritual knowledge, is nourished by the preaching and writing of people of holiness, and most especially by scripture. All great spirits derive sustenance from some source of truth external to themselves. St. Francis of Assisi was steeped in the four Gospels; George Fox, in the sweep of the Old and New Testaments; Gandhi and Thomas Merton, in the great scriptures of both the East and the West. Rufus Jones found intense and living nourishment in the church fathers and in certain of the women and men of towering spirituality who flourished in medieval times, and he in turn spoke inexhaustibly to the condition of modern humanity. He was an activist, too, and a key founder of the American Friends Service Committee.......

The burden of evidence is that seeking an authentic realization of the Gospel of Hope in our activism without providing for periodic, programmed reaffirmations of the content of our faith is highly risky. Most of us, unless we are extraordinarily far advanced in spiritual realization, need some outside reinforcement, some upliftment. — *Daniel A. Seeger, 1983.*

NOW, MOTHERS of families, that have the ordering of children and servants, may do a good deal of good or harm in their families, to the making or spoiling of children and servants; and many things women may do and speak amongst women, which are not men's business. So men and women become helpmeets in the image of God.

And the elder women in the truth were not only called elders, but mothers. Now, a mother in the church of Christ, and a mother in Israel, is one that nourishes, and feeds, and washes, and rules, and is a teacher in the Church, and in the Israel, of God, and an admonisher, an instructor, an exhorter. So the elder women and mothers are to be teachers of good things, and to be teachers of the younger, and trainers up of them in virtue, in holiness, in godliness and righteousness, in wisdom, and in fear of the Lord, in the Church of Christ......

*   *   *

Surely such a woman is permitted to speak, and to work the work of God, and to make a member in a church; and then as an elder, to oversee that they walk according to the order of the Gospel.

And women are to keep the comely order of the Gospel, as well as men, and to see that all have received Christ Jesus, do walk in Christ Jesus; and to see that all that have received the Gospel, do walk in the Gospel, the power of God which they are heirs of.— *George Fox, 1672.*

"That ye might walk worthy of the Lord unto all pleasing, being fruitful in every good work, and increase in the knowledge of God."— Col. 1:10.

ALL OF US HAVE occasion to fear the unknown. The thought of departing from known habits and rewards is so threatening that we cling to them, even when they cause pain. At least they are familiar....The unknown contains risk, possible loss, maybe even death.

But somewhere in us a voice whispers, "Go." It says that there is a fuller calling for us, that there is much to be gained by venturing forth. It says that there are resources within ourselves that we have ignored. It says that external validations are empty unless they are responses to what we actually are, rather than to the roles we carefully play.

Playing these roles is hard work. We become known for the traits that we have cultivated thus far in our lives: our punctuality, perhaps or our productivity, or our generosity, or even our spirituality. But what might have started out as genuine impulses now feel like burdens, mere reputations to maintain....We have sacrificed our inner urges in order to make ourselves acceptable to others. Like a child, we feel that if we do not do certain things, "They won't like us anymore...."

The underlying fear is the fear of the unknown within ourselves. What if there is no reservoir of strength to call upon? *What if there is nothing there?* Or what if we have to confront those things that we have successfully suppressed from our consciousness for so long?.......

As we put aside the encumbrances and see them for what they are, we will see what was there, unnoticed and untapped, all along....Our commitment is to notice the stirrings within ourselves and to let them carry us to new levels of expression and service.— *Paul Niebanck, 1981.*

THE QUAKER OF OLDEN TIME

The Quaker of the olden time:—
  How Calm, and firm, and true!
Unspotted by its wrong and crime,
  He walked the dark earth through!
The lust of power, the love of gain,
  The thousand lures of sin
Around him, had no power to stain
  The purity within.

With that deep insight, which detects
  All great things in the small,
And knows how each man's life affects
  The spiritual life of all,
He walked by faith and not by sight,
  By love and not by law;—
The presence of the wrong or right,
  He rather felt than saw.

He felt that wrong with wrong partakes,
  That nothing stands alone,
That whoso gives the motive, makes
  His brother's sin his own.
And pausing not for doubtful choice
  Of evils great or small,
He listened to that inward voice
  Which called away from all.......
                — *John Greenleaf Whittier.*

IF AN INDIVIDUAL thinks that war is evil, we are so simple-minded, so naïve, as to say "If war is evil, then I do not take part in it", just as one might say, "If drunkenness is evil, then I do not drink; if slave holding is evil, then I do not hold slaves." I know that sounds too simple— almost foolish.— Henry J. Cadbury.

* * *

Today there are millions of men in nearly every great nation who have taken part in war and they still believe that that war, or their part in it, was justified. As long as they hold that view, they seem to me to be a risk against world peace. Those people who have once believed that war is justified can readily be persuaded that it will be justified again....

I believe it is true that this tendency to believe that war is justified creates in itself a danger to peace, and it is not lessened by what men have learned or experienced of the terrible damage that war can do materially, morally or spiritually, or by what we know now that another war could do. I believe the greatest risk of war is in the minds of men who have an unrepentant and unchanging view of the justification of past wars.— *Henry J. Cadbury, 1948.*

Speech made at the presentation of the Nobel Peace Prize to the Friends' Service Council and to the American Friends' Service Committee, 1948.

I AM HAPPY to say that I do not write as a "disciple" of John Woolman or of Mahatma Gandhi or of any of those great teachers who have helped me to understand more about God and Man— and myself. The world will be no better for people who can recite chunks from Woolman's Journal, even if they try to apply them to personal and social problems, unless they have drunk from the spring which was the inspiration of Woolman's life. "Seek ye first the Kingdom of God" is not a counsel of "other-worldliness," but a simple suggestion that you may as well get your bearings if you intend to reach the harbor.

Men fear the Kingdom of God more than anything else, though Christians pray regularly for its coming. That was what the Athenians feared, though they had no such name for it when they gave Socrates his last drink. I would rather ask awkward questions myself than provide slick answers. It came to me at Pendle Hill after having seen the turmoil in the minds of adolescents last summer— the rich fertile confusion of young minds shaken from

> "The comfortable ways
> Of men's consent and praise."

I saw it suddenly as a new beatitude; though for all I know it was new only to myself, but none the less a shattering vision of a new purpose. And I said: "Blessed are the confused, for they *may* see the light. And beware of those who know all the answers, for they are wrong."— *Reginald Reynolds, 1958.*

WE ARE PEOPLE who can hardly ever be quiet. We travel to work with the roar of traffic in our ears, we spend our days in the presence of clanging machinery, or chattering people, and our evenings in the continuous flow of sound through the facility of broadcasting. Even in the countryside we find it difficult to avoid pollution by noise. We are conditioned by our age to be noisy, so much so that we are almost afraid to be silent....

In obedience to [western society's] demands we forget to stand still for a while and ask what it is all for, and whether we should not be paying more attention to the quality of life. Instead, we drive ourselves to the limits of our...capacities. We become tired and bored with our occupations: but such weariness is the sign of failure, so, in efforts to conceal this from ourselves, we camouflage the dreadful fact by plunging even more ferociously into further strenuous activity....

Despite our engagement in the strenuous and noisy activity of life, and our frequent but causal encounters with people...we are basically lonely and isolated....

[Perspective] can only be rediscovered by our willingness to recognize that there is a natural balance between work and rest, and, that the constant striving for perfection is probably the surest way of missing the mark altogether. We have to recognize that there is an inbuilt rhythm in life to which we need to adjust so that we can respond to its ebb and flow. Such a recognition and adjustment will come about as we stop and stand still in silence....

That in learning to be quiet and still, modern men will find, as did the first Friends...a way to rediscovery of their identity as real people.— *George H. Gorman, 1973.*

NO QUAKER would suggest that Quaker worship, in its private or public aspects is a panacea for the ills of modern life. They would, nevertheless, want to affirm most strongly that their regular participation in silent worship is, at the very least, a vital and necessary form of therapy. By and large Quakers tend to be busy people, and you rarely find them wondering how to occupy their time. They would, however, be the first to recognize how essential it is for them to have periods of disinvolvement, even from the activities which express their continuing concern to care for people....In our disinvolvement two elements will be present. First is a kind of detachment that while standing back, accepts all experience in the hope of transcending it—seeing beyond it creatively. Secondly a cessation from all mental activity so that the body and mind are as still and quiet as possible.

The Society of Friends has always encouraged its members to seek a daily opportunity to withdraw from the necessary affairs of life, and, "in inward retirement", to renew their resources, and also to ensure that they get their priorities right. There is no hard and fast rule about how this should be done, and Friends will set about it in the manner most helpful and natural to them....It is, of course, an individual discipline, but it has a two-fold objective. The first is to enable a person to be in touch with the inner core of his being so that his whole life may be renewed. The second is to help to prepare him to enter more fully into the corporate worship which is the central activity of the Society of Friends...[Yet] the uniqueness of the Quaker approach lies in its emphasis on the role of silence.— *George H. Gorman, 1973.*

SOMETIMES when the fugitives came to us destitute, we kept them several days, until they could be provided with comfortable clothes. This depended on the circumstances of danger....Sometimes fugitives have come to our house in rags, foot-sore and toil-worn, and almost wild, having been out for several months traveling at night, hiding in canebrakes or thickets during the day, often being lost and making little headway at night, particularly in cloudy weather, when the north star could not be seen, sometimes almost perishing for want of food, and afraid of every white person they saw, even after they came into a free State, knowing that slaves were often captured and taken back after crossing the Ohio River....

When they first came to us they were generally unwilling to tell their stories, their names, or the names of their masters, correctly, fearing that they would be betrayed. In several instances fugitives came to our house sick from exhaustion and exposure, and lay several weeks....

[Slavehunters] often threatened to kill me, and at various times offered a reward for my head. I often received anonymous letters warning me that my store, pork-house, and dwelling would be burned to the ground, and one letter, mailed in Kentucky, informed me that a body of armed men were then on their way to Newport to destroy the town....I had become so accustomed to threats and warnings, that this made no impression on me....The most of the inhabitants of our village were Friends, and their principles were those of peace and non-resistance. They were not alarmed at the threat to destroy the town, and on the night appointed retired to their beds as usual and slept peacefully.— *Levi Coffin, 1876.*

THE EARLY ASCETICS were driven out into the desert because they believed that there they could find God, and learn to love and serve him effectively. They looked to the desert because it was, so to say, all around them, near at hand to the narrow strips of cultivable land on either side of the Nile, or around the great oases. They also went there because they knew that it was the place where Jesus had gone, and where many of the great Jewish leaders— Moses and Elijah, for instance— had sought God. The attraction of the desert and the liberation it brought them...meant the possibility of facing the many aspects of an individuals' life which kept him from God....

Among the second or third generation of desert dwellers the wisdom of the beginnings was somewhat narrowed and accentuated; just the kind of development which can be observed in the history of our own Society, where, for example, the concern for plainness became an obsession with particular styles in garments and furnishing. As for the permanence of their retreat, it is probably natural for us to think that they mistook their guide; we would prefer that they, like Jesus, had returned to the world to serve it, after a time in the desert had prepared them to serve it better. Yet the stories make two things very clear; that the world was never far away, rarely more than a day's walk, and that those who dwelt in the desert, on the fringe of society, were constantly receiving visitors and helping them with advice....

Our world is a very different place, and yet I do not doubt that we need the witness from the desert and to find some equivalent in our own lives.— *Christopher Holdsworth, 1985*

MANY OF US LIVE at such a pace, where we almost boast that we never have a spare moment, that we can go for long periods without ever having time for solitude and the challenges which it brings. The lure of activity may be peculiarly hard for Friends to resist, because so often we are, apparently, capable people who have much to do and to give, both in our work and in our service to the Society. A public Friend, as they used to be called, can very easily spend most of his or her time dashing from one good cause to another, but I doubt whether any of us can in fact do without some solitude. It is abundantly clear that Jesus needed it, and I see no reason why we should not. Sometimes it needs some accident, or personal disaster, a bereavement for instance, to bring us to our senses, and to the place where we can take stock. Quite what form solitude will take for each of us, surely will vary; for one it may be as a solitary walk, for another a time alone at home: some will need to make a desert in each day, others may make spaces in holidays or at some weekends.

If we go out into our desert the layers of ourselves which are obscured during our busyness will come to the surface; it is stupid to pretend that they won't. All the stupid, unsatisfactory, unlovely sides of ourselves which we often think are not there, will work their way up and have to be faced.......

Solitude should not produce people who worry about judging others, but instead should create individuals who are full of compassion, just because they have come face to face with their own weaknesses.— *Christopher Holdsworth, 1985.*

I THEN BEING sixteen years of age and four months, in the 10th month, 1654...I received knowledge of God and the way of his blessed truth, by myself alone in the field, before I ever heard anyone called a Quaker preach, and before I was at any of their meetings. But the First Day that I went to one, which was at Pardshaw, the Lord's Power in the meeting so seized upon me, that I was made to cry out in the bitterness of my soul...and the same day at evening, as I was going to a meeting of God's people, even those people scornfully called Quakers, [on] the way, I was smitten to the ground with the weight of God's judgment for sin and iniquity, that fell heavy upon me; and I was taken up by two Friends.

And, Oh! the godly sorrow that did take hold of me, and seized upon me that night in the meeting; so that I thought in myself, everyone's conditions was better than mine. So a Friend (as he told me some time after) being touched with a sense of my condition, (and did greatly pity me) was made willing to read a paper in the meeting (there being but a very few words spoken) which was suitable to my condition, that it helped me a little, and gave me some ease in my spirit....For I was by nature wild and wanton; though there was good desires stirring in me many times, and something that judged me and reproved me....But not being sensible what it was, got over it....

So about six years after I had received the Truth...the Lord opened my mouth with a testimony... Oh! then a great combat I had through reasoning: I was but a child, and others were more fit and able to speak than I. But the Lord...wrought me into willingness, and with fear and trembling I spoke in our blessed meetings.—*John Banks, 1696.*

THE ETERNAL love of my father is to thee, and because he loves thee and would entirely enjoy thee, therefore doth he so grievously batter and break down that which stands in the way. What he is doing towards thee, thou canst not know now, but thou shalt know hereafter. Only be still and wait....The great thing necessary for thee at present to know is the drawings of his Spirit, that thou mayst not ignorantly withstand or neglect them, and protract the day of thy redemption.

Oh! look not after great things; small breathings, small desires, after the Lord, if true and pure, are sweet beginnings of life. Take heed of despising "the day of small things," by looking after some great visitation, proportionable to thy distress, according to thy eye. Nay, thou must become a child, thou must lose thy own will quite by degrees. Thou must wait for life to be measured out by the Father and be content with what proportion, and at what time, he shall please to measure.

Oh! be little, be little; and then thou wilt be content with little. And if thou feel now and then a check or a secret smiting— in that is the Father's love; be not over-wise or over-eager in thy own willing, running and desiring, and thou mayst feel it so and by degrees come to the knowledge of thy Guide, who will lead thee, step by step, in the path of life and teach thee to follow and in his own season, powerfully judge that which cannot or will not follow. Be still, and wait for light and strength and desire not to know or comprehend, but to be known and comprehended in the love and life which seeks out, gathers, and preserves the lost sheep.— *Isaac Penington, c. 1679.*

SO AT LAST there was something revealed in me, that the Lord would teach his people himself. And so I waited, and many things opened in me....And sometimes I would have heard a priest, but when I heard him, I was moved by the Lord, and his word in me spoke to oppose. And often as a fire I burned, and a trembling fell on me. Yet I feared reproach, and so denied the Lord's motion....Still my mind ran out, and out of fear into carelessness....

And so I went up and down, preaching against all the ministry; and also ran out with that which was revealed to myself, and preached up and down the countryside of the fulness that was in the old bottle, and so was wondered after, and admired by many...and we fed one another with words....

And immediately, as soon as I heard [Fox] declare...that the Light of Christ in man was the way to Christ, I believed the eternal word of truth, and that of God in my conscience sealed to it. And so not only I, but many hundred more who thirsted after the Lord...were all seen to be off the foundation, and all mouths were stopped in the dust....

My eyes were opened, and all the things I had ever done were brought to remembrance...and there was thunder and lightning and great hail. And then the trumpet of the Lord was sounded, and then nothing but war and rumor of war, and the dreadful power of the Lord fell on me: plague, and pestilence, and famine, and earthquake, and fear and terror for the sights that I saw with my eyes....And in the morning I wished it had been evening, and in the evening I wished it had been morning and I had no rest, but trouble on every side.— *Francis Howgill, 1656.*

THE FIRST QUAKER MEETING I ever attended was in Virginia Beach, Virginia. It is home port for much of the navy's Atlantic aircraft carrier fleet, and the Friends meetinghouse happened to be located under the flight pattern of the navy's main runway. It was normal for the meeting to be interrupted by the roar of jet aircraft coming or going. The interruption was the more noticeable because pacifism is one of the basic tenets of Quakerism and the noise of military aircraft right during meeting for worship was a constant reminder of "the world."

Absolute silence is artificial. We can create it only by building elaborate rooms that shut out the world completely. And even there we hear the sound of our own heartbeat. Absolute silence is a scientific... curiosity, apart from the world in which we live.

We were not meant to live apart from the world. Without it we lose our center and become "eccentric." The world may seem at times to hold us back, but it is like the ballast in a ship. With ballast a ship can proceed in a straight line. Without it any storm can blow it off course.

So I am grateful for the splashing waves, the wiggles of small Friends, and even for jet engines. They remind me of the world in which I live, out of which I draw sustenance, and to which I must return after any retreat within myself. They remind me that anything I find in the silence must be tested against a larger reality than myself.

The purpose of retreat into silence is to be able to cope better with the world in which I live. As I must take the fruit of silence back into the world, so it is well that the world be present in the silence. — *Dwight Ericsson, 1988.*

THE DUTY of many of us lies very much in scenes of active life, and various occupations may take up a considerable part of our time; but in this hurry and bustle, without setting apart proper seasons of retirement, the mind is very apt to get bewildered, and too often settles in a false rest.

*   *   *

This I at times experience to be my own case, and though I would by no means make the path of virtue appear dismal or gloomy, yet I confess I could never yet find it to be strewed with roses, but have been rather inclined to embrace the saying of our Saviour to his disciples: "In the world ye shall have tribulation, but in me peace."

A great part of our happiness, while in this present state of being, arises from a well-grounded hope of a glorious immortality; and though we are to receive with thankfulness the various undeserved blessings that are bestowed upon us in terrestrial things, yet the uncertainty of their duration makes it improper that we should set our affections on them; but using the things of this world and not abusing them, we should endeavor to maintain an equal mind in prosperity or adversity, and with humble resignation of heart, say, "Thy will, O God, not mine, be done;" trusting that all things will work together for our good, being anxiously solicitous about nothing, but that we may be established in righteousness, and gain admittance into that Kingdom which will never end.— *Margaret Woods, 1774.*

"DEAR FRIENDS," writes Fox to his groups, "keep close to that which is pure within you, which leads you up to God." John Woolman, the Quaker tailor of Mt. Holly, New Jersey, resolved so to order his outward affairs, so to adjust his business burdens, that nothing, absolutely nothing would crowd out his prime attendance upon the Inward Principle. And in this sensitizing before the inward altar of his soul, he was quickened to see and attack effectively the evils of slave-holding, of money-loaning, of wars upon the Indians.

But the value of Woolman and Fox and the Quakers of today for the world does not lie merely in their outward deeds of service to suffering men, it lies in that call to all men to the practice of orienting their entire being in inward adoration about the springs of immediacy and ever fresh divine power within the secret silences of the soul. The Inner Light, the Inward Christ, is no mere doctrine, belonging peculiarly to a small religious fellowship, to be accepted or rejected as a mere belief. It is the living Center of Reference for all Christian souls and Christian groups—yes, and of non-Christian groups as well—who seriously mean to dwell in the secret place of the Most High. He is the center and source of action, not the end-point of thought. He is the locus of commitment, not a problem for debate. Practice comes first in religion, not theory or dogma. And Christian practice is not exhausted in outward deeds. These are the fruits, not the roots. A practicing Christian must above all be one who practices the perpetual return of the soul into the inner sanctuary....— *Thomas Kelly, 1941.*

HUMILITY is a form of inner strength, a kind of dignity that makes it less necessary for a person to pretend.

We cannot help but be humble when we look beyond the appearances of things and contemplate the vast reaches of the unknown. The more we grow in understanding, the more we realize how much there is that yet lies hidden.

When we seek to realize the meaning of our own emotions, we cannot help but be humble. We are baffled by the play of love and hate in our lives. We cannot penetrate the clouds of anxiety that move across the horizons of our inner world. We are perplexed by conditions that sometimes move us toward depths of longing. We are bewildered by the complexity of our feelings, which lead us at times to accept what we should reject and to reject what by rights we should accept.

We cannot help but be humble when we consider the poignancy of our grief; the weight of our melancholy on occasion; the inexpressible quality of the joy that sometimes wells up in us; the ominous waves that threaten to engulf us as we stand on the brink of despair; and the thrill that surges through us as we taste in advance a happy fulfillment of our hopes.......

When we are humble, we are able to wait and be silent. We can wait, for we do not expect that we should immediately understand each question from within or have a response to each query from without...

Being able to wait enables us to listen. We are good listeners when others have something to say, and we will hear them out if we think it fit or timely to do so. But even more, we are good listeners to our own inner voices which often speak slowly and indistinctly.— *William O. Brown, 1978.*

I HAVE WONDERED what it would take for a Meeting to be able to "weary out all contention." What is it that makes loving confrontation so difficult? Is it because we don't know what to do with our negative, angry, hateful feelings in the Quaker context? Are there ways in which we can clear the emotional pathways so that the positive and constructive can find expression?... Friends from the beginning have voiced sensitive concerns about nearly imperceptible to major violations of integrity, have eldered each other in the Light, have prayed together for understanding and vision, have held threshing sessions to clear the air, have held open the hope for redemption and transcendence, have tried what love can do and when all else failed, have suffered defeat and separation. If we are to face up to the complexities of who we are and what we are about as a people and not be overwhelmed, then where better to work out the complexities of building community than in this microcosm of our local Meeting?

A dimension much needed in the process of loving confrontation and in meeting challenges in all their complexity is perhaps a gift like that of grace—the gift of humor. There is a particular kind of Quaker humor that is gentle and dry and we chuckle when we are privy to it. It is a humor that nourishes, that saves the day, that delights and reaches down to some deep, needful core of self. It is a humor that has the universal appeal of holding up the mirror for us to unthreateningly see ourselves and the human condition in wonderful clarity. Thank God for the grace of humor, without which we would be less than human and less aware of the signals of transcendence within ourselves and others.— *William O. Brown, 1978.*

THROUGHOUT OUR LIFE we need faith and the realization of God's love, but in the stress and rush and haste of the active years we have not so much time to be aware of its presence—or its absence.

Age comes, and without jobs, without the energy to fill all our hours with activity, with decreased ability to read, to travel and sometimes even to knit, we have much more time to think. We lie awake for hours at night. And we find, some of us, that what we thought was faith was not much more than well-being, that our realization of God and his love was academic, unreal, unconvincing. The words used so easily by spiritual writers and the devout seem empty and perfunctory. The little books on our bedside tables have been read and re-read until all the juice has gone out of them. What now? How do I re-write this prayer? Not necessarily as I would write it for myself, but how would I like younger people to express it, for all of us past sixty-five, with all of our differences and gradations of age? Might this do?

CONSIDER THY OLD FRIENDS, O GOD, WHOSE YEARS ARE INCREASING. PROVIDE FOR THEM HOMES OF DIGNITY AND FREEDOM. GIVE THEM, IN CASE OF NEED, UNDERSTANDING HELPERS AND THE WILLINGNESS TO ACCEPT HELP. DEEPEN THEIR JOY IN THE BEAUTY OF THY WORLD AND THEIR LOVE FOR THEIR NEIGHBORS, GRANT THEM COURAGE IN THE FACE OF PAIN OR WEAKNESS, AND ALWAYS A SURE KNOWLEDGE OF THY PRESENCE.
— *Elizabeth Gray Vining, 1982.*

AS IT IS COMMON for Friends on such a visit to have entertainment free of cost, a difficulty arose in my mind with respect to saving my money by kindness received from what appeared to me to be the gain of oppression. Receiving a gift...brings the receiver under obligations to the benefactor, and has a natural tendency to draw the obliged into a party with the giver. To prevent difficulties of this kind, and to preserve the minds of judges from any bias, was that Divine prohibition: "Thou shalt not receive any gift; for a gift blindeth the wise, and perverteth the words of the righteous." (Exod. 23:8.) As the disciples were sent forth without any provision for their journey, and our Lord said the workman is worthy of his meat...yet in regard to my present journey, I could not see my way clear in that respect.......

The way in which I did it was thus: when I expected soon to leave a Friend's house where I had entertainment, if I believed that I should not keep clear from the gain of oppression without leaving money, I spoke to one of the heads of the family privately, and desired them to accept of those pieces of silver, and give them to such of their negroes as they believed would make the best use of them; and at other times I gave them to the negroes myself, as the way looked clearest to me. Before I came out, I had provided a large number of small pieces for this purpose and thus offering them to some who appeared to be wealthy people was a trial both to me and them. But the fear of the Lord so covered me at times that my way was made easier than I expected; and few, if any manifested any resentment at the offer and most of them, after some conversation, accepted of them. — *John Woolman, 1757.*

ALL THE SOCIAL DOCTRINES can be derived directly from the primary doctrines of the Inward Light and the teachings of Jesus. The Inward Light interprets the teachings of Jesus and enables men to apply them to situations which did not exist when Jesus lived. The teachings of Jesus act as a check on what may be considered to be revelations of the Inward Light but which are often obscured by wrong thoughts and actions. The Christian social gospel is of course by no means peculiar to the Quakers. However, it is probable that this particular sequence of primary producing secondary and the secondary conditioning the form of the tertiary testimonies occasions social action in the form which is characteristic of the Society of Friends. Such social action is more than a logical deduction from the fatherhood of God, the brotherhood of man, and the ethics of the New Testament. It grows out of actual experiences in meetings for worship or business over a period of time. The silence of the meeting permits the worshiper to be faced with problems which are peculiarly his. This has often led to social pioneering. Problems faced directly and intimately are most likely to lead to action. The individual becomes slowly sensitized to the world's needs. The tender plant is first nurtured in the seed-bed of the meeting. When it is strong enough it can be set out to grow in a less favorable environment.

Social testimonies may evolve slowly. Actions which seem right today may seem wrong tomorrow in the light of further insight. The Society of Friends is still far from discovering all that is implied in these divine-human communities.— *Howard H. Brinton, 1949.*

NOW I FEEL a concern in the spring of pure love, that all who have plenty of outward substance, may example others in the right use of things; and carefully look in the condition of poor people, not abridging them of their due with regard to wages. While hired laborers may, by moderate industry and the Divine blessing, live comfortably, raise up families, and give them suitable education, it appears reasonable for them to be content with their wages. If they who have plenty, love their fellow-creatures in that love which is Divine, and in all their proceedings have an equal regard to the good of mankind universally, their place in society is a place of care, an office requiring attention. The more we possess, the greater is our trust, and with an increase of treasures, an increase of care becomes necessary.

When our will is subject to the will of God, and in relation to the things of this world, we have nothing in view but a comfortable living, equally with the rest of our fellow-creatures, then outward treasures are no farther desirable than as we feel a gift in our minds equal to the trust, and strength to act as dutiful children in His service, who hath formed all mankind, and has appointed a substance for us in this world. A desire of treasures from any other motive appears to be against that command of our blessed Saviour, "Lay not up for yourselves treasures on earth," Matt. 6:19.—*John Woolman, 1774.*

"Charge them that are rich in this world, that they be not highminded, nor trust in uncertain riches, but in the living God, who giveth us richly all things to enjoy."—1 Tim. 6:17.

THE QUESTION constantly arises: To what extent can a type of behavior, developed within a small community, such as a meeting or a school, become a standard for action outside that community? Some would say what is right in one place is right in another and that there can be no compromise. Some would proceed by a double standard....Whatever the Quaker theory may be on this matter, Quakers have, in practice, first built up the small community of the meeting or school, in which they can be fairly consistent. From that point they have gone out into the world depending on divine guidance to indicate how much consistency is in each instance required of them. According to Quaker autobiographies many have been enabled to live lives which they believed were consistent for long periods of time, lives which resulted in prolonged inner peace and serenity...consistency [being] made easier by a large degree of isolation in a simple type of society....But it is not so easy today to decide to what extent Quakers can take part in business and other large scale activities and still adhere to the standards of their religion. They do not completely withdraw from society in order to achieve consistency as is done by members of some monastic orders but they take part in society and attempt like most other Christians to be a leaven in the lump. If we cannot be wholly consistent we can at least take an unconventional stand on some issues such as a refusal to take part in war or in discrimination because of race. Each, in view of the immense complexity of modern social and business relations, must answer this problem of consistency according to his own light and leading.— *Howard Brinton, 1949.*

WE MUST UNDERSTAND religion not just as an intellectual exercise but as something which involves the whole personality. Our attitudes, emotions, behavior and values are all involved and our thinking must be concerned with them. We cannot separate theology into a separate box that neither draws on our personal experience and ways of life nor contributes to them. This means in particular, that theology should be moral. Our Quaker principles that the light leads out of sin and into unity also imply this. It should be moral towards people. That is, it must take seriously their deepest concerns and try to avoid facile answers. Thus, the problem of suffering has to be taken into account and the values of freedom, justice, equality and concern for others.

Theology must also be concerned with the ethical results of its activities. We may not make on religious grounds a statement we would regard as wrong on moral or social grounds, or encourage cruelty or oppression or hatred. On the contrary, it should give guidance towards the practical ways of living which should result from its conclusions.

It must also be moral towards God. It may not make any statement about God that is unworthy, or that implies that God does not reach our highest moral standards, or that allows God to be used as a justification for immoral action.

Our theology must also be inclusive towards other faiths and towards atheism. This is that it must take them seriously, respect their principles and concerns, and seek to find them a place which justifies and does not condemn them...and try to avoid judging others.— *Janet Scott, 1980.*

TAKE HEED of judging the measures of others, but every one mind your own; and there ye famish the busy minds and high conceits, and so peace springs up among you and division is judged. And this know, that there are diversities of gifts but one spirit, and unity therein to all who with it are guided. And though the way seems to thee diverse: yet judge not the way, lest thou judge the Lord, and knowest not that several ways (seeming to reason) hath God to bring his people out by, yet all are but one in the end. This is, that he may be looked to from all the ends of the earth, to be a guide and lawgiver; and that none should judge before him. Deep is the mystery of godliness!— *(1653)*

* * *

Above all things take heed of judging one another, for in that ye may destroy one another, and leave one another behind, and drive one another back into the world, and eat out the good of one another...so go on in the Truth, answering it in every one in the inward parts and in the power of God...in that is your life.— *(1662)*

* * *

Let your lives and conversation preach, that with a measure of the spirit of God you may reach to that of God in all.— *George Fox, 1675.*

SO OFTEN each one of us begins to feel insecure or concerned about a particular source. Perhaps we are worried about the source of our income or our job, perhaps we are worried that we will not be loved enough, that we will not have enough food, or that we don't have enough strength for a particular situation.

George Fox spoke of a Light Within. Other Christians speak of the Christ within, which is a constant within each one of us, coming from an Eternal Source. That Light or Love never fails, doesn't come in quantities, is not "rationed" to some and not to others. "Consider the lilies, how they grow. They toil not, neither do they spin." Are any one of us less than the lily or sparrow that have been provided for? There is a Source of Everything, that is constantly there for us all. When Jesus fed the multitudes, there was not just enough bread for a chosen few; there was unconditional bread for all, with plenty left over....

Sometimes in our fear of lack we forget our plenty, or our believing that only one other person or thing is our *only* source of what we believe we need, we may become dependent upon that particular person or thing and lose sight of the real Source. In fearing our needs will not be met, we often block out the real Source of all we have, all that is given us, all that is available for us, preventing it from reaching us through any ready channel or source which may express or reflect or provide that which we need. Thus, in our fear and blindness, we block that Source from working through and in us.— *Sylvia Messner, 1980.*

AN EPISTLE TO FRIENDS.— All ye friends of the Light, though we, who are your ministers and messengers of light, be cast into *prisons, holes and dungeons*, and kept there by the devilish corrupted will of man, and it be suffered by God, the Father of Light, for the fulfilling of the Scriptures upon that generation, which was prophesied of by the ministers and messengers of Light in the days of old, who suffered in the same nature, by the same generation, for the same testimony, and though the Lord yet suffers the same generation to act in their nature against us, and fill up their measure of wrath, it is for the manifestation of His truth and exaltation of His name.

And through all this are we known and made manifest unto you who are in the Light, and the heathen come to know and confess that He is greater that is with us, than all they that can rise up against us. And in all this we do rejoice, and through our sufferings are crowned and get the victory over the world, without [as well] as within. And though we are kept [in prison, yet it is for] the Lord's appointed time; therefore, Friends, eye the Lord in all these things, and look not out at man, nor at what man can do, either for or against us; but eye God in all his works and in all his instruments, and there will be no cause for discouragement; for discouragement and fears, doubts and questionings, spring from the carnal mind.— *James Parnell, (1636-1656)*

A fiery teenager whose preaching drew large crowds and wrote many epistles, James Parnell died as a result of falling from a little cell in the dungeon wall, called "the hole," reached by a rope which in his state of weakness and exposure he failed to hold, with the words, "Here I die innocently."

WHAT has light meant in my life? Increasingly, as I have moved deeper and deeper into Quakerism, it has meant, internally, a warming and enlargement of the heart, or so it seemed at times. At other times, in revelations of the mind, light almost seemed to break literally when a new thought or concept revealed itself to me. But only since coming to the mountains have light and darkness had such good *physical* connotations. There are no street lights where I live, so that, aside from the few darkness-phobic people who have placed arc lights outside their homes, a kind of impersonal velvety blackness settles over everything when the sun's rays have left the hills....

But the mountains of southern Appalachia, my home for the past year, have disclosed a new and unexpected revelation. Gravel roads and wooded paths here take the place of concrete and asphalt; fellow travelers, either human or animal, are rare. Coursing these roads and paths by daylight, I tried to savor their curves and contours, their dips and hollows....I rarely use a flashlight on Celo community roads and paths...I walk these paths confidently, sometimes quickly, sometimes meditatively....To my feet, gravel roads are like highways; they stride confidently along, undeterred by pebbles and puddles alike. They find the worn tracks almost by themselves....

In this life, no course we take is unobstructed, free of the errors of self-will, the snares of unforeseen happenstance. Some of us at times may well feel "led," certainly guided, often nudged and prodded internally and externally. We move best only "as way opens."

A light unto my feet is symbol indeed. To the whole, to the inner-directed person, its impulses are to be taken seriously.— *James S. Best, 1980.*

ALTHOUGH we use silence as the medium through which we become aware of the divine presence...it is our way of communion, [and] there are many indications...that we do not make a quiet place in our daily lives. Certainly we...live in an environment which is polluted by noise. The roar and honking of traffic, the invidious [music] in shops, offices and factories, the clatter of machinery. Thanks to the wonders of modern batteries and the silicon chip, transistors can suddenly be produced from a pocket or a handbag, filling a lonely beach or a high hill with noise. We are in danger of drowning in noise. And we are assailed on every side by words, not always spoken out loud, but leaping at us from hoardings and newspapers, from television and radio. Both tire, and also...bore, so that many of us are not easily able to stand silence, or to still the incessant chatter within our minds....

In the desert, where most of the sounds which we take as normal were lacking, and where people deliberately refrained from talking to each other for long periods, the nature of silence was certainly realized. Aba Poemen, for instance, once said,

"There is one sort of person who seems to be silent, but inwardly criticizes other people. Such a person is really talking all the time. Another may talk from morning to night, but says only what is meaningful, and so keeps silence."

What was their aim in seeking silence? They wanted to find it so that they could hear, to attend to the voice of God which normally they were too busy, too disturbed, too bathed in noise to hear. In this sense becoming quiet was a crucial part of that form of exploration of inner space which is called prayer.— *Christopher Holdsworth, 1985.*

SOMETHING CAN HAPPEN, when we are silent. We notice, first perhaps, the sounds in the room where we sit—the crackling of logs on the fire, the ticking of the clock, the wind at the window. Then we may hear ourselves—the gentle hiss of our breaths, in and out...the beating of our heart, a sound which may be particularly frightening as we grow old. But gradually, if we persist in the quiet, in the exploration of inner space, the strains may fall away, and we become aware of something which we may recognise as a sense of the presence of God, or to which we may give another name, but which is at the time, somehow alive with a silent word for us. This kind of experience was described by George Fox in some of the loveliest and deepest advice which he ever gave:

"Be still and cool in thy own mind and spirit from thine own thoughts, and then thou wilt feel the principle of God to turn thy mind to the Lord God..."

The desert fathers were clear, too, that the silence may help to keep and preserve afterwards the opening given us in quiet, in other words, to learn when to speak and when to keep silent...

Henri Nouwen remarks how awkwardly the emphasis on "sharing" fits with this side of the teaching of the desert. We should ask ourselves, he suggests, "whether our lavish ways of sharing are not more compulsive than virtuous; that instead of creating community they tend to flatten out our life together. Often we come home from a sharing session with a feeling that something precious has been taken away from us...or holy ground...trodden upon."

Perhaps we need to learn when to be reticent, when to keep silent and to tend the fire silently, and then there may be a word to share.— *Christopher Holdsworth, 1985.*

OUR STATE in this life is a state of probation. Such was the state of man originally, and such it is now. And in order that man at first, or ever after, might be able to conquer, or be justly punishable for desertion or defeat, he was, is, and must be, armed with armor invincible against all the powers that were or are suffered to assail him. This is just our ground, our state and situation: subject to vanity, or to many and various temptations, yet, being inwardly armed with the spirit of Omnipotence, so far as we stand faithful and fight valiantly in the strength afforded us, we are sure of victory. Our strength or help is only in God; but then it is near us, it is in us— a force superior to all possible opposition— a force that never was nor can be foiled. We are free to stand in this unconquerable ability, and defeat the powers of darkness; or to turn from it, and be foiled and overcome. When we stand, we know it is God alone upholds us; and when we fall, we feel that our fall or destruction is of ourselves.

*   *   *

Many there are who put light for darkness, and darkness for light; bitter for sweet, and sweet for bitter. They call the divine light, "which lighteneth every man that cometh into the world," a natural light, an *ignis fatuus*, or by some other ignominious epithet, though the Scriptures declare it to be the very life of the holy Word, that was in the beginning with God, and truly was God.— *Job Scott. (1751-1793)*

I HAVE BEEN THINKING over my life and the survey has not been encouraging. Alas! if I have been a servant at all, I have been an unprofitable one. And yet I have loved goodness and longed to be good, but it has been so hard to bring my imaginative, poetic temperament into subjection. I stand ashamed and almost despairing before holy and pure ideals. As I read the New Testament I feel how weak, irresolute and frail I am and how little I can rely on anything save Our Lord's mercy, and infinite compassion, which I reverently and thoughtfully own have followed me through life, and the assurance of which is my sole ground of hope for myself and for those I love and pray for. — John Greenleaf Whittier, letter, 1880.

*   *   *

I am grateful for thy generous estimate of my writings...but I fear the critics will not agree with thee. Why not anticipate them, and own up to the faults and limitations which everybody sees, and none more clearly than myself?   Touch upon my false rhymes, and Yankeeisms: confess that I sometimes "crack the voice of Melody, and break the legs of time." Pitch into Mogg Megone.   That "big Injun" strutting around in Walter Scott's plaid, has no friends and deserves none. Own that I sometimes choose unpoetical themes. Endorse Lowell's *Fables for Critics* that I mistake occasionally, simple excitement for inspiration. In this way we can take the wind out of the sails of our ill-natured cavaliers. I am not one of the master singers and don't wish to pose as one. By the grace of God I am only what I am, and don't wish to pass for more. — *John Greenleaf Whittier, letter, 1883.*

NOW THE OBVIOUS tendency of a vivid first-hand perception of truth, or light, is to render the possessor of it so far independent of external teachers. And we all know such [persons] show a disposition to go their own way, and to disregard, if not renounce, traditional teaching, which has brought them into frequent collisions with ecclesiastical and other authorities.

It is the easier to do this because of the two marked characteristics of mystics—quietness and independence. Mystics are naturally independent, not only of ecclesiastical authority, but of each other. This is necessarily implied in the very idea of first-hand reception of light. While it must always constitute a strong bond of sympathy between those who recognize it in themselves and in each other, it naturally indisposes them to discipleship. They sit habitually at no man's feet, and do not as a rule greatly care to have anyone sit at theirs.

Mysticism in this sense seems naturally opposed to tradition. No true mystic would hold himself bound by the thoughts of others. He does not feel the need of them, being assured of the sufficiency and conscious of the possession of that inward guidance, whether called light, or voice, or inspiration, which must be seen, heard, felt, by each other in his own heart, or not at all. But the duty of looking for and of obeying this guidance is a principle which may be inculcated and transmitted from generation to generation like any other principle. Its hereditary influence is very perceptible in old Quaker families, where a unique type of Christian character resulting from it is still to be met with.— *Caroline Stephen, 1890.*

I LOVE THEE, Friend, for all those Friendly ways
That speak to my condition: for the plan
To let the routine pattern of our days
Give witness to our love of God and man.
I love thee, Friend, for showing me the face
Of strength is neither harsh nor bleak nor lined
But, in the house of man, a window-place
With panes through which the inner light has shined.
I love thee, Friend, for teaching me to hear
And see and feel and know myself akin
To what affects my touch, my eye, my ear,
And all that comes by welling up within.

O Friend, I knew not that-of-God in me
Until entwined with that-of-God in thee.

The actual experience of God is not unique to Quakers, but the procedural method whereby we repeat the experience gives us some sense of common identity. We worship in silence. We search within ourselves and within others. We seek that-of-God in every man. We increase our sensitivity to everything about us— to what affects our touch, our eye, our ear, to all that comes welling up within us. We stress the importance of our routine patterns of daily life. We recognize that the interaction between people provides one of the most fruitful areas for coming into contact with God. These are our principles. They are not a creed, but a way. They are not to be believed but to be lived. When we accept these principles we are not convinced, but converted.— *Martin Cobin, 1961.*

AS ONE query admitted with unanimity was, "Are any concerned in buying or vending goods unlawfully imported, or prize goods? I found my mind engaged to say that as we profess the truth, and were there assembled to support the testimony of it, it was necessary for us to dwell deep and act in that wisdom which is pure, or otherwise we could not prosper. I then mentioned their alteration, and referring to the last-mentioned query, added, that as purchasing any merchandise taken by the sword was always allowed to be inconsistent with our principles, so negroes being captives of war, or taken by stealth, it was inconsistent with our testimony to buy them; and their being our fellow-creatures, and sold as slaves, added greatly to the iniquity. Friends appeared attentive to what was said; some expressed a care and concern about their negroes; none made any objection, by way of reply to what I said, but the query was admitted as they had altered it.

As some of their members have heretofore traded in negroes, as in other merchandise, this query being admitted will be one step further than they have hitherto gone, and I did not see it my duty to press for an alteration, but felt easy to leave it all to Him who alone is able to turn the hearts of the mighty, and make way for the spreading of truth on the earth, by means agreeable to his infinite wisdom.— *John Woolman, 1758.*

THE APPLICATION of this way of life to situations of tensions lies in the ability of Friends to move into such situations without altering their lives, without losing the capacity for love and calm.... To develop this ability, Friends must grow....But we should do only as we are led.... Otherwise it will not work. There is no gain in driving ourselves or one another.

Let us remember that we have different talents, different needs, different leadings. Let us remember our humility should be collective as well as personal....Let us give our best. But we need not be always right. The Society of Friends need not be always in the vanguard. Let us use our talents. When our talents are those best suited to meeting the needs of men at a particular point in their development, then we will offer leadership. At other times, we will not be greatly influential....There are those among us who are sensitive to the desperate nature of our situation. They walk not in peace but in tension. Their love for us is so great they are pained by our lethargy; they would hurry us along. The Friends Meeting is a slow way to conduct business, a slow way to move— so slow that neither God nor our inner peace are ever left behind. Let us move as quickly as we can, as slowly as we must. Let those who are gifted with individual insights and abilities— let these Friends run ahead. We all run ahead at one place or another. Those of us who need new strength for our running will keep returning to the Meeting. I see no calamity in those who find the Meeting no longer provides the necessary nourishment and who come to turn elsewhere for it. But it would be a calamity if the Meeting no longer existed as a place of nourishment.— *Martin Cobin, 1961.*

HE UTTERED the following prayer: "O Lord, my God! the amazing horrors of darkness were gathered around me, and covered me all over, and I saw no way to go forth; I felt the depth and extent of misery of my fellow-creatures separated from the Divine harmony, and it was heavier than I could bear, and I was crushed down under it: I lifted up my hand, I stretched out my arm, but there was none to help me; I looked round about, and was amazed. In the depths of misery, O Lord! I remembered that thou art omnipotent; that I had called thee Father; and I felt that I loved thee, and I was made quiet in my will, and I waited for deliverance from thee. Thou hadst pity upon me, when no man could help me; I saw that meekness under suffering was showed to us in the most affecting example of thy Son, and thou taught me to follow him, and I said, "Thy will, O Father, be done!"— *John Woolman, 1772.*

* * *

In silent protest of letting alone,
The Quaker kept the way of his own.—
A non-conductor among the wires,
With coat of asbestos proof to fires.
And quite unable to mend his pace,
To catch the falling manna of grace,
He hugged the closer his little store
Of faith, and silently prayed for more.
And vague of creed and barren of rite,
But holding, as in his Master's sight,
Act and thought to the inner light,
The round of his simple duties walked,
And strove to live what the others talked.
    — *John Greenleaf Whittier*
    (from "The Preacher")

TO BECOME a nonviolent society, a basic change we need to make is in the way we think. We need to stop dividing people, ideas, situations, countries, etc. into separate categories while failing to recognize their interconnectedness. We need to seek resolutions of conflict that result in all sides "winning" rather than in one side winning and the other losing. The changes needed are fundamental, and all of us need to reflect on how we might be contributing to a violent culture....

The tendency to divide people and ideas into conflicting groups was.....evident at a threshing session.... One participant said that there are two ways to approach a problem— the way of the heart, or the way of the intellect...one can do things out of political interest or out of humanitarian concern. The paradox is that the purer the act— the more devoid of politics— the more effective the act will be....

V.H. spoke of the whites who helped the blacks with the underground railroad in the 19th century. Someone asked him how to choose the most effective course of action. His reply went something like, "I don't think Harriet Tubman worried much about effectiveness. We are not called to be effective— we are called to be faithful."

Faithfulness and effectiveness. Humanitarian and political. These are not really separate divisions. Humanitarian concerns can lead to political action. And surely the path God wants us to choose to effectiveness is faithfulness....

We can create a nonviolent society. It will mean changing the way we think...the way we raise children...in our economic system; it will mean changes in the way we resolve conflicts.— *Deb Sawyer, 1987.*

IS IT NOT delightful to find so many fine minds and good people in the world? I am constantly combatting the "human depravity" doctrine and preach instead the innate purity of man.— *(Letter)*

*   *   *

I long for the day my sisters will rise, and occupy the sphere to which they are called by their high nature and destiny.— *(1841)*

*   *   *

I confess to you, my friends, that I am a worshipper after the way called heresy, a believer after the manner many deem infidel. While at the same time my faith is firm in the blessed, the eternal doctrine preached by Jesus and by every child of God since the creation of the world, especially the great truth that God is the teacher of his people himself; the doctrine that Jesus most emphatically taught, that the kingdom is with man, that there is his sacred and divine temple.— *(1849)*

*   *   *

In the true marriage relationship the independence of the husband and wife is equal, their dependence mutual, and their obligations reciprocal.— *(1855)*

*   *   *

Within thirty or forty years there has been more remarkable success than before in all reforms. The people are learning that the weapons of our warfare are not carnal, to the pulling down of strongholds.— *(1875)*

*   *   *

I want that there should be a belief that war is wrong, as everyone must, then we ought to believe that by proper efforts on our part it may be done away with.— *Lucretia Mott. (1793-1880)*

I AM SOMEWHAT like Zaccheus of old, who climbed the sycamore tree, his Lord to see. I climb the pulpit, not because I am of lofty mind, but because I am short of stature that you may see me.

Weep not for me, rather let your tears flow for the sorrows of the multitude. My work is done. Like a ripe fruit I await the gathering. Death has no terrors, for it is a wise law of nature. I am ready whenever the summons may come.— *Lucretia Mott, 1876, age 83.*

* * *

The little graveyard is a still-green oasis in one of the worst sections of north Philadelphia. All around are houses that look as though they have been bombed, doors and windows gaping open or temporarily boarded up with sheets of metal. Abandoned cars sit on their axles at the curbs. Garbage, trash, and graffiti are everywhere. In the midst of the desolation a few black and Puerto Rican children play. A pregnant teen-ager stands at the corner, drinking a soda, watching the intruder with dull eyes.

O Lucretia, what would you say to this? Whatever became of that bright vision of radical reform, just down the road a bit, which kept you going all those years? Where is that progress that seemed to you so natural, so inevitable, when men and women turned to the Inward Guide?

The grass stirs, the children shout. Otherwise there is nothing, only that clear light that she loved pouring down upon me. Only the memory, out of the silence, of the many, many times she said it: The Light is as available today as it was yesterday as it has been everywhere, for all eternity. Only after a bit, a gentle nudging. "What is thee doing about it?" Lucretia wants to know.— *Margaret Hope Bacon, 1980.*

IF WE ARE CALLED to any station or situation in life, I do not know that we ought to reject it, merely because responsibility is attached to it; for if we can do good, we should not shrink from labor because it is unpleasant to us; but if duty points the path, set our hands and our hearts cheerfully to work.

There is scarcely anything in life to which some degree of responsibility is not annexed. If we are blessed with sound limbs, we ought to use them according to their office; if with a good understanding, we are bound to cultivate it. If we are possessed of riches, we should use them as good stewards who are to account for them. If we have servants, we are responsible for our care and good treatment of them; and if children, much more so and likewise to labor for their benefit in various respects. No relationship or situation in life can be exempt from responsibility; and though we may not covet those situations where it is increased, to endeavor to escape it wholly will be in vain, because in the nature of things impossible. To be content whatever we are, or in whatever circumstances we are placed, filling up the measure of our duties as well as we are able, is the only wise and safe plan— the plan which will most promote our happiness in the present life, and give us a well-grounded hope that we shall receive the welcome sentence of "Well done, thou good and faithful servant, enter thou into the joy of the Lord."— Margaret Woods, 1818.

"Whatsoever thy hand findeth to do, do it with thy might."— Eccl. 9:10.

IN MY NINTH YEAR...my dear mother took me to London Yearly Meeting...and there for the first time, I had the privilege of listening to that eminent servant of the Lord, Elizabeth Fry. I shall never forget the impression she made upon my young mind by her sweet voice, beautiful face, and her earnest pleading, as she spoke of the prisoners, the suffering and the outcast. I was too young to understand one half of what she said, yet good seed was sown then and there which led to active labour in after years. In the solemn silence that followed, after she took her seat, my childish heart was lifted in the prayer that I might grow as good as she was, and work in the same way.... I expressed to my mother a fear that [God] would not care for a little child like me...She replied by lifting me up to see a bird's nest in the hedgerow, and explaining to me that God taught the little bird to build its nest, and to rear its young; and then bade me pluck a little flower at my feet, and pointed out how nothing was so small to escape His notice....

My dear father took great delight in seating me on his knee, and talking to me of the truth and beauty of the distinguishing views of the Society of Friends, which he had joined when quite a young man. Many an hour I have listened with great interest as he told me of the cruel persecutions and great sufferings of the early Friends. He took pains to impress upon me the utter uselessness of water baptism and other outward ceremonies, telling me that he was once baptised with water, and was much disappointed to find that it did not wash away a single sin, or help him at all, in his efforts to be good. Of the horrors of war, he often spoke, and of the sinfulness and cruelty of slavery.— *Elizabeth Comstock (1815-1890).*

I BELIEVE that preaching is one great and powerful agency by which God is pleased to arouse, awaken, and convert man. That now, as formerly, He is "pleased by the foolishness of preaching to save them that believe." There is a joy and rejoicing in my heart when visiting the sick and the prisoners, the suffering and dying, to hear "the blessing of him that is ready to perish" in my ear.

I know that I have a gift to comfort the afflicted, and for this power I do thank God, and strive to exercise it whenever and wherever I can. I would not give away this precious gift for a large property. I have no unity with that sort of preaching that says "I have tried to be excused," "I am reluctant to occupy the time of this meeting," "I have spoken because I dared not keep silence." But I rejoice in my gift, and it is willingly that I use it, attending to the injunction "Whatsoever thy hand findeth to do, do it with thy might."

I rejoice that to me is given a dispensation of the gospel, and I rejoice in the "the recompense of the reward...."

The [Indiana] Yearly meeting is a wonderful sight. Friends in the thousands, crowding into the meeting-house yard, which covers...many acres, in their various styles of carriages, from the neat glass coach to the tilted wagon, and the open lumber wagon....Friends, seated fifty in a row...and 3,000 holding meeting in the open air, outside the meeting-house, are enough off for the faint sound of the voice of the distant preacher now and then to be heard within the walls. Enos Pray, the most popular preacher in that Yearly Meeting, with a stentorian voice, electrifies with his eloquence the thousands out of doors.— *Elizabeth Comstock, 1861.*

WE HAVE NOW reached a terrible crisis in this land. Fearful accounts reach us daily of war and bloodshed.... The latest account tells us of the total defeat of the Northerners at Manasses Junction, with a loss of 3,000 men....The poor wounded soldiers claim our earnest sympathy, where, upon the space of one square mile, 3000 dead are lying, with multitudes of wounded mixed up with them...in that warm country....The effect of the excitement in the country is disastrous. Trade and commerce are almost at a standstill; forty per cent of the shopkeepers in New York and many other cities have failed. Many of the manufactories are closed. Taxes and rates rising...Farm produce very low...My dear husband and other farmers around here sensibly feel these things. We ought to be thankful for the abundance of our harvest just gathered...so that we have plenty of provisions, but money we seldom see....John is always willing to go with me to all the meetings, and to take me anywhere in the work of the ministry where my mind seems drawn....But if this fearful civil war goes on, I do not know what we shall do. We shall not be able to go out thus, nor shall we have the means. More than this, the way will not be clear before us, or the minds of the people be open to receive us. A strong prejudice against our Society seems springing up, because of our testimony against war; people look upon us as a sort of half-secessionists, because we will not fight for the Union, and oppose all war...We begin to apprehend that the balance of power between the North and South is more equal than we had supposed...and now our eyes seem suddenly opening to perceive...that they may prevail and punish us, at least for awhile.— *Elizabeth Comstock, 1862.*

FIRST DAY THOUGHTS—

IN CALM and cool and silence, once again
I find my old accustomed place among
My brethren, where, perchance, no human tongue
Shall utter words; where never hymn is sung,
Nor dim light falling through the pictured pane!

There, syllabled by silence, let me hear
The still small voice which reached the prophet's ear;
Read in my heart a still diviner law
Than Israel's leader on his tables saw!

Let me strive with each besetting sin,
Recall my wandering fancies, and restrain
The sore disquiet of a restless brain;
And, as the path of duty is made plain,
May grace be given that I may walk therein,
Not like the hireling, for his selfish gain,
With backward glances and reluctant tread,
Making a merit of his coward dread,—

But, cheerful, in the light around me thrown,
Walking as one to pleasant service led;
Doing God's will as if it were my own,
Yet trusting not in mine, but in his strength alone!

— *John Greenleaf Whittier*

THIS MORNING a troop of beggar children came to my gate. They brought a woman, a beggar wrapped in a torn sari, and a tiny baby covered with sores. The children wanted me to show the woman how to treat her wee son. They ran for water, and they explained each step in Bangla, while I showed her how to bathe and medicate the child. As I knelt there I thought of the story Jesus told about poor Lazarus outside the gate, covered with sores, and the rich man inside who ignored his need. Here was I— comparatively rich, well clad, well fed— privileged to bathe the bleeding feet of a small Lazarus, beloved of God.

As I write this, a small boy comes. He is about nine, with no parents or family. He survives by begging and scavenging here and there. He too is covered with sores; my gardener tenderly treats his wounds. When I noticed him and asked him in, I learned that my Buddhist gardener had given him some of his own food, and perhaps a small coin. How often the poor help the poor, while we who are rich fail even to see, or see and turn away!— *Carol Urner, Dhaka, Bangladesh, 1984.*

God's ways seem dark, but, soon or late,
  They touch the shining hills of day;
  The evil cannot brook delay,
The good can well afford to wait.
  Give ermined knaves their hour of crime;
Ye have the future grand and great,
  The safe appeal of Truth to Time!
    — *John Greenleaf Whittier*

WHERE people are sincerely devoted to follow Christ, and dwell under the influence of his Holy Spirit, their stability and firmness...is at times like dew on the tender plants round them, and the weightiness of their spirits secretly works on the minds of others. In this condition...they feel a care over the flock, and way is opened for maintaining good order in the Society. And though we may meet with opposition from another spirit, yet as there is a dwelling in meekness, feeling our spirits subject, and moving only in the gentle, peaceable wisdom, the inward reward of quietness will be greater than all our difficulties. Where the pure life is kept to, and meetings of discipline are held in the authority of it we find by experience that they are comfortable and tend to the health of the body.......

Dear young people, choose God for your portion; love his truth, and be not ashamed of it; choose for your company such as serve him in uprightness; and shun as most dangerous the conversation of those whose lives are of an ill savor; for by frequenting such company some hopeful young people have come to great loss, and been drawn from less evils to greater, to their utter ruin. In the bloom of youth no ornament is so lovely as that of virtue, nor any enjoyments equal to those which we partake of in full resigning ourselves to the Divine will.

These enjoyments add sweetness to all other comforts, and give true satisfaction in company and conversation, where people are mutually acquainted with it; and as your minds are thus seasoned with the truth, you will find strength to abide steadfast to the testimony of it, and be prepared for services in the church.— *John Woolman, 1758.*

"SPEAK TRUTH TO POWER" became a resounding call among us Quakers in the 1950s. It brought with it a sense of vast possibilities. It is still a significant call and demands courage and presence in its practice— but it's only half the equation.

Recently I've been thinking about and experiencing the other half: "Listen to power to discover the Truth it speaks......."

I feel we meet as human beings across the wide spaces in thought, philosophy, and belief between us. Way is open for us to continue to explore each other's approaches to life.

My experiences have persuaded me that some of us must begin thoughtful acts of listening to people in power *with no thought of trying to speak our truths.* And I believe we must meet them on their home ground.

There are so many we can meet with. We can meet with the pro-nuclear people, with those who live down our street. We must get out of our safe forums and our seminars and sit down face-to-face with our opposition— with whomever God sends our way. This is how we will know there are *people* on the other side of these terrible questions, and so will they.

Then we must listen. We must listen and listen and listen. We must listen for the Truth in our opponent, and we must acknowledge it. After we have listened long enough, openly enough, and with the desire to really hear, we may be given the opportunity to speak our truth. We may even have the opportunity to be heard.

For no one and no one side is the sole repository of truth. But each of us has a spark of it within.— *Gene Knudsen-Hoffman, 1981.*

THE RAYS OF LIGHT from within and from without are not indeed always precisely distinguishable from one another...It is only in proportion to our openness to both that we can have the humble yet well-founded assurance of having rightly interpreted Divine Guidance....By the outer light I mean all the abundant instruction of experience, history and observation— reaching us partly through our own and partly through other minds...But in the central inner-most region of our minds there shines one pure ray of direct light from the very throne of God; one ray which belongs to each one individually....

I believe it to be as truly a duty to submit every impulse to the discipline and test of reason as it is to keep burning the pure flame of devotion to the Most High by which alone Reason can be raised to the level of Wisdom...

If we are to have even a glimpse of the innermost and unspeakable joys of the spirit— if we are to rise above pain and sorrow and bitterness into the pure serenity of the heaven within— if we are to "know that He is God"— we must be still....

Quietness and obedience are in truth one. We may of course talk of obeying anything, even our whims; but it is only the unchanging, the unseen and eternal things which can truly and permanently rule us, and give us that "quietness and confidence" which is our strength. To be faithful to the Light we have is the one certain way to have more....

This light does not run counter to the dictates of reason, of conscience, of common sense, propriety or wisdom. It inspires, harmonises and transfigures them all.— *Caroline Stephen, 1908.*

GEORGE FOX preached a different gospel. He claimed that churches of his day were preaching a Christ who could save us in our sins but not from our sins. He maintained that Christ is able not only to forgive but also to deliver us from captivity to sin and enable us to gain the victory over the evil in our lives....Fox also saw that the church is, or should be, a community of disciples who are taught by Christ and who learn *together*, obey *together*, and suffer *together*....

The early Friends felt that God had drawn very near to them and through them....A new apostolate was being raised up and the hearts of men and women were being made tender to the word of life that they preached. What they experienced 300 years ago is being experienced again today. A new apostolate is being raised up, and in places where Friends could hardly bear to hear the name of Christ a few years ago, people are experiencing an encounter with the living Christ.... Fox wrote to Francis Howgill and Edward Burrough, "Stir abroad while the door is open." Today the door seems to be more open among Friends than it has been for generations. This is an exciting time to be a Quaker....

Since the New Foundation preaching mission began ten years ago, there has been no lack of people who want to come together to hear the gospel that Fox preached. But the laborers are few....

I am thankful that by keeping to the simplicity of the gospel, early Friends bore witness to the gospel foundation that stands sure....Through the writings of Fox many are rediscovering this gospel and some are preaching it. The world-overcoming faith of the Valiant Sixty is being experienced again.— *Lewis Benson, 1985.*

A FIRST STEP for developing a truly nonviolent sensibility is to stop being judgmental. Everyone is familiar with the advice "Judge not, that ye be not judged," and with the stricture against casting the first stone.   Rarely do we think very much about judgmentalism, and especially do we fail to understand its full implication. To end judgmentalism is to help realize nonviolent social change....

We must never sit in judgment of the poor who may react violently to the violence of their oppressors. This part of the "judge not" equation is usually readily accepted by American social-change activists. The more difficult part of the equation is that we must not sit in judgment of their oppressors either.......Condemnation has no part in a truly peaceable outlook....

Contemporary social activists, including pacifist, are often willing to heap condemnation on others, not only on prominent individuals in political life, but on whole categories of humanity: the oppressor class, the military industrial complex, the Establishment.

To develop an effective nonviolent witness it is not enough simply to obey the commandment "Thou shalt not kill." The emotion of hatred can in its own way be as deadly as the act of killing. We may pretend to ourselves that it does not matter what our emotions are as long as we act rightly, but when the test comes we always betray ourselves, for our thoughts and emotions control our acts. If our minds are full of hatred and condemnation, this ultimately will be expressed in acts of violence and destruction and murder. We will eventually find that we seem to have no other choice.— *Daniel A. Seeger, 1986.*

THE AVOIDANCE of judgmentalism, a key to the development of a nonviolent character, involves more than eschewing the condemnation and hatred of others. For passing a sentence on others is not the only form of judgmentalism there is; self-congratulation for having found the truth one tries to live by is judgmentalism in another form. A feeling of pride at having come to understandings which are not yet widely grasped is corrupting....For how can one take credit for the experiences one has been given... all of which have led one...[to] some splinter of the truth which has been proclaimed by sages since the beginning of human history? Can we be sure that if we were in another's shoes we would not have the same opinions and be behaving exactly the same way that he or she is doing?

The sparks of truth we find in others and in ourselves are occasions for joy and for thanksgiving, but no more than we are to condemn those of less perfect understanding are we to congratulate ourselves or each other for superior wisdom....

Guilt is another form of judgmentalism which is equally fatal. It is judgmentalism turned inward on ourselves. Often, social-change advocates who are free in their condemnation of others are also mountains of guilt....

It is not necessary to feel guilty for not having been tortured...[or] for having been born an American citizen. It is not even necessary to be morosely preoccupied with one's own past lapses from virtue....Rather, we must turn wholly away from evil, not dwell upon it, and do good.

What, then are we left with as we choose not to criticize others, congratulate ourselves or feel guilt? We are left with an overwhelming feeling of solidarity...with all human beings.— *Daniel Seeger, 1986.*

WE ARE very much engaged from 9 a.m. to 5 or 6 p.m. in visiting the prisons, hospitals, almshouses, poorhouses, orphan, blind, lunatic,and other asylums, etc... Yesterday we went to the "Tombs," a large prison in the very heart of [New York], a sort of Newgate. It was a mournful sight to me to see the hardened, depraved, degraded countenances of some of the poor women there; yet there was evidence during our meeting with them that they were not wholly lost to feeling....It is a blessing if we can do anything to encourage, to comfort, to soothe these poor outcasts and wanderers; if we may only be the favoured instruments of leading a few of them to seek to walk in a happier and better course.

There are thousands of children in this city from three to eighteen or nineteen years, in houses of refuge, houses of correction, reform schools, and asylums of various kinds.   We saw about two thousand; had meetings with them last First-day. They were classified, the Nurseries containing those under seven. I spoke to them a short time, trying to give them a little lesson on the goodness of God in taking care of them, as manifested in the different parts of their bodies, the eyes, ear, foot, and hand. When I told them of a little boy of six years old I had seen a few days before in a hospital, who had gone too near some machinery and had his hand so injured that it had to be taken off, some of the pretty little creatures held up their hands and looked at them, and I think rejoiced for once in their lives over their two useful hands, their eyes, and their feet. It is very touching to go to the hospitals and see the suffering there.— *Elizabeth L. Comstock, 1862.*

I AM a convinced Friend since 1950 when I became a member of a meeting. [A] working artist, I loved books and I had always wanted to do them. So maybe the fact that that came first...made it possible that being a Friend did not conflict with my creative work....

I think you must obey your inner drives and inner urges; they are God-given. If you are obeying those and listening to the voice within you which tells you to paint this picture, to write this book, to make this pot or sculpture, then it will respond to that of God in other people, because I believe that God is directing this creative urge.

I think out of chaos, and only out of chaos, can come creativity. If you begin to order things and put them in pigeonholes, you may organize things until there is no creativity left in them. I think this is a true danger. I think people should trust this divine chaos: the things falling apart, the things not working. I have found in my own experience that very often out of this comes some most unexpected and surprising results....

I think people are Friends, at least convinced Friends, perhaps mostly because they are unselfish people who are very caring and concerned about other people the world over. I think the difficulty is that the artist must be selfish.....And if I create anything, it's because I obey that inner drive...I don't really try to do good in my books at all. I've been told they are moral...and that a course in Quaker psychology apparently has recommended my *Obadiah* books as being very sophisticated psychologically...I am interested in doing something that fills my needs and also entertains children. — *Brinton Turkle, 1981.*

TO ME, the concepts of "stewardship" and "simplicity" have always seemed so closely related as to be almost identical: to practice one properly, it seems, one must always also practice the other. Nevertheless, there are differences. Simplicity deals with the ownership of property, stewardship with the use of it. Simplicity tells us to ask for no more than we need; stewardship reminds us that we need less if we take care of what we have. Simplicity insists that we get rid of encumbrances; stewardship helps us decide what are encumbrances and what are not. It does this in a very straightforward way. If a possession, or a task, is an encumbrance, using it properly rapidly becomes much more trouble than it is worth, and the possession falls into disrepair, or the task remains constantly undone. It is at this point that stewardship says: "Wait a minute—we have too much to take care of here," and it becomes time, in the good Quaker phrase, to lay something down.

But here a warning must be raised: stewardship and simplicity must themselves remain subject to the queries on stewardship and simplicity. We must keep our stewardship simple and husband our simplicity: it is too easy for pride to allow us to overdo either one. We must avoid that "simpler than thou" feeling on the one hand, while striving also to steer clear of that all-too-common feeling that if we can AFFORD to own something, then we DESERVE to own it.— *Bill Ashworth, Oregon, 1986.*

FRIENDS speak of "right sharing of the world's resources," rightfully connecting the concept to both simplicity and stewardship, but primarily to stewardship. Use is necessary for stewardship, but it is not itself stewardship. Citizens of the United States today can afford to use considerably more of the world's resources than the citizens of other nations— and we do use them— but that is not stewardship, that is greed. It has not led us to care for the things we use, but to be careless with them. The waste dumps of our industrial society suggest just how much.

Perhaps the real problem is not how we use our possessions, but how we interpret that phrase "our own possessions.' Are the things we "own" really ours? Does this make any difference in how we use them? There is a well-known saying in the environmental community to the effect that we do not own the world; we are merely borrowing it from our children. How do we use our children's world, and that of our children's children?

How do we use our neighbor's world, and the world of the raccoon and the squirrel and the pine and the butterfly? Do we remember that they need to use their worlds, too? The query on stewardship reminds us that all of this— our world, our children's world, the world of the raccoon and the squirrel and the pine— is really all one world, the world of God. How do we use God's world?— *Bill Ashworth, Oregon, 1986.*

TAKE HEED, dear Friends, to the promptings of love and truth in your hearts, which are the leadings of God. Resist not his strivings within you....

Seek to know one another in the things which are eternal. Live in love as Christian brethren, entering with sympathy into the joys and sorrows of each other's daily lives. Be ready to give help, and to accept it. Bear the burden of each other's failings and pray for one another.

Be constant in the private reading of the Bible and other writings which reveal the ways of God. Seek to know an inward retirement, even amid the activities of daily life. Make a quiet place wherein you may learn more of the meaning of prayer and the gladness of communion with God our Father. Encourage in your family life the habit of dependence upon God's guidance and on his help for each day's needs. Treasure opportunities for corporate worship. Throughout the week think prayerfully of your meeting and its members.

In worship, we enter with reverence into communion with God, surrendering our whole being to him and to his purpose. Worship becomes sacramental as we receive the spirit of the living Christ in our midst, and offer ourselves to his service. Come with heart and mind prepared. Pray silently as you gather together that you may all be drawn into the spirit of adoration and communion in which fellowship with one another becomes real. Yield yourselves and all your outward concerns to God's guidance, that you may find the evil weakening in you and the good raised up.— *Advices, London, 1964.*

REMEMBER that to every one is given a share of responsibility for the meeting for worship, whether that service be in silence or through the spoken word. Do not assume that vocal ministry is never to be your part. If the call to speak comes, do not let the sense of your own unworthiness, or the fear of being unable to find the right words, prevent you from being obedient to the leading of the Spirit. Ask wisdom of God that you may be sure of your guidance and be enabled humbly to discern and impart something of his glory and truth. Pray that your ministry may rise from the place of deep experience, and that you may be restrained from unnecessary and superficial words. Faithfulness and sincerity in speaking, even very briefly, may open the way to fuller ministry from others....Wait to be sure of the right moment for giving the message. Beware of making additions towards the end of a meeting when it was well left alone.

The spirit of prayer will be active in the truly gathered group. Vocal prayer may wonderfully draw those present into communion with God and with one another, though it may be expressed in hesitating and imperfect words. In a difficult or divided meeting, prayer may bring healing and unity as nothing else can. Prayer should spring from a deep place in the heart; let it be offered with reverence.

Receive the ministry of others in a tender and understanding spirit and avoid hurtful criticism. As servants of the same Lord, with diversities of gifts, receive and give faithfully in the service of truth, remembering that ministry which to one may seem to have little value, to another may be a direct word from God.— *Advices, London, 1964.*

I AM indeed prepared to sympathize by experience
with the most faint and feeble of my fellow-travellers.
Yes, I can cordially take the poorest of the mental poor
by the hand, and say, my brother, or my sister though
thou mayst not be able to rejoice in thy tribulations, yet
endeavor to be thankful; and low or weak as thou art
ready to apprehend thyself, yet count it a great mercy to
have been preserved thitherto, through the shocks and
shades and other vissitudes of thy probationary
course....

*   *   *

I unite with thee in the sentiment, that there is more
of spiritual life in society than in solitude; and that
there is more of this society in towns than in fields and
in woods, is equally true; yet we cannot but love rural
scenes; and impressed perhaps with the feeling that
"God made the country, and man made the town," we
find the latter suffer greatly by comparison, as all
artificial things must do, when placed in contrast with
the workmanship of a perfect Creator. Yet, on the
whole, both the quantity and quality of active or positive
virtue is found to rise higher in social than secluded life;
and this fact I think applies in a remarkable manner,
though I can scarcely tell why, to our religious society;
still I love the country; and the life of a farmer, such as
I could imagine, though it might seem a little Arcadian,
has charms even for my age, which no other employment
possesses.— *Jonathan Hutchinson, 1827.*

JUST as it is easiest to ford a stream during the dry season and in a temperate climate, it is easiest to practice Quakerism in peaceful times from the suburbs. There are fewer threats to our footing. But John Woolman offered guidance when he said, *"Oppression in the extreme appears terrible, but oppression in more refined appearances remains oppression; and where the smallest degree of it is cherished it grows stronger and more extensive. To labor for a perfect redemption from this spirit of oppression is the great business of the whole family of Christ Jesus in this world."*

Because oppression, or the lack of universal justice, is so insidious, we must labor constantly to bring about our great hope, the commonwealth of God. We do this not only because oppression limits the ability of the disinherited to use their talents but also because it can easily make them doubt the goodness, if not the very existence of God. Finally, in due time oppression will almost invariably lead the victims to resort to violence and many of the superficial to blame the victims because they could no longer bear a pain not experienced by their critics....

We are called to promote justice. This is our duty. There is no escaping it. Should an oppressed group— whose cause we favor— take up arms, we do not take up arms. But neither do we become neutral. We continue working for justice in our own way. We must not compromise Truth. We are not for a party, whether it be Paul or Apollos, reactionary or revolutionary. We are for Truth. Never must we condone violence, but always we must seek to understand it.— *Dwight Spann-Wilson, 1981.*

AS THERE CAN be nothing more opposite to the natural will and wisdom of man than this silent waiting upon God, so neither can it be obtained, nor rightly comprehended by man, but as he layeth down his own wisdom and will, so as to be content to be thoroughly subject to God. And therefore it was not preached, nor can it be practiced, but by such as find no outward ceremony, no observations, no words, Yea, not the best and purest words, even the words of the scripture, able to satisfy their weary and afflicted souls....Such, I say, were necessitated to cease from all externals, and to be silent before the Lord; and being directed to that inward principle of life and light in themselves, as the most excellent teacher...thereby to be taught to wait upon God in the measure of life and grace received from him, and to cease from their own forward words and actings, in the natural willing and comprehension, and feel after this inward seed of life....

And so from this principle of man's being silent, and not acting in the things of God of himself, until thus actuated by God's light and grace in the heart, did naturally spring that manner of sitting silent together, and waiting together upon the Lord. For many thus principled...did not apply themselves presently to speak, pray, or sing, etc., being afraid to be found acting outwardly in their own wills; but each made it their work to retire inwardly to the measure of grace in themselves, not being only silent as to words, but even abstaining from all their own thoughts, imaginations and desires; so watching in a holy dependence upon the Lord, and meeting together not only outwardly in one place, but thus inwardly in one Spirit.— *Robert Barclay (1648-1690).*

IT OFTEN HAPPENS that in carrying out my good intentions I find myself embroiled in a controversy....

Insight might be gained by comparing mutual care with the eastern idea of compassion. As I understand it, compassion in the eastern context is an inner experience that abides regardless of external circumstances. That is, the feeling is never sacrificed for expediency. In acting out of true compassion one does what one can to help others while maintaining the spirit of compassion. If controversy arises which threatens the feeling of   compassion, one chooses the course...that maintains the feeling even if it means backing off from helping someone.

By contrast, the idea of mutual care as we in the western culture think of it seems to be more tied in with results. Our idea is that if we are convinced of a need we will do something about it. Controversy is taken for granted. The greater the obstacles become the more effort required....The idea here is that caring of the heart does not count unless it expresses itself in a material way. The difficulty here is that heartfelt caring is wrung out of the situation long before help reaches its intended target. The further difficulty is that as true caring seeps out, arrogance enters in.

I believe that if a person is living a balanced life where mind, body and soul are in harmony, one will care about others because it is one's nature. If we see in our reaction to this the element of compulsion we can take this as a prompting to look at our life and see how it might in some way be out of balance. In my experience nothing done out of compulsion brings about the desired end. On the other hand...a life in balance can be by its very existence a help to others.— *Vince Oredson, 1986.*

BE FAITHFUL; be patient; be in earnest to fulfil your service as messengers of truth. Feel the power of God in one another, drawing you together as he draws you to himself.

Watch with Christian tenderness over the opening minds of your children. Seek to awaken in them the love of Jesus Christ and an understanding of his teaching. Uphold in your own conduct, and thus encourage in theirs, truthfulness and sincerity. Through example and training help them to recognize and obey the voice of God in their hearts that they may be joyful and willing in his service. Remember, at the same time, that there is a unique potentiality in each human being as a child of God, and that the Holy Spirit may lead your children along paths which you have not foreseen.

Endeavour to make your home a place of peace and happiness where the presence of God is known. Try to live simply. Remember to value beauty in all its forms. Encourage the appreciation of music, literature and the other arts and the development of a taste that will reject the worthless and the base. God's good gifts are for all to enjoy; learn to use them wisely.

Choose recreations that do not conflict with your service to God and man, and in that service, be willing to lay them aside. Be discriminating in the use of radio and television and other means of information, persuasion and entertainment. Give thought to the right use of Sunday with its special opportunities for both service and leisure.— *Advices, London, 1964.*

I BELIEVE it is not safe for me to be trusted with health and strength, under some plea or other I am so apt to use them for my own purposes. Lately I have lost my hold on the pearl; in my attempts to promote the comfort of my family, the quiet of my spirit has been disturbed. Some of this is doubtless owing to physical weakness; but with every temptation, there is a way of escape; there is never any *need* to sin.

Another thing I have suffered loss from— entering into the business of the day without seeking to have my spirit quieted and directed. So many things press upon me, this is sometimes neglected; shame to me that it should be so.

Some things I must bear in mind. First, always to seek this daily retirement, and earnestly search into my faults. Second, to talk less, and carefully to weigh my words, so that they may minister grace to the hearer. Let me be careful, without display or pretension, when I do speak, to do some good, if it is only to manifest kind feeling toward others.   Third, and this is of great importance, to watch carefully— now I am so weak— not to over fatigue myself, because then I cannot contribute to the pleasure of others; and a placid face and a gentle tone will make my family more happy than anything else I can do for them. Our own will gets sadly into the performance of our duties sometimes. Fourth, almost above everything else, to agonize for a loving spirit toward all.— *Elizabeth Taber King, 1856, aged 35.*

HE is an accountant who can cast up correctly the sum of his own errors.

As the stream, so the ship; canoes for shallows, and vessels of burden for deep waters.

We are too apt to imagine that contentment may be found almost anywhere than at home.

In religious disquisitions, the tongue does not always represent the mind.

Thieves are as liberal as honest men; but then it is with other people's property.

Those who have had the most forgiven them, should be the least addicted to slander.

Others sometimes appear to us more wrong than they are, because we ourselves are not right in judging them.

A lottery, which is confessedly a species of gambling, is an unsafe corner-stone to erect a place for worship upon.

Ingratitude to a benefactor naturally indisposes him to continue his benefits.

Company which does not help to improve us, will certainly have a contrary effect.— *George Dillwyun.*

WE WESTERN PEOPLES are apt to think our great problems are external, environmental. We are not skilled in the inner life, where the real roots of our problem lie. For I would suggest that the true explanation of the complexity of our program is an inner one, not an outer one. The outer distractions of our interests reflect an inner lack of integration of our own lives. We are trying to be several selves at once, without all our selves being organized by a single, mastering Life within us. Each of us tends to be, not a single self, but a whole committee of selves. There is the civic self, the parental self, the financial self, the religious self, the society self, the professional self, the literary self. And each of our selves is in turn a rank individualist, not co-operative but shouting out his vote loudly for himself when the voting time comes. And all too commonly we follow the common American method of getting a quick decision among conflicting claims within us. It is as if we have a chairman of our committee of the many selves within us, who does not integrate the many into one but who merely counts the votes at each decision, and leaves disgruntled minorities. The claims of each self are still pressed. If we accept service on a committee on Negro education, we still regret we can't help with a Sunday-school class. We are not integrated. We are distraught. We feel honestly the pull of many obligations and try to fulfill them all.— *Thomas Kelly, 1941.*

SEEK FOR YOURSELVES and for your children that full development of God's gifts which is true education. Realize that it should be continued throughout life and that its privileges should be shared by all. Study the Bible intelligently, using the help available from modern sources. Make every effort to understand the Christian faith. Be ready at all times to receive fresh light from whatever quarter it may come; approach new theories with discernment. Remember our testimony that Christianity is not a notion but a way.

Throughout life, rejoice in the power and beauty of those friendships which grow in depth, understanding and a mutual respect. At all times love and value "that of God" in your friend. No relationship can be a right one which makes use of another person through selfish desire.

In looking forward to the lifelong comradeship of marriage, remember that happiness depends on an understanding and imaginative love on both sides....Consider together the responsibilities of parenthood. Remember the help which you may draw from older and more experienced people, including your parents. Ask God's guidance continually; and when difficulties arise remind yourselves of the value of prayer, of perseverance, and a sense of humor.— *Advices, London, 1964.*

IN MY PRESENT arduous labors, way has been remarkably made for me by the most influential members of our Society in the cities where Friends reside, and by the prison authorities....In every institution I have been kindly received, and in most my visits have been encouraged by those in authority. Way has been made, not only for holding meetings with the prisoners collectively, but for me to visit them from cell to cell, and labor with them in private, which visits have seemed very acceptable to the poor prisoners, who seldom see the face of one whom they feel to be their friend, or hear the voice of sympathy.

In visiting the Penitentiary here I found a fine, intelligent man, about thirty-five years of age, sentenced for forty-five years for helping a slave with his wife and family to escape. They were nine, father and mother and seven children, and five years' imprisonment was the penalty for each. The prisoner had "harbored" them, given them food, and shown them the way to Pennsylvania.

Another man, a colored preacher, a very respectable man, is under sentence for fifteen years for having [the book] "Uncle Tom's Cabin" in his house....During the past year, I have travelled 5,750 miles, have visited and had meetings with 52,850 sick and wounded soldiers, 17,100 prisoners, 16,060 inmates of almshouses, 520 blind, 1,125 widows, 3,250 insane, 5,450 orphans, 5,850 children in refuges and asylums, 1,987 poor fallen women, 6,900 coloured people; I have had twelve meetings with Hicksite Friends, twenty-six with citizens in large cities....With children altogether, from the little ones in infant schools to the young aspirants for collegiate honors, I have visited or had meetings with 26,500.— *Elizabeth Comstock, 1863.*

MY FRIENDS, the world situation is grave. Humanity, with fearful, faltering steps, walks a knife-edge between complete chaos and a golden age, while strong forces push toward chaos. Unless we, the people of the world, awake from our lethargy and push firmly and quickly away from chaos, all that we cherish will be destroyed in the holocaust which will descend.

This is the way of peace: overcome evil with good, and falsehood with truth, and hatred with love. The Golden Rule would do as well. Please don't say lightly that these are just religious concepts and not practical. These are laws governing human conduct, which apply as rigidly as the laws of gravity. When we disregard these laws in any walk of life, chaos results. Through obedience to these laws this frightened, war-weary world of ours could enter into a period of peace and richness of life beyond our fondest dreams....

I maintain that personal problems should be seen as having a real purpose. They are sent to us by God and we are given the means to deal with them, and in so doing the strength and growing power is engendered.

I shall not accept more than I need while others in the world have less than they need......

Worry is not concern. It is the useless mulling over the past and/or being apprehensive of the future. This is obviously a lack of faith. If you will do all you humanly can to improve a situation and then will leave the rest to God, you are exercising your faith.

— *Peace Pilgrim, 1980.*

Her only possessions the clothes she wore, Peace Pilgrim walked over 25,000 miles across the United States by 1964, speaking to thousands on nuclear disarmament.

I BESEECH YOU, in the love of Jesus Christ, wisely to consider the force of your examples, and think how much your successors may be thereby affected....

As moderate care and exercise, under the direction of true wisdom, are useful both to mind and body, so by these means in general the real wants of life are easily supplied, our gracious Father having so proportioned one to the other that keeping in the medium we may pass on quietly....

Treasures, though small, attained on a true principle of virtue, are sweet; and while we walk in the light of the Lord there is true comfort and satisfaction in the possession; neither the murmurs of an oppressed people, nor a throbbing, uneasy conscience, nor anxious thoughts about the events of things, hinder the enjoyment of them.

When we look towards the end of life, and think on the division of our substance among our successors, if we know that it was collected in the fear of the Lord, in honesty, in equity, and in uprightness of heart before him, we may consider it as his gift to us, and, with a single eye to his blessing, bestow it on those we leave behind us. Such is the happiness of the plain ways of true virtue. "The work of righteousness shall be peace; and the effect of righteousness, quietness and assurance forever." (Isa.32:17.)

Dwell here, my dear friends; and then in remote and solitary deserts you may find true peace and satisfaction. If the Lord be our God, in truth and reality, there is safety for us; for he is a stronghold in the day of trouble, and knoweth them that trust in him.— *John Woolman, in Virginia, 1757.*

WHAT IS THEOLOGY? It is a response—a pondered human response to the presence of God among us. It is also a response to the concerns and strivings of people who seek richer, better-integrated lives.

Theology starts with revelation, with the active self-disclosure of the One called God, Elohim, Sustainer, Ruah, Spirit. A person can experience revelation through worship, prayer, existential searching, Bible study, thoughtful reading and everyday existence. The crucial point is that the first movement in theology is not a human one....

Theology thus starts with human limitation. This limitation has other aspects beside the need for patient waiting. Divine truth can never be expressed by humans except from a human perspective.......

Each of us can be a theologian. We can enrich our spiritual lives and those of people around us by articulating our spiritual experiences. In drawing on theological writings from the past, we can find continuity and wipe out feelings of isolation. We can define answers to our toughest concerns....We can dare to find out what God is saying to us.

Once I sat in meeting for worship absolutely certain that I had a message which needed to be shared. However, I felt no leading whatsoever that I was the one to give the message. I waited and waited, feeling I would burst from the tension, until a woman across the room got up and gave my message much better than I could ever have given it. What was happening here? What did this mean in terms of the movement of the Spirit in our lives? These are questions for theology.— *Shirley Dodson, 1980.*

HEARING SOME persons mention that their preference of silent meetings was increasing, I was led to consider the happiness of having bread in our own houses, and water in our own cisterns; where we need not the help of man, but can worship in solemn silence the Father of spirits, in spirit and in truth.

For my own part at present I feel far from this desirable attainment; clouds and darkness seem to overshadow me. In this state of mind, outward help is frequently necessary; and if the spring lies deep, and we have no strength to dig, the joint labor of others assists us in coming to that refreshment which we know not how to obtain. Nevertheless, I am well convinced, that a dependence on outward help will avail us nothing. If we are nourished by the bread of life, it must be by sinking deep into our own hearts, and experiencing the living powerful word to be near us, which will guide us into all truth.

We are too apt to let a careless negligence take hold of our minds when assembled together for the purpose of worship; instead of keeping them diligently fixed on the supreme Author of our being, and endeavoring to wait in the silence of all flesh, to hear that inspeaking word which would not only show us our states and conditions, and inform us what we ought to do; but, in His own good time, prepare a sacrifice acceptable to himself, and cause us to rejoice in the overshadowing of his love.— *Margaret Woods, 1774.*

"Thus saith the Lord, cursed be the man that trusteth in man, and maketh flesh his arm, and whose heart departeth from the Lord."—Jer. 17:5.

CEASING THE PRACTICE of condemnation and self-congratulation, and developing a bond of solidarity with all people, does not mean that one fails to discern truth from error, or greater truth from lesser truth, nor does one cease to act vigorously for the realization of the principles of truth in human society.

To disagree with a person is not to interrupt our solidarity with him or her, to thrust her away, or to judge ourselves better than he is. Once it is clear...that our love for our fellow human beings is not a function of their beliefs and attitudes, it no longer becomes necessary to betray the truth by pretending that the diverse ideas of everyone within some arbitrarily defined "in-group" are equally valid.

The practices of avoiding judgmentalism and of affirming solidarity with all our fellow creatures have a liberating influence in terms of our search for Truth. We know that the human order which surrounds us is but a disorder, and that the reason for this disorder lies in confusions of intellect and spirit which are widespread. At the same time, our healthy instinct not to be "holier than thou" or to isolate ourselves...tends to cloud our own hearts and minds, so we search for Truth half-heartedly, wishing not to separate ourselves from too many other people....

Seeking the Truth with impartiality, trying to live the Truth...and speaking the Truth without ego investment, hostility, or selfish involvement, is always a service. It means that we can collaborate...with people who do not understand fully what we know, and that we need not "preach" at people in the unhelpful way which is so justifiably and widely feared by nonviolent advocates. — *Daniel A. Seeger, 1986.*

THE ETERNAL GOODNESS

O FRIENDS! with whom my feet have trod
  The quiet aisles of prayer,
Glad witness to your zeal for God
  And love of man I bear.

I trace your lines of argument;
  Your logic linked and strong
I weigh as one who dreads dissent,
  And fears a doubt as wrong.

But still my human hands are weak
  To hold your iron creeds:
Against the words ye bid me speak
  My heart within me pleads.

I walk with bare, hushed feet the ground
  Ye tread with boldness shod;
I dare not fix with mete and bound
  The love and power of God.

I see the wrong that round me lies,
  I feel the guilt within;
I hear, with groan and travail-cries,
  The World confess its sin.

And so beside the Silent Sea
  I wait the muffled oar;
No harm from Him can come to me
  On ocean or on shore.
                — *John Greenleaf Whittier*

INWARD PEACE is both an end and a means. As a means it becomes an evidence of divine approval while lack of it is an evidence that some divine requirement is not being fulfilled. In a Quaker meeting for the business the expression is frequently heard: "I would feel most easy," or "I would feel comfortable" if...an action were carried through or not carried through, indicating that the inward peace of the speaker would be attained [then] only.   Throughout Quaker journals we find frequent reference to the absence of inward peace as a sign that some "Concern," possibly to undertake a journey [or] engage in some effort for social reform, had been laid upon the individual. When that concern has been carried through there is reference to the return of peace. It is not essential that the undertaking be successful for inward peace to result.   It is only necessary that the individual feel that he has done all that he is able to do to carry out the requirement. God does not require more than is possible.   He only demands that we live up to our capacity....

If inward peace is to be used as a test of guidance two conditions must be honestly met— first the feelings must be sensitized through prayer, worship, or meditation, so that they may be trustworthy for ascertaining moral or religious truth.   Second, the guidance of the individual must be checked with the guidance of others— the guidance of the group to which he belongs and the guidance of inspired utterances of the past and present. The guidance of the group is not always superior to the guidance of the individual, but it must be taken into account. The presence or absence of inward peace, whether in the individual or the group, is a useful test.— *Howard H. Brinton, 1948.*

WHEN YOU come to your meetings, both preachers and people, what do you do? Do you gather bodily only and kindle a fire, compassing yourselves about with the sparks of your own kindling, and so please yourselves and walk in the light of your own fire and the sparks which you have kindled, as those did in the time of old whose portion was to lie down in sorrow? Or, rather, do you sit down in true silence, resting from your own will and workings, and waiting upon the Lord, with your minds fixed in that Light wherewith Christ has enlightened you, until the Lord breathes life in you, refresheth you and prepares you and your spirits and souls, to make you fit for His service, that you may offer unto Him a pure and spiritual sacrifice?

*   *   *

Above all he is often retired to the Lord, loves fellowship with Him, waits for daily bread, which he asks not in his own words, strivings or will; but as one empty of his thoughts and jealous of the peace or comfort that is drawn from thence, he silently waits to feel the heavenly substance brought into his soul by the thought, or remembering the other passage in Scripture, or designedly calling to mind what has been formerly known that gives right peace, but every immediate word that proceeds out of the mouth of God that can satisfy him.— *William Penn (1644-1718).*

STAYING CLEAR in my purposes, which involves not setting goals only because they're satisfying and recognizable to others, has required a great deal of effort in the past two months. I do not want to go after things too great, nor marvels beyond me. But the world is excitable, and the pressures from others to come down from the mountaintop with a vision, or at the least with a set of clay tablets, are stronger than I would have believed.

Not only do I have to struggle against the expectation of others, I have had to face my own expectations. There is no doubt about it, I had fallen into a way of thinking about the spiritual life which involved hitting upon some special set of practices which would be a sure recipe for holiness. By mid-March I wrote in my journal: "An underlying, slow growing realization for me in recent days is that there is no *Way*, no magic Key that will Open the Door."

That which we are born remembering, then, is not a "how to." It is God as presence. All of prayer, all of meditation, seeks that from which we came, that toward which we move:

> Word not to be heard
> Love not to be known
> God beyond calling
> Be thou my God.

The wisdom of solitude is not easy to translate into the world. If we arrive in the midst of the old busy scene with all our being open and vulnerable, we can easily be destroyed. There is a way— and it is my task this year to learn it— to be present both to God and to the world, and yet stay shielded.— *Elise Boulding, 1975.*

THE CONCLUSIONS which I am trying to reach [on simplicity] are good mainly for me. God forbid that all Friends should think alike...and in the present state of the Society, it is not likely that they will....

Would it not be useful for each Friend to compose for himself his own idea of simplicity? Discussion groups may want to exchange views of the simple life. Here are some Queries:

1. How do I stand in the Light? Do I dream of God? Am I led by love? or duty? What is God's will for me?

2. How did I actually spend my time yesterday? Last week? Last year? Are there ways of spending my time God and I would prefer?

3. Do I do my job in a Godly way? Do I moonlight to do extra service? Do I answer to my family? My friends? How do I find recreation? Do I earn money in an honest way?

4. Do I spend money to get what I really need? Am I grateful for food, shelter and clothing? Am I wasteful? How important are things to me?

5. What are my favorite ways of avoiding truth in speech?

Though we are all individuals and will all give different answers, we will find in our seeking that we have much in common, for we are all the children of light.

One day many years ago, I was credibly informed that I would be shot the next day. This knowledge, as Dr. Johnson predicted, had the effect of concentrating my mind. When the fullness of my time comes, I pray that my mind and life may be so clarified and simplified that I shall step easily over the boundary between life and death in the presence of God.— *George Peck, 1973.*

NOR IS A RECLUSE LIFE (the boasted righteousness of some) much more commendable or one whit nearer to the nature of the True Cross; for if it be not unlawful as other things are, it is unnatural, which true religion teaches not. The Christian convent and monastery are within, where the soul is encloistered from sin. And this religious house the true followers of Christ carry about with them, who exempt not themselves from the conversation of the world, though they keep themselves from the evil of the world in their conversation. That is a lazy, rusty, unprofitable self-denial, burdensome to others, to feed their idleness; religious bedlams where people are kept up lest they should do mischief abroad; patience per force, self-denial against their will...and out of the way of temptation than constant in it....

Not that I would be thought to slight a true retirement, for I do not only acknowledge but admire solitude. Christ himself was an example of it; He loved and chose to frequent mountains, gardens, seasides. They are requisite to the growth of piety and I reverence the virtue that seeks and uses it, wishing there were more of it in the world; but then it should be free, not constrained. What benefit to the mind to have it for a punishment and not a pleasure? Nay, I have long thought it an error among all sorts that use not monastic lives that they have not retreats for the afflicted, the tempted, the solitary and the devout, where they might undisturbedly wait upon God, pass through their religious exercises and, being thereby strengthened may with more power over their own spirits, enter into the business of the world again; though the less the better, to be sure. For divine pleasures are found in a free solitude.— *William Penn (1644-1718).*

TO INDIVIDUAL lives, now, as to the world, there comes the stale time when we are neither young nor old, neither looking back on great achievements nor looking forward to them; when the early dreams and aspirations have lost their freshness or failed to materialize and the new ambitions have not got the same hopeful certainty about them. Talents may have shrivelled through lack of husbandry, loyalty lost its keen edge, pretense crept in—the star we hitched our wagon to long ago still seems very far away, and the wagon wheels don't turn as they used to.

Still we go on, trying so hard, working so hard, believing in the importance of putting a good face on it, keeping integrated, never allowing ourselves to go to pieces; until it happens on a time, to some, that one more jar to our self-respect breaks us up. Perhaps it is a financial calamity, an insult, a disagreement, a temptation embraced instead of ignored...a disappointment—whatever form it takes, we think: "Now this is the end, I can't do a thing right. At last I see what I really am, absolutely no good at all."

Our carefully built defences are down....Finding some quiet corner, we gather it all about us, making a bed in hell of our sins and failures and injuries and lost hopes....So we dare to look upwards from the pit...and forgetting all our polite prayers and cry out, "Look, God, what's happened!"

It is zero, blessed state when all is lost, even self. We could have arrived here through beautiful self-giving, but folly and pride chose the hard way, and it does not matter now, for into the...present comes peace from striving.—*Leila Ward, East Kent, 1980.*

RELIGION is a feeling of infinite dependence upon God, to paraphrase the German Protestant theologian Scheiermacher, leading to an understanding of the relatedness of all things and the concatenation of all events.

Quakerism is a religion with an open end; it is always amenable to further revelations. The Quaker spirit, therefore, is prophetic rather than priestly. A Friend with an inspired message speaks to the whole meeting, like prophets of old who revealed God's will to their people.

Centering down is like letting oneself sink slowly into the vast, unexplored ocean of the inner self— as vast and unexplored as the trackless spaces of the cosmos. When one has completely submerged oneself in that silent depth, one can begin the interior dialogue in which a stilled mind encounters the silence of the soul. When the silence of the mind has merged with that of the soul, it is ready to listen to the silence of eternity.— *Peter Fingesten, 1985.*

"In that day the remnant of Israel and the survivors of the house of Jacob will no more lean upon him that smote them, but will lean upon the Lord, the Holy One of Israel, in truth." And: "Thou dost keep him in perfect peace, whose mind is stayed on thee, because he trusts in thee."—Isa 10:20, 26:3.

TO THEE I would hand more than a cup of cold water in the name of a disciple, if I had it to give. We are very emphatically called *Friends*; and friends we should be to one another, not sparing friendly advice and reproof, and taking willing oversight of one another as keepers of one another, and so profitably conjoined in harmonious labor. If, then, we should not withhold reproof and correction in proper season, why should we withhold encouragement, and the expression of strengthening unity? If I have anything to write to thee, my dear, at this time, it is in this line—the line of encouragement to hold on thy way.

Continue in the littleness of self, and thou wilt continue to witness an enlargement in the service of thy great Master. And be not weary in well-doing; *consider* whose cause it is in which thou art engaged, of infinite importance and consequence; and how much depends on every one who is sent on any expedition, or who has any part to maintain, faithfully and firmly discharging their duty. Farewell. Mayst thou take deeper and deeper root in humility and in the experience of the Divine life, for thy own preservation and nourishment, the more thou advancest in religious stature and spreadest wide thy fruit-bearing branches.

By faithfulness in matters comparatively small, accumulated strength and encouragement accrues. Clean hearts and clean hands give boldness and confidence.— *Richard Shackleton, 1789.*

BY DAY I sat in the Gandhi library reading the writings that had poured from Gandhi's pen in his life. As I read his passionate words about sarvodaya (welfare)— and not wanting what the least of his brothers and sisters could not have— I knew that these were my brothers and sisters too, and that I also could not want what they could not have. I wrote long letters home about stripping ourselves of what we did not need.......

I saw how we all had chained ourselves to daily rhythms that were bound to defeat us. Day after day we recapitulated the old cycle of effort, irritation, impatience and anger— softened by small epiphanies of love and remorse. The spirit had to break through from time to time, because spirit is our very nature, but...how heavy-handed our daily behavior. For how many millenia had this gone on? Was the human race never to discover its self-forged chains?

The snapping of my chains was my signal that the human race was indeed to be freed— in theological language— from the bondage of sin and death. My experience is one of the simplest and oldest religious experiences that come to humans....Was the leap an act of the will or an invasion of grace?...God does not carry us as so much baggage...

Solitude is the most beautiful condition of the human spirit. I understand now what St. Augustine really meant when he said, "Every time I go out among men I return less a man." He was trying to say that in solitude he understood humanness, but easily lost track of it when confronted with his fellow specimens....I love humans now as I never loved them before when I depended on them. It is in solitude that I am learning to truly remember what I have lived forgetting.— *Elise Boulding, 1975*

EACH STAGE OF OUR LIVES offers its own fresh opportunities. Face with courage the approach of old age, both for yourselves and for those dear to you, realizing that it may bring wisdom, serenity and detachment. As far as possible make arrangements in good time which will avoid laying an undue burden on others. Dwell with thankfulness on the blessings and happiness that life has brought you. Try throughout life to discern the right moment to relinquish responsibilities which should pass to those younger than yourselves. As outward activity lessens, your thought and prayer may liberate love and power in others.

Bring the whole of your daily life under the ordering of the spirit of Christ. Live adventurously. In every situation seek to be aware of the presence of God, praying that spiritual energies in yourself and in others may be released for the furtherance of God's kingdom. Life brings many conflicting responsibilities and choices. To one, the summons may come to apply himself with fresh energy and vision to his present work; to another, to make a complete change, perhaps even to retire early or to limit his engagements, so that he may be free for new service of God's appointing. When you have a choice of employment, choose that which gives the fullest opportunity for the use of your talents in the service of God and your fellow-men.— *Advices, 1964.*

LET US THEN TRY what love will do, for if men did once see we love them we should soon find they would not harm us.

Force may subdue, but love gains, and he that forgives first wins the laurel...

Love is the hardest lesson in Christianity, but for that reason it should be most our care to learn it. *Difficilia quae pulchra.*

It is a severe rebuke upon us that God makes us so many allowances and we make so few to our neighbor, as if charity had nothing to do with religion or love with faith, that ought to work by it....

Did we believe a final reckoning and judgment, or did we think enough of what we do believe, we would allow more love in religion than we do, since religion itself is nothing else but love to God and man.

He that lives in love lives in God, says the beloved disciple. And to be sure a man can live nowhere better....

What we love we'll hear, what we love we'll trust, and what we love we'll serve, ay, and suffer for too. If you love me (says our blessed Redeemer) keep my commandments. Why? Why then He'll love us; then we shall be His friends; then He'll send us the comforter; then whatever we ask, we shall receive; and then where He is we shall be also, and that forever. Behold the fruits of love: the power, virtue, benefit and beauty of love!

Love is above all, and when it prevails in us we shall all be lovely and in love with God and one with another.— *William Penn (1644-1718)*

BEING PEACEMAKERS is essentially an affair of the heart, rather than of the mind. For whether a person decides to use the energies of his body and mind for building weapons and thinking the unthinkable, or whether a person dedicates herself wholly to a search for peace, is probably ultimately determined by a quality of the heart for which the mind is but a servant.

It is unlikely, therefore, that we shall debate each other, or our fellow citizens, into the ways of love. For we touch people's hearts not by what we debate with them about, but rather by the quality of our being— by who we are, and by how we live, and by what we do. Thus, all of our merely verbal efforts in education or politics have meaning only insofar as they spring out of our own very direct experience of joyfully seeing what love can do in practice....

Indeed, there is a profound sense in which the higher capacity of human nature...is beyond the power of manipulation. We cannot devise legislative programs, military campaigns, or rational debates to awaken in people these higher capacities; there is absolutely no way we can *force* others, whether our contemporaries or those in future generations, to be better human beings. No revolutionary campaign we can devise will assure that the people of the future will be more "awake," more virtuous, than we are....

The past is but a memory; the future but a dream. The present moment is every person's equal possession. Each moment affords a choice between life and death, between good and evil. All to which we aspire can find expression in time present. Indeed, there is no time but this present.— *Daniel A. Seeger, 1986.*

IN YOUR relations with others, exercise imagination, understanding, and sympathy. Listen patiently, and seek whatever truth other people's opinions may contain for you. Think it possible that you may be mistaken. In discussion, avoid hurtful and provocative language; do not allow the strength of your convictions to betray you into making statements or allegations that are unfair or untrue.

Remember that no one can live to himself; and be ready to seek counsel and help from one another. Let not failure discourage you. When tempted to do wrong, or to despair, call upon God for help, confessing to him your weakness and your need.

Remember your responsibility as citizens for the government of your own town and country, and do not shirk the effort and time this may demand. Do not be content to accept things as they are, but keep an alert and questioning mind. Seek to discover the causes of social unrest, injustice and fear; and try to discern the new growing-points in social and economic life. Work for an order of society which will allow men and women to develop their capacities and will foster their desire to serve.— *Advices, 1964.*

A spiritual revolutionary has a hard time in our society. The structures of violence and habits of oppression must be destroyed, but by means that we do not yet understand very well. We have only begun to explore non-violence....— *Elise Boulding, 1975.*

DO WE PRAY, or does God pray through us? I know not. All I can say is, prayer is taking place, and we are graciously permitted to be within the orbit. We emerge from such experiences of infused prayer shaken and deepened and humbled before the Majesty on High. And we somehow know that we have been given some glimpse of that Life....

I have tried, in these words, to keep very close to the spirit and practice of my three dearest spiritual friends and patterns, outside of Jesus of Nazareth. They are Brother Lawrence,and St. Francis of Assisi, and John Woolman.

Of these, Brother Lawrence, who lived in Lorraine three hundred years ago, is the simplest. He spent his life in the practice of the presence of God, and a priceless little book of counsels, by that name, has come down to us.

John Woolman, A New Jersey Quaker of two hundred years ago, really so ordered his external life as to attend above all to the Inner Teacher and never lose touch with Him.

But greatest of all is Francis of Assisi, whose direct and simple and joyous dedication of soul led him close to men and to God till he reproduced in amazing degree the life of Jesus of Nazareth. It is said of St. Francis not merely that he prayed, but that he became a prayer.

Such lives must be reborn to-day, if the life of the Eternal Love is to break through the heavy encrustations of our conventional church life, and apostolic life and love and power be restored to the church of God. He can break through any time we are really willing.— *Thomas R. Kelly, 1939.*

Like most true mystics William Penn in the end came to the simplicity and power of love. If any seeker, wanting to know where Friends stand on the question of the immortality of the soul, combs the Quaker anthologies and the indexes of Quaker books, he is sure to find Penn's words on love and death, taken from "Some Fruits of Solitude," some of the most beautiful words ever written on the subject. They have been of comfort to sorrowing souls far beyond the borders of his own communion.

THEY THAT LOVE BEYOND THE WORLD cannot be separated by it.

Death cannot kill what never dies.

Nor can spirits ever be divided that love and live in the same Divine Principle, the root and record of their friendship.

If absence be not death, neither is theirs.

Death is but crossing the world, as friends do the seas. They live in one another still.

For they must needs be present that love and live in that which is omnipresent.

In this divine glass they see face to face, and their converse is free as well as pure.

This is the comfort of friends, that though they may be said to die, yet their friendship and society are in the best sense ever present, because immortal.— *William Penn (1644-1718).*

AND THIS WE OWE our beloved dead, whether young or old: to wipe from our memories all that was less than their best, and to carry them in our hearts at their wisest, most compassionate, most creative moments. Is that not what all of us hope from those who survive us—that they will remember us "at the meridian", "soaring, and never setting...?"

And if we owe it to our beloved dead, we also owe it to our beloved living, not to dwell on their faults and lesser moments. In seeing them whole, we help them become more fully themselves.

Time does restore to us our quiet joy in the spiritual presence of those we love, so that we learn to remember without pain, and to speak without choking up with tears. But all our lives we will be subject to sudden small reminders which will bring all the old loss back overwhelmingly.......

When we pause in the daily round of cogs meshing into one another, the trivial busyness that makes up so much of our lives, we can become aware of the great wheel of the Universe turning with its circumference in the far reaches of space...

And on the circumference of my world [Emily Dickenson] remains. She taught me that grief is a time to be lived through, experienced fully, and that the heavens will not fall if I give voice to my anger against God in such a time. When we accept the unacceptable, it has no more power over us. We can move through and beyond the experience.—*Elizabeth Watson, 1979.*

WE THEN secured our horses, and gathering some bushes under an oak we lay down; but the mosquitoes being numerous and the ground damp I slept but little. Thus lying in the wilderness, and looking at the stars, I was led to contemplate on the condition of our first parents when they were sent forth from the garden; how the Almighty, though they had been disobedient, continued to be a father to them, and showed them what tended to their felicity as intelligent creatures, and was acceptable to him.

To provide things relative to our outward living, in the way of true wisdom, is good, and the gift of improving in things useful is a good gift, and comes from the Father of Lights. Many have had this gift; and from age to age there have been improvements of this kind made in the world. But some, not keeping to the pure gift, have in the creaturely cunning and self-exaltation sought out many inventions. As the first motive to these inventions of men, as distinct from that uprightness in which man was created, was evil, so the effects have been and are evil. It is, therefore, as necessary for us at this day constantly to attend on the heavenly gift, to be qualified to use rightly the good things in his life amidst great improvements, as it was for our first parents when they were without any improvements, without any friend or father but God only.— *John Woolman, Goose Creek, South Carolina, 1757.*

THIS IS THE POINT of prayer, then. When we pray we affirm our hope and intention of coming closer to God. We work to deepen our trust in and love for God, and...change as the intimacy of this relationship with our Divine Parent grows. As we pray and change in this relationship we become better equipped to be God's friends, to be better servants and instruments of God's love.

It is important to ask, even though we know God knows what we need, because in the asking we sharpen and express our own appreciation of God's attentiveness to us and care for us, and in this we enhance our relationship.

It is important to offer thanksgiving even though we know God knows we are grateful, because in this we affirm and confirm our appreciation of the unique and special grace our relationship with God brings.

As we grow through the dialogue of prayer in "the life of intimacy with God to which we are called", our willingness to trust in and depend on God will develop naturally, and with this development our capacity to serve God and our sisters and brothers in the fullness of love grows as well....

In the end, then, the...relationship with God which prayer offers is, as well, an entrance into paradox. We may need to ask and to thank and to pray in all variety of ways, in order to develop and nurture a relationship of intimacy with God; but as that relationship does develop, the desire and need to pray will be one of its first fruits. As we grow in the life of intimacy with God to which we are called we will come naturally to be, as Paul suggest we should, "joyful always, praying continually, and giving thanks in all circumstances, for this is God's will."— *Thomas H. Jeavons, 1984.*

IN HEARING William Savery preach, he seemed to me
to overflow with true religion, and to be humble, and yet
to be a man of great abilities; and having been gay and
disbelieving only a few years ago, makes him better
acquainted with the heart of one in the same situation.
If I were to grow like him, a preacher, I should be able
to preach to the gay and unbelieving better than to any
others, for I should feel more sympathy for them, and
know their hearts better.

Today I have felt all my old irreligious feelings. My
object shall be to search, try to do right, and if I am
mistaken, it is not my fault; but the state I am now in
makes it difficult to act. What little religion I have felt
has been owning to my giving way quietly and humbly
to my feelings; but the more I reason upon it, the more
I get into a labyrinth of uncertainty, and my mind is so
much inclined to both scepticism and enthusiasm, that
if I argue and doubt, I shall be a total sceptic; if, on the
contrary, I give way to my feeling, and as it were, wait
for religion, I may be led away.

But I hope that will not be the case; at all events,
religion, true and uncorrupted, is all that comforts the
greatest; it is the first stimulus to virtue; it is a support
under every affliction. I am sure it is better to be so in
an enthusiastic degree, than not to be so at all, for it is
a delightful enthusiasm.— *Elizabeth Gurney, 1798.*

"For all these things do the nations of the world seek after;
and your Father knoweth that ye have need of these things.
But rather seek ye the Kingdom of God; and all these things
shall be added unto you."— Luke 12:30,31.

WE LIVE IN an ambiguous world, which can be interpreted as happening by design or by chance; which can be seen as full of beauty and goodness, or suffering and evil; in which we can find divine purpose or complete absurdity. We experience ourselves in this world in a conflict between responsibility and impotence; in a situation of creation and destruction, anxiety and hope. We are finite creatures with a knowledge of our finitude, but with immortal longings. We know ourselves subject to time, and with it, to change, growth, decay, frustration, pain and death. Perhaps above all we wish to be saved from being meaningless.

We know ourselves as individuals but only because we live in community. Love, trust, fellowship, selflessness are all mediated to us through our interdependence. Just as we could not live physically without each other, we cannot live spiritually in isolation. We are individually free but also communally bound. We cannot act without affecting others and others cannot act without affecting us. We know ourselves as we are reflected in the faces, actions and attitudes of each other.

We can only separate ourselves from the community after it has formed us and we cannot think of ourselves except by reference to the community and its ways of thought and speech.

Both the individual and the community are free to go wrong and to learn from their mistakes, but the community differs from the individual in that its wrongdoings are magnified in their effects, but its powers of self-renewal are greater....

But our subjection to time is a condition of growth. We cannot change without time.—*Janet Scott, 1980.*

ARGUMENTS that convince our intellect alone leave us merely with questions answered, but they do not bring us to our knees in humble, joyful submission into His hands of all that we are. They do not bring the unutterable joy that makes Paul and Silas sing hymns at midnight in prison. Even though moments of the experience of Presence may dawn upon us, and then fade, we are thereafter new men and women, ploughed through to our depths, ready to run and not be weary, and to walk and not faint. We love God with a new and joyous love, wholly and completely. It is no commanded love, it is the joyful answer of our whole being to His revealed love....

I believe the real vitality of religion rests upon the fact that religious experience is universally taking place. It isn't creeds that keep churches going, it is the dynamic of God's life, given in sublime and intimate moments to men and women and boys and girls.

Let us notice that the experience seems to come from beyond us. It doesn't seem to be a little subjective patch in our consciousness. It carried a sense of objectivity in its very heart, as if it arose from beyond us and came in a revelation of a reality out there. If I may use a philosophic term, it is realistic. Just as my experience of that wall out there doesn't seem to be a subjective state of my mind, but a disclosure of a real wall out there beyond me, so the experience of God has in its inner nature a testimony that an Object is being disclosed to us. We do not make it, we receive it...And in glad discovery we know that God is dynamically at work in the world, and at work in us, pressing in upon us, knocking at the door of our minds and doing things to us which arise in His own initiative.— *Thomas Kelly, 1939.*

THE DILUTED WILBURITE tradition that survives today...may be described as a kind of nonverbal Christianity. Although the Wilburite tradition has generally held the same Quaker Christian faith enunciated by George Fox, it has scrupulously avoided overemphasizing the intellectual at the expense of genuine religious experience. Precious as the Christ-reality is to the Wilburites, they have feared an intellectual or emotional dependence on words.

As George Fox taught us long ago, the word is not the reality, nor is properly speaking the religious slogan the same as the glorious truth and transformation it represents. Thus, although Wilburites may use a Christ-language that sounds orthodox, theirs is a non-verbal orthodoxy quite aware of the limitations of language and of the danger of making faith merely a matter of intellectual propositions....It is no accident that Friends still generally refrain from calling the Bible the "Word" or "The Word of God," since we hold that only Christ is the Word of God, not as a closed intellectual formula but as a fluid, creative, open-ended, personal, and living power.......

It is good to remember two things when dialoguing or worshiping with a Wilburite. The first is that it is good to allow time for plenty of quiet spaces in the discussion or the worship, for some Wilburites are slow to verbalize about the precious inward reality and can appear to be silenced or out-argued by people who are verbally more facile. Wilburites returning from a wider Quaker gathering occasionally comment that by the time they are ready to speak, the meeting had moved on to another subject!— *William Taber, 1984.*

A READING of Quaker journals from George Fox onward makes it clear that this inward work takes time and may cause us to make painful changes in our life as we become more and more sensitive and obedient to the inward guide. Although this inward work continues as long as we live and remain open to new learning, there is a sense in which seekers do become finders through the inward work of Christ. There is a point when we can feel a perceptible freedom from our former materialism, individualism, and warped ways of viewing reality; a point when, through the mystery of grace, our former individualism becomes a rich and creative individuality; a point when our senses are widened and we feel and know that we are in some mysterious way in living union with the Divine, as well as with others who have travailed through the inward work of Christ.

It is this inward work of Christ, and not our verbal statements about Christ, that can produce that amazing unity in a gathered meeting for worship, a gathered meeting for business, or a gathered opportunity between two people. And finally, it is this inward work of Christ that leads inevitably to the important *outwardness* of Quakerism: to a life able to behave in all those ways which Jesus taught and in which he led the way, to a living equality of men and women, to a radiant and supple pacifism that comes not merely from books or movements or anger but that wells up from deep inner springs.

The Wilburite contribution to the current Quaker dialogue, then is the evidence that it is still possible— even in the analytical 20th century—for a Quaker middle way to exist. — *William Taber, 1984.*

FROM THE STEADY opposition which faithful Friends in early times made to wrong things then approved, they were hated and persecuted by men living in the spirit of this world, and, suffering with firmness, they were made a blessing to the church, and the work prospered. It equally concerns men in every age to take heed to their own spirits; and in comparing their situation with ours, to me it appears that there was less danger of their being infected with the spirit of this world, in paying such taxes, than is the case with us now. They had little or no share in civil government, and many of them declared that they were...separated from the spirit in which wars were, and being afflicted by the rulers on account of their testimony, there was less likelihood of their uniting...with them in things inconsistent with the purity of truth. We, from the first settlement of this land, have known little or no troubles of that sort. The profession of our predecessors was from a time accounted reproachful, but...their uprightness being understood by their rulers, and their innocent sufferings moving them, our way of worship was tolerated, and many of our members in these colonies became active in civil government....Our minds have been turned to the improvement of our country, to merchandise and the sciences, amongst which are many things useful...but in our present condition I believe it will not be denied that a carnal mind is gaining upon us. Some of our members, who are officers in civil government, are in one case or other, called upon in their respective stations to assist in things relative to the wars....Thus, by small degrees, we might approach so near to fighting that the distinction would be little else than the name of a peaceable people.— *John Woolman, 1757.*

IT REQUIRES great self-denial and resignation of ourselves to God, to attain that state wherein we can freely cease from fighting when wrongfully invaded, if, by our fighting, there were a probability of overcoming the invaders. Whoever rightly attains to it does in some degree feel that spirit in which our Redeemer gave his life for us; and through Divine goodness many of our predecessors, and many now living, have learned this blessed lesson; but many others, having their religion chiefly by education, and not being enough acquainted with that cross which crucifies to the world, do manifest a temper distinguishable from that of an entire trust in God. In calmly considering these things, it hath not appeared strange to me that an exercise...which, with respect to the outward means, is different from what was known to many of those who went before us...

The calamities of war were now increasing; the frontier inhabitants of Pennsylvania were frequently surprised; some were slain, and many taken captive by the Indians; and while these committees sat, the corpse of one so slain was brought in a wagon, and taken through the streets of the city in his bloody garments, to alarm the people and rouse them to war.

Friends thus met were not all of one mind in relation to the tax, which, to those who scrupled it, made the way more difficult. To refuse an active payment at such a time might be construed into an act of disloyalty, and appeared likely to displease the rulers, not only here but in England; still there was a scruple so fixed on the minds of many Friends that nothing moved it. It was a conference the most weighty that ever I was at, and the hearts of many were bowed....—*John Woolman, 1757.*

THE MEETING

THE elder folks shook hands at last,
Down seat by seat the signal passed.
To simple ways like ours unused,
Half solemnized and half amused,
With long-drawn breath and shrug, my guest
His sense of glad relief expressed.
Outside, the hills lay warm in sun;
The cattle in the meadow-run
Stood half-leg deep; a single bird
The green repose above us stirred.
What part or lot have you," he said,
"In these dull rites of drowsy-head?
Is silence worship? Seek it where
It soothes with dreams the summer air,
Not in this close and rude-benched hall,
But where soft lights and shadows fall....

"Dream not, O friend, because I seek
This quiet shelter twice a week,
I better deem its pine-laid floor
Than breezy hill or sea-sung shore.....
"And so I find it well to come
For deeper rest to this still room,
For here the habit of the soul
Feels less the outer world's control;
The strength of mutual purpose pleads
More earnestly our common needs;
And from the silence multiplied
By these still forms on either side,
The world that time and sense have known
Falls off and leaves us God alone.

        — *J.G. Whittier.*

A LEADING does not come to us simply so we may have one. Eventually its inwardness takes outward form and affects the rest of the human community. When we are led to the truth it is so we may live *by* it and do something *with* it. But as the examples of seasoned Friends often show, the struggles over leadings do not cease, nor do the possibilities of outrunning one's lead. The private leading must be tested against the experience and collective leading of the worshipping community, not only to check the excesses of the wilful or the mistaken, but also to give the support and strength of the religious community to what might otherwise be a lonely, ineffective witness. At its best, such testing strengthens the testimony of both the individual and the group. Very early in Quaker history, therefore, the community of faith had to find means to discern the true from the false leading and help the individual test [its] validity....

In *The Quakers in Puritan England*, Hugh Barbour describes four major tests which Friends came to apply to leadings: moral purity, patience, the self-consistency of the spirit, and bringing people into unity....

Not every leading demands such self-abnegation, but patience is a sound test, since "self-will is impatient of tests." So our church structures evolved to deal with the authoritarian Friend, who gives his meeting the ultimatum, "love me, love my leading," and the apocalyptic Friend, so sure that she alone knows the urgency of the times, as well as with those too at ease in Zion....The networks of meetings and committees became channels for the individual to submit leadings to the scrutiny of more seasoned Friends and to wait for clearness to proceed.— *Paul A. Lacey, 1985.*

THERE is a striking analogy between little children by nature, and those who are born from above. In the infant state of religion the child of God cries for something, it does not well know what; it does not desire to know, but it wants to be fed; its growth and its strength are *acquired* by its feeding, not by its increase of understanding, which yet, as it is necessary and useful, arrives in its season, and is added by degrees. And as we cannot add one cubit to our stature as natural men, so neither by taking much thought can we add to our religious growth: this is the work of God, as saith the Scriptures. In this day there is so much revolting from the genuine spirit of Christianity, and the few that are found in the faith and alive in the root are so rejoiced at the prospect of any of the visited youth coming forward in stability and service, that there is sometimes a danger lest such youth should be carried off their feet, and pulled forward into action beyond their proper strength, and the right requirings of duty. Only let us be inward and diligent in our spirits, keeping to our own particular exercise, and attending to the account current which is between the great Lord of the household and our own souls respectively, making short reckonings, and giving up no false rest till Infinite Mercy forgives the debt; so shall we, though poor, witness content, and though not abounding, yet have a little sufficiency. — *Richard Shackleton, 1783.*

I HAVE been learning...that when we accept our finiteness realistically and without bitterness, each day is a gift to be cherished and savored. Each day becomes a miracle. I am learning to offer to God my days and my nights, my joy, my work, my pain, and my grief. I am striving to keep my house in order, and my relationships intact. I am learning to use the time I have more wisely, so that death will not catch me with too much undone, too many projects incomplete. But I am learning to work without fretting, and I am finding a sense that there is time "for every purpose under heaven........"

I do not know whether human personality survives physical death. I am content to wait and see what comes after death, open to any possibility. If it should turn out to be eternal sleep, that too is a gift after a full life.

But I know that we live in the lives of those we touch. I have felt in me the living presence of many I have loved and who have loved me. I experience my daughter's presence within me daily. And I know that this is not limited to those we know in the flesh, for many of the guests of my life shared neither time nor space with me....

Life, then, is a gift of time. For each of us the days are numbered. I am grateful for each day I have to walk this beautiful earth. And I do not fear the return to the earth, for I know, like Whitman, that it is part of myself.— *Elizabeth Watson, 1979.*

I bequeath myself to the dirt to grow from the grass I love,

If you want me again look for me under your boot-soles.

You will hardly know who I am or what I mean,

But I shall be good health to you nevertheless. (*Whitman*)

Toward the end of her life Josephine Duveneck wrote:

A FEW PAGES BACK I used the word Immanence to describe a state of mind—I cannot account for the sharpened awareness which has come to clarify my perceptions. The episodes of every day life have a sacred quality. Sleep, dreams, waking in the morning, the breaking of bread, sunlight and shadow, meeting with friends or strangers, children, dogs, music and fragrances, my beloved hills and the sky, mid-day weariness, even petty annoyances, bring dual impressions—a tangible reality and an intangible aura—which is more real. Once in a public meeting Jung was asked, "Do you believe in God?' He answered, I do not believe—" He paused and then he added, "I know."

I, too, know.

There are no words to express this inner certainty, but it is based on the evidence of unity within all things, on the creative power of love and the pervasive energy of the Spirit flowing through and transcending human endeavors.

This is what I mean by Immanence—a merging of the outer and the inner. No longer two levels of life, but a reconciliation of opposites—a conclusion of my quest.—*Josephine Whitney Duveneck.*

Born in Boston in 1891 to a socially prominent family, lonely as a child, Josephine Duveneck kept notebooks in her late teens in which she wrote of her search for God, her desire for independence, her urge to write, and the need to love and be loved. Along the way she and her husband, Frank Duveneck, shared their wealth and their lives with other men, women and children, and tried in countless ways to combat the social ills of their times.

IF IT WERE necessary for every member in the meeting to feel equally happy about the decision reached, we should be presuming to be settling matters in an angelic colony and not among flesh and blood members of a local Quaker meeting! From my point of view as a member...the kind of unanimity that is refered to is a realization on my part that the matter has carefully and patiently been considered....Even if the decision finally goes against what I initially proposed, I know that my contribution has helped to sift the issue...and I may well have...come to see it somewhat differently from the point at which I began....I have also come to realize that the group as a whole finds the resolution that seems best to them. When this point comes, if I am a seasoned Friend, I no longer oppose it...and I emerge from the meeting not as a member of a bitter minority...but rather as one who has been through the process of the decision and is willing to abide by it....

Without this kind of participative humility, the Quaker business meeting process is seriously hampered. I have seen a clerk in my own meeting tenderly defer to one member who felt strongly opposed to an action that the group was ready to accept, and after a matter of a few months' time this person was no longer unwilling....

Speaking of seasoned Friends, it is almost impossible to exaggerate the assistance that Friends in a business meeting can often give to the clerk in helping at critical junctures by rephrasing an issue...by suggesting that perhaps we have reached a point where we could unite on a part of the issue or in proposing that we have gone as far with a matter that we can perhaps go until another meeting of the group.— *Douglas V. Steere, 1982.*

ORDERS CAME to some officers in Mount Holly to prepare quarters for a short time for about one hundred soldiers. An officer and two other men, all inhabitants of our town, came to my house. The officer told me that he came to desire me to provide lodging and entertainment for two soldiers, and that six shillings a week per man would be allowed as pay for it. The case being new and unexpected I made no answer suddenly, but sat a time silent, my mind being inward. I was fully convinced that the proceedings in wars are inconsistent with the purity of the Christian religion; and to be hired to entertain men, who were then under pay as soldiers, was a difficulty with me. I expected they had legal authority for what they did; and after a short time I said to the officer, if the men are sent here for entertainment I believe I shall not refuse to admit them into my house, but the nature of the case is such that I expect I cannot keep them on hire; one of the men intimated that he thought I might do it consistently with my religious principles. To which I made no reply, believing silence at that time best for me.

Though they spake of two, there came only one, who tarried at my house about two weeks, and behaved himself civilly. When the officer came to pay me, I told him I could not take pay, having admitted him into my house in a passive obedience to authority. I was on horseback when he spake to me, and as I turned from him, he said he was obliged to me; to which I said nothing; but thinking on the expression, I grew uneasy; and afterwards, being near where he lived, I went and told him on what grounds I refused taking pay for keeping the soldier.— *John Woolman, 1758.*

IN ALL [Uncle Eli's] work for the betterment of man at home and abroad, I never saw him discouraged or in doubt about the final issue. He was always full of hope and courage, and radiantly happy to be able to work at human problems...and seemed to have a kind of inward peace....

I felt that the way to become good was to go to work in the power of God to help make others good, and to help solve the problems of those among whom we live.

I got a further impression of this truth from an event which came at first as a calamity. I went out one morning in early winter to feed our cattle and horses in the barn, and found to my horror that a fearful storm in the night had blown the barn down with almost everything we possessed in it....The news carried fast, and before the day was over men from near and far gathered in our yard. They were all hard-working people like ourselves, with little wealth beyond their own strong hands. But before they separated they had decided to go to work at once and replace what the storm had destroyed. The entire neighbourhood went to work, and a new structure rose....

It was a simple deed, which perhaps many towns could parallel, but it affected me in a strange way. I saw, as I had not seen before, that the religion of these men was not merely an affair of the meeting-house; not merely a way to get to heaven. It was something which made them thoughtful of others and ready to sacrifice for others. I saw how it works itself out in practical deeds of kindness and righteousness. During those days that I worked in the cold of a Maine winter, among those men with their rough clothes and hard hands, I was helping build more than a barn; I was forming a wider view of the religion which such men as these were living by. — *Rufus Jones, 1926.*

THE WORLD talks of God, but what do they do? They pray for power but reject the principle in which it is. If you would know God and worship and serve God as you should do, you must come to the means He has ordained and given for that purpose. Some seek it in books, some in learned men; but what they look for is in themselves, though not of themselves, but they overlook it. The voice is too still, the seed too small and the light shineth in darkness; they are abroad and so cannot divide the spoil. But the woman that lost her silver found it at home, after she had lighted her candle and swept her house. Do you so too and you shall find what Pilate wanted to know, viz. *truth*, truth in the inward parts, so valuable in the sight of God....

Therefore, O friends, turn in, turn in, I beseech you; where is the poison there must be the antidote. There you want Christ and there you must find Him.

*   *   *

To have religion upon authority and not upon conviction is like a finger watch, to be set forwards or backwards as he pleases that had it in keeping. It is a preposterous thing that men can venture their souls where they will not venture their money; for they will take their religion upon trust but not trust a synod about the goodness of half a crown.

*   *   *

Don't bow down thyself before thy old experiences but behold the arm that has helped thee and that God who has often delivered thee. Remember that the manna descended from heaven daily; that it daily must be gathered and eaten, and that manna that was gathered yesterday cannot serve today for food.— *William Penn (1644-1718).*

IN THE VERY nature of things emotions are more or less variable, while convictions, where they are really convictions, and are not purely notions or ideas, are permanent...I learned in time, therefore not to seek emotions, but to seek only for convictions, and I found to my surprise and delight that my convictions brought me a far more stable and permanent joy than many of my more emotional friends seemed to experience. In the time of stress, with many of them, their emotions flagged...and they had hard fights to prevent utter failure and despair, and some of them have been thankful at last to struggle back to the stable ground of conviction, which in their emotional days had seemed so barren and comfortless.......

I am convinced it is a great art to know how to grow old gracefully, and I am determined to practice it...I always thought I should love to grow old, and I find it is even more delightful than I thought. It is so delicious to be done with things, and to feel no need any longer to concern myself much about earthly affairs...I am tremendously content to let one activity after another go, and to await quietly and happily the opening of the door at the end of the passage way, that will let me in to my real abiding place. *(1903)*

Once my Divine Master sent me on His errands, and I knew His will was good, and was happy in trying to do it. And now He has shut me up to an invalid life, and tells me to sit in my wheeled chair, and to be content to let others do His errands and carry on His work, and I know His will is good just the same, and am happy in trying to accept it.— *Hannah Whitall Smith, three days before her death, 1911.*

SHOULD a Quaker always seek amicable resolution of disputes, or is a Quaker ever justified in bringing legal action? Should a Quaker practice law and enter a profession where contention rather than consensus is the norm? Should a Quaker serve as a judge, even if it involves imposing a sentence contrary to Quaker beliefs..?

Feeling that suing another only aggravated differences, early Quakers refused to go to law against those who had wronged them.......

The concern not to aggravate a grievance by prosecuting is in keeping with the Query, "Are love and unity maintained amongst you?" This Query dates from 1682, and, as noted by Howard Brinton in *Friends for 300 Years*, it is the Query which has been in longest continuous use by Quakers. Reflecting the concern of the Query, the Discipline forbade any Quaker to sue another. If a dispute arose, the parties were to appeal to the meeting.

Because the Quakers were required to resolve disputes within the meeting, they were reluctant to use the courts....

At the same time they were loath to use the courts for their own benefit, early Quakers recognized the power of the courts to correct injustice...and the Meeting for Sufferings supported persecuted Quakers who turned to the law for relief....

Should Quakers go to law? A Quaker professor of political science is unsure, saying, "The basic question, is what does turning the other cheek mean in everyday life?" There is no pat answer. On the one hand there is the right to defend your won integrity. On the other hand, in the act of defense, you must make sure you aren't injuring the other person."— *Anne Farrer Scott, 1982.*

THOUGH I HAD faced death with quiet acceptance, I now found myself delighted to be alive again....I was deeply moved and felt overwhelming gratitude to God, who— through the study, hard work, skill, and dedication of so many, some of whom I had never seen— had given me back the incomparable gift, the many-faceted bundle of miracles, of human life. I vowed never again to take that gift for granted....

I recalled how hard I had worked trying to climb the organizational ladder for 38 years, how I never quite made it to the top, and how depressed I had been when I was passed over at the time appointments for higher positions were made. I now saw that all that energy was wasted, and I shall never again strive for such goals.

Two conclusions emerged from these reflections, and I decided that the remaining time alloted to me should be concentrated on these. First, so far as possible I shall try to be always aware of the marvels, mysteries, and beauties of God's world and to thank and praise God for the privilege of conscious enjoyment of them all. Second, I shall try to spend my days in caring helpfulness for all God's creatures, as I had been cared for in this crisis.

That's it. Later it occurred to me that this is what the New Testament— all great religion for that matter— is all about. Praise God and serve your neighbor. Nothing about making it to the top of your organization or being elected president of your professional society. Just love God and all God's works, and your neighbor as yourself.— *Richard D. Cooper, 1982.*

IT IS HIGHLY necessary for mortals to show mercy in all their words and actions one to another; and also to the creatures which God hath made for the use of man.

It is usually said, that a merciful man is merciful to his beast, which generally is true; and if men are merciful to their beasts, how much more ought they to be merciful one to another. Where mercy is to be extended, it ought not to be done sparingly, since thereby, according to Christ's blessed doctrine, we are to obtain mercy. That servant who showed no mercy to his fellow, had no mercy showed to him from his Lord. It is also recorded in the name of the Lord, "He hath shown unto thee, O man? what is good, and what doth the Lord require of thee, but to do justly, love mercy, and walk humbly with thy God."

By which it appears that we are not just in the sight of God, if we are cruel and unmerciful one to another. And we ought not only to be merciful, but to love it, which if we are truly humble, we shall certainly do.

Mercy will lessen, and not magnify weakness, failings or small and trivial things, one in another; and sometimes, as the case may require, larger things. Yet there is room for seasonable reproof and correction; but mercy must be mixed with justice, else the correction may end in tryranny. We ought to be gentle to all men, which is a token of true gentility; so to be truly merciful, is to be blessed, and to obtain mercy.— *Thomas Chalkley (1675-1741)*.

"Blessed are the merciful; for they shall obtain mercy."— Matt. 5:7.

IT IS ONE amongst the numerous moral phenomena of the present times, that the inquiry is silently yet not slowly spreading in the world: *Is War compatible with the Christian religion?*   There was a period when the question was seldom asked, and when war was regarded almost by every man both as inevitable and right. That period has certainly passed away; and not only individuals but public societies, and societies in distant nations are urging the question upon the attention of mankind.

It is not unworthy of remark, that whilst disquisitions are frequently issuing from the press, of which the tendency is to show that war is not compatible with Christianity, judicious attempts are made to show that it is. Whether this results from the circumstance that on individual peculiarity is interested in the proof—or that there is a secret consciousness that proof can not be brought—or that those who may be desirous of defending the custom rest in security that the impotence of its assailants will be of no avail against a custom so established and so supported—I do not know: yet the fact is remarkable, that scarely a defender is to be found. It can not be doubted that the question is one of the utmost interest and importance to man. Whether the custom be defensible or not, every man should inquire into its consistency with the moral law.—*Jonathan Dymond, London, 1852.*

"They shall beat their swords into plough shares, and their spears into pruning-hooks: nation shall not lift up sword against nation, neither shall they learn war any more."— Isa.2:4.

THE FREEDOM of the kingdom of God involves membership one of another and responsibility towards God and man. Check in yourselves and discourage in others those tendencies which lead to gambling and speculation. Do not, out of the spirit of emulation or through the offer of easy terms, buy what you do not need or cannot afford; and do nothing to encourage others in these practices. In view of the evils arising from the unwise use of alcohol, tobacco and other habit-forming drugs, consider how far you should limit your use of them or whether you should refrain from them altogether. Do not let claims of good fellowship, or the fear of seeming peculiar, influence your decision. All users of the road should constantly remember that danger can arise from lack of patience and courtesy, and that any use of alcohol or drugs impairs alertness and so may imperil the lives of others.

Be faithful in maintaining our witness against all war as inconsistent with the spirit and teaching of Christ. Seek, through his power and grace, to overcome in your own hearts the emotions which lie at the root of conflict. In industrial strife, racial enmity and international tension, stand firmly by Christian principles, seeking to foster understanding between individuals, groups and nations....

Use your abilities and possessions not as ends in themselves but as God's gifts entrusted to you. Share them with others under his guidance and to his glory. Use them in humility and with courtesy. Guard against the love of power; be considerate of the needs of others and respect their personalities.   Show a loving consideration for all God's creatures.   Cherish the beauty and variety of this world. — *Advices, London, 1964.*

ALL TRUTH is a shadow except the last, except the utmost; yet every Truth is true in its kind. It is substance in its own place, though it be but a shadow in another place (for it is but a reflection from an intenser substance); and the shadow is a true shadow, as the substance is a true substance. *(1653)*

*   *   *

Are there not different states, different degrees, different growths, different places?..What wisdom and spirit is that, which doth not acknowledge this, but would make all equal?..Therefore, watch every one to feel and know his own place and service in the body, and to be sensible of the gifts, places, and services of others, that the Lord may be honoured in all, and every one owned and honoured in all, and every one owned and honoured in the Lord, and no otherwise. *(1667)*

*   *   *

Even in the Apostles' days, Christians were too apt to strive after a wrong unity and uniformity in outward practices and observation, and to judge one another unrighteously in those things; and mark, it is not the different practice from one another that breaks the peace and unity, but the judging of one another because of different practices. He that keeps not a day may unite in the same Spirit, in the same life, in the same love, with him that keeps a day...but he that judgeth the other because of either of these errs from the Spirit, from the love, from unity, in the Spirit, in the inward life, and not in an outward uniformity...Men keeping close to God, the Lord will lead them on fast enough...for He taketh care of such, and knoweth light and what practices are most proper for them.— *Isaac Penington, 1659.*

WHAT WOULD happen were we to share more of our good-natured presence with our friends and neighbors where we live—in our work places, our homes, our meetings, our communities? At a gathering such as the one at Berea we do that with one another. We dissolve our fears in taking time with each other to feel the presence of God alive and well and moving among us. How widespread is that need in our society as a whole and the world at large.

Can we go forth acknowledging God, accepting God, and answering God? Can we content ourselves for a change in reflecting and blending with the goodness we find around us, helping our sisters and brothers feel God alive and at work in themselves? In sharing these thoughts with you I do not mean to diminish our historic Quaker testimonies or to suggest that we no longer need to engage in Quaker service and witness against the evils of our day.

But surely if we are to remain faithful to our doctrine of continuing enlightenment, and discover God's will and way for Quakers today, in these times, then we must seize our God-given freedom to fly out of the cage of our historic cultural conditioning and rediscover the presence and power of God, life, and love face to face for ourselves.

If we are to find our way home to the Kingdom together and discern the true nature of reality, we must honor the experience of life that God has given each of us by embracing it fully for ourselves and sharing it boldly with others. Let us continue to proclaim to one another our experience of what we know of God, of what we know of life and its goodness!— *Ross Flanagan, 1982.*

THEREFORE be not discouraged, O thou tossed as with tempest, nor dismayed in thyself; because thou seest such mighty hosts of enemies rising up against thee, and besetting thee on every side; for not was so beset, and tried, and tempted as the true Seed was, who was a man of sorrows, and acquainted with grief. But be thou still in thy mind, and let the billows pass over, and wave upon wave; and fret not thyself because of them, neither be cast down, as if it never should be otherwise with thee: sorrow comes at night, but joy in the morning; and the days of thy mourning shall be over, and the accuser will God cast out forever. For therefore was I afflicted, and not comforted, and tempted, and tried for this end, that I might know how to speak a word in due season, unto those who are tempted and afflicted as I once was, as it was said unto me in that day, when sorrow lay heavy upon me. Therefore be not disconsolated, neither give heed unto the reasonings and disputings of thy own heart, nor the fears that are therefrom; but be strong in the faith, believing in the light which lets thee see them, and his grace thou will know to be sufficient for thee, and his strength to be made perfect in weakness. And so thou will glory in thy infirmities and his power to rest upon thee.— *John Crook, 1660.*

"Why art thou cast down, O my soul; and why are thou disquieted in me? hope thou in God; for I shall yet praise him for the help of his countenance."— Psalm 13:5

"Then He arose and rebuked the winds and the sea, and there was a great calm."— Matt. 8:26.

"HIS FACE did shine, and he wist not that it did shine."

Here is the secret of "the Quaker face." It was once very evident. On a visit to Philadelphia Yearly Meeting, fifty years ago...I, an Indiana Quaker pastor...sitting on the "facing seats" and looking into the faces of hundreds of Friends, I was suddenly aware that I knew them— that I knew them all.

THERE was a common practice among Friends, toward the weekend, to prepare themselves, hours before "First Day" morning meeting for worship, for that coming gathering, in the quiet closet of personal devotion— to cleanse the mind of selfish motives (can that ever be fully done?) and then gather with others equally prepared in spirit. How different from the modern scene where, at the last minute, we hastily dispatch our corn flakes and "go to meeting" at fifty miles an hour!

There are still Quaker concerns which are alive with contemporary relevance, but the calm, confident, serene facade, reflecting inner poise and depth, actually composed of faith and suffering, is today likely to be colored by tension and nervous fears, in spite of confident words...Do not mistake— the Quaker face, so unperturbed, so peaceful, so staid and serene never had any taint of resignation. It was calm and stern and confident, and lest you mistake, meant serious business. That by-product of Quietistic intimacy with Spiritual Truth which was raised to its highest in John Woolman, had its imprint in varying degrees across the Society, so that calm confidence in God who is in control of things, was revealed in the countenance of individuals, and the group.— *Elden H. Mills, 1981.*

WE MUST BE as frank as we can over this business of loving, accepting and forgiving another person. While I am absolutely convinced that this is what we must strive for, I am equally convinced that it is one of the hardest things we are called upon to do. However hard we try we shall find, all too frequently, that we fail. Sometimes when we are really honest we shall be able to admit that the grudge we hold against someone, because of some disservice, or outright nastiness they have perpetrated against us, is not one that we even want to relinquish.

Even those who strongly interpret their experience as a direct communion with God, and...seek his help in enabling them to achieve the act of reconciliation, willingly admit that it is not an easy activity....

First, harboring a grudge against life in general, or a particular circumstance or person brings about a bitter, unhealthy state in our personality and tends to diminish us as a person. Second, the fact that we recognize this is, at least, one positive sign that we are moving in the right direction. Third, one thing I have found helpful is to try to avoid a hasty confrontation with the person concerned as this can so often lead to hurtful unconstructive recriminations, when we say things we later bitterly regret. At the same time I am fully aware of the damage done by bottling up one's outraged feelings, quite apart from the fact that the unwillingness to tell people when they have hurt us indicates a lack of integrity which is destructive of real human relations. Of course, there are people, so loving and perfectly in control of themselves, that they can handle positions of direct confrontation with delicacy and constructiveness.— *George H. Gorham, 1979.*

THE DAY DAWNING, the night retires, and the substance comes, the shadow vanishes.   My dear, though unknown friend, when the beloved of thy soul appears, if the world and the things and friendship and glory of it, be not thy beloved, thou will not then mind His picture, if it were His picture, nor mind His shadow, though He had even said, Look upon this till I come. It is true, thou wilt not then condemn His picture when He is with thee; no more do I; but have a due esteem for all He commandeth, in their times, dispensations, and ends.

Nor do I lightly esteem those who use that in imitation with a good intent and sincere mind, but pity them that they are come no nearer the kingdom; which though at hand seventeen hundred years ago, is not yet come unto those who are set down contented under the shade of night, and dreaming of things of which they have no knowledge or enjoyment.

Go into the sunshine, and turn thy face towards the sun, and the shadow will be behind thee; but turn thy back on the sun, and the shadow will be before thee; and the more thou followest it, the more it will flee thee; and the more thou goest after it, the further from the sun. The kingdom of heaven is within, and stands not in eating and drinking, nor comes with outward observation, but in righteousness and peace, and joy in the Holy Ghost.— *Thomas Story, 1690.*

I AM now sitting with my dear little cares, watching them in their evening's repose. They (as thou justly observest) attach us strongly to life; and without a guard over ourselves, we are in danger of centering too much of our happiness in them. They may, indeed, in various ways, be deemed uncertain blessings; their lives are very precarious, and their future conduct proving as one could wish not less doubtful. I already often look forward with anxiety, and the most ardent wishes for their welfare, in a state of permanent felicity. They are now pretty play-things, and pleasing calls of attention, and should be received with grateful hearts as additions to our present comfort; but we should consider that they may be only lent for a time.

We are so incapable of judging with regard to our own happiness, or that of others, that it should lead us to a patient acquiescence in the Divine will; a resignation which would not only enable us to say, "Thy will be done," but to feel that submission of mind which would preserve us in calm composure. Things which appear to our present unhappiness and disadvantage have frequently at a future period proved a benefit, and we have been led to acknowledge that the Lord only knows what is best for us. Suffer us to beseech, O Lord, more and more to enlighten us with divine knowledge, and having made us sensible of thy will, enable us to obey it.— *Margaret Woods, 1777.*

"Lo, children are an heritage of the Lord."— =Psalm 127:3.

IT IS UNFORTUNATE that, so often, it is only in times of great crisis and despair— when we are laid so low that our pride and ego can no longer be a refuge— that we allow ourselves to call out to that unseen presence and yield our will to God's.

Our will! That precious free will that we were given. We fight against giving it up to anyone— even to God. We don't want some force to dominate us. Yet, if God is Love and all that is God, how much better to be dominated by Love than by our petty egos and conceits. Only when we are open and vulnerable to God can we allow ourselves to be led in the Light.

I spent a good part of my life fighting off "Thy will be done." It was only when I was faced with the possibility of not realizing what I had worked so long and hard for that I found myself kneeling for the first time in my life in earnest prayer and revealing to God my acceptance of whatever direction I was led to go. I felt calm, serene, confident, and filled with a sense of the Spirit. I have tried since then always to make sure that God was included in every aspect and direction of my life.

We are indeed fortunate to find as Friends a faith that cherishes a communion with God and with each other— in silence, in ministry, and in service— that meshes the concepts of faith and practice into an integrated whole. Perhaps our awareness and gratitude can give us the courage to both seek and find.— *Betty-Jean Seeger, 1982.*

THERE'S the whole matter of having a meaningful attitude for the problems that life may set before you. If only you could see the whole picture, if only you knew the whole story, you would realize that no problem ever comes to you that does not have a purpose in your life, that cannot contribute to your inner growth. When you perceive this, you will recognize problems as opportunities in disguise. If you did not face problems, you would just drift through life and you would not gain inner growth. It is through solving problems in accordance with the highest light that we have that inner growth is attained. Now, collective problems must be solved by us collectively, and no one finds inner peace who avoids doing his share in the solving of collective problems, like world disarmament and world peace. So let us always think about these problems together....

There is [another] preparation, and that is the simplification of life to bring inner and outer well-being— psychological and material well-being— into harmony in your life. This was made very easy for me. Just after I dedicated my life to service, I felt that I could no longer accept more than I needed, while others in the world have less than they need. This moved me to bring my life down to need-level. I thought it would be difficult. I thought it would entail a great many hardships, but I was quite wrong. Now that I own only what I wear and what I carry in my pockets, I don't feel deprived of anything. For me, what I want and what I need are exactly the same, and you couldn't give me anything I don't need...anything beyond need tends to be a burden....There is great freedom in simplicity of living.— *Peace Pilgrim, 1980.*

"Save Me, God! The water is already up to my neck! I am sinking in the deepest swamp, there is no foothold; I have stepped into deep water and the waves are washing over me. Worn out with calling, my throat is hoarse, my eyes are strained, looking for my God." Psalm 69:1-3.

ALL OF US know this feeling, times of distress that seem overwhelming, cutting us off from the feeling of God's presence. Whether the distress is one due to personal health, fear, sorrow, loneliness, pressure we do not feel able to live up to, or whatever, this cry is ours.

We all know of people, perhaps ourselves at some other period of time, who have coped with equally distressing things by turning to God and finding peace and strength for endurance. When I find myself uttering David's cry, I find myself also asking, ""What is wrong with me? Why should I feel cut off?" I answer it with "My faith is not good enough," adding a large burden of guilt to the distress I already feel, I tend to think, in my agony, "Other people, with better faith, would handle this correctly."

Adding a burden of guilt to an already overwhelming distress is not useful or necessary. In fact, I rather think it is doing ourselves an injustice that can be very harmful....Why should we have these times when we feel cut off from God in our distress? I suspect none of us really knows...I suspect that everyone we know who seeks after God has been through it and just does not talk about it....If we feel cut off from God, we should continue to remember in faith that God is still there anyway and still loves us. We should continue to seek a divine response, believing God is there. — *Ruth Ellison, 1982.*

BEING THUS fully convinced, and feeling an increasing desire to live in the spirit of peace, I have often been sorrowfully affected with thinking on the unquiet spirit in which wars are generally carried on, and with the miseries of many of my fellow-creatures engaged therein; some suddenly destroyed; some wounded, and after much pain remaining cripples; some deprived of all their outward substance and reduced to want; and some carried into captivity. Thinking often on these things, the use of hats and garments dyed with a dye hurtful to them, and wearing more clothes in summer than are useful, grew more uneasy to me, believing them to be customs which have not their foundation in pure wisdom. The apprehension of being singular from my beloved friends was a strait upon me, and thus I continued in the use of some things contrary to my judgment....

Though my mind was thus settled in relation to hurtful dyes, I felt easy to wear my garments heretofore made, and continued to do so about nine months. Then I thought of getting a hat the natural color of the fur, but the apprehension of being looked upon as one affecting singularity felt uneasy to me. Here I had occasion to consider that things, though small in themselves... become great things to us...

I had several dyed garments fit for use which I believed it best to wear till I had occasion for new ones. Some Friends were apprehensive that my wearing such a hat savored of an affected singularity; those who spoke with me in a friendly way I generally informed, in a few words, that I believed my wearing it was not in my own will, trusting...the Lord...would open the hearts of Friends towards me.—*John Woolman, 1761.*

JOHN WOOLMAN experienced the mystical Presence of God long before it ever occurred to him that slavery was unethical. Then one day in his retail office someone asked him to write out a receipt for a slave. Something revolted in Woolman's conscience because, as a result of his spiritual consciousness, he was terribly present to that moment—awake, mindful. He didn't write the receipt. It was a personal matter for him. Gradually thereafter, he began speaking to his friends, to his meetings, to other meetings, about freeing the slaves. His ethics spontaneously grew from his spiritual sensitivity. No one pressured him to join any committees. He did not start with an ethical ideal of human rights and go to meeting in order to talk about it. It happened the other way around. He went to meeting to be present before God. His ethic was the flowering of Silence....

So ethics begin in awareness, in a heightened consciousness of the present, which is where we meet God. When you are fully present to the present, it is holy ground. You are naked. Your mind is naked. Time is naked, there is no past or future. You are just there. But you bring to the present a certain quality that is not of the mind, not fabricated by thought, a quality of pure awareness, like a deep clear mirror...And that is how God addresses you. If you can handle it, if you do not flee, but simply answer, "Here I am," then wherever you are becomes holy ground.

Real values are not learned. They form. They form from *inside out*. They cannot be imposed....So the essence of our ethical development *must* be the meeting— the meeting with its silence. How else can we learn, with such intensity, how to be here now?— *Alfred K. LaMotte, 1982.*

GREAT INDEED has been the travail of my soul in secret for six months past. I could copy many things from my little diary which would convince my friends that I have not been idle, and I have thought sometimes, if it was my Master's good pleasure to remove me from my troubles here, the account of my time spent from day to day would witness for me; for indeed I have been a mournful Jeremiah in and near London, and but little can I do but wait for those days to be over and to hear this language.

It is enough I have not drawn back from any labor which was clearly pointed out in my own land, neither do I find this charge against me here, though of late it has been a time of as deep searching of heart as ever my soul experienced. Yet after all, with deep humility I acknowledge I have not been faultless.

What a hard thing it is, when plunged into the deeps, to be content in the will of God; what a hard thing for the unsubjected will, wit, and reason of man to become a fool—one of no reputation. Truly I have thought my soul never was made so sensible of what the patriarch, prophets, and mournful sufferers in their day and generation passed through, and of the agonizing pangs of Him unto whom the heathen was given for an inheritance, and the uttermost parts of the earth for a possession, who also gave his cheeks to the smiter and His face to them that pluck off the hair, who hid not His face from shame and spitting.— *Thomas Scattergood, London, 1798.*

"These are they which came out of great tribulation, and have washed their robes and made them white in the blood of the Lamb."— Rev. 7:14.

WE WISH those getting married a lifetime of happiness together, but few lives are full of joy. Sorrow and pain come to all of us. Problems can divide us, or we can grow together through them. Facing economic reverses, disasters, serious illness, and death honestly and supportively can strengthen a relationship. Much of life consists, however, of going on day after day, without making much visible progress, doing our work as faithfully as we can, with no special reward or recognition. Our mate's understanding of the need for encouragement, of a break— sometimes in the form of a special treat or gift or night out— can make an enormous difference. If, however, we expect our mates to support us in idleness or carry a disproportionate share of the load or smooth out all our difficulties and shield us from disaster, we are doomed to disappointment.   No marriage can grow into wholeness unless both work at it with mutual forbearance and trust and caring. If we can help a couple see something of this beforehand, we will fulfill part of our role of providing clearness.

We can wish young people joy together, but we should also wish them courage, patience, and a sense of humor. It takes all three to make a good marriage. We can also tell them how important it is to keep talking and listening to one another and not to let things get bottled up inside, unresolved....

Finally, perhaps the most important thing members of clearness committees can do is to "let their lives speak." If our marriages are loving and supportive, we become role models of a rewarding relationship. Our examples are inviting and encouraging to those embarking on the adventure.— *Elizabeth Watson, 1981.*

TOLSTOY wrote a story called *What Men Live By.* At the end he states clearly the answers to three great questions:

* The most important time in all eternity is this moment, now.
* The most important person in all the world is the person I am with now.
* The most important task in all the world is to do good to that person....

The most exciting possibilities open up when we try to reach out in love to the person, of all those in our circle, most difficult to love or reach....

The love of which I have been speaking is amazingly contagious. But one of the wonders is that you absolutely never know where the seeds will sprout....

It is predictable enough when you think about it, but still always unexpected, that the seeds sprout where God has tilled the soil and not particularly where we have been doing all the gardening....

There are so many more subtleties one could look at. One is how human power relationships enter into it. It is a very different thing trying to love someone in a more powerful position than you, on an equal footing, and below you in the system. We Friends need to examine ourselves more thoroughly for our failure to transcend human power structures with the greatest power of all: Divine Love.

Every moment, we need to ask ourselves: Who is there in my life most difficult to love, toward whom God is calling me to share this kind of love? How can I find creative ways to express that love?— *Ruth Morris, 1982.*

JESUS' life was manifestation of the Light. His birth was signalled by the bright star which penetrated the darkness. At his death darkness returned. A long tradition of paintings show light radiating from his shoulders and head. When the child Jesus was brought to the temple in Jerusalem, the old man, Simeon, saw the light. Speaking to Mary and Joseph he said, "I have seen with my own eyes...a light that will be a revelation to the heathen and glory to thy people Israel." (Lk 2:30-32)

Through actions that he considered much less important than his teaching, Jesus repeatedly demonstrated his oneness with the Light. Irritated by constant demands for convincing miracles, he berated the doubters...[and] reluctantly he finally did say, "I am the light of the world. No follower of mine shall wander in the dark, but shall have the light of life."(John 8:12)

Jesus spent his life turning us toward the Light. Sometimes he spoke of it directly. Often he spoke in metaphors. Always he asked us to dig deeply within ourselves for understanding. But once we learn that worldly light...is metaphor for the living light of God's presence, we can follow Jesus where few Christians have dared to go....

"You are light for all the world," he said, placing us on a level with himself. "When a lamp is lit, it is not put under the meal tub, but on the lamp stand, where it gives light to everyone in the house. And you, like the lamp, must shed your light among your fellows." (Mt. 5:14)

This, then is the promise, that as we come to dwell more closely within the Light, we become agents of the Light...[and can] change the world....— *Barry Morley, 1981.*

PEACE is the farm in Iowa
Fields which stretch clear to the horizon
Covered with snow and no mountains in sight.
Me rising early, rolling over like a snowball
Out of Grandma's too soft bed.
The crisp warm smell of bacon comes up from
    downstairs
Mingled with women's voices.
I touch my feet to the cold hardwood floor,
Am quick to pull on pants and shirt,
Tiptoe downstairs to the warmth of the kitchen
Where Grandma in her purple dress
Stands no taller than me,
Reminds me of the rolls she bakes, warm and soft
With layers we peel off like leaves of an artichoke.
My grandmother's a Quaker
So was Nixon's
But sometimes it makes a difference.
A picture of her father and mother hangs on my wall.
Sitting there on a piece of cardboard
At the turn of the century, surrounded by greyish white
As if taken on a smog-filled morning
Their faces and shoulders peer out, stiff and frozen
Albert with his mustache, short hair
Suit jacket and no tie,
Effie a bit below him, her hair in tight curls
To match the ruffles on her dress.
They stare out from their Quaker straightness
at me
A great-granddaughter they never knew.

            — *Vicky Aldrich, 1980.*
            from SOME QUAKER ROOTS...

HISTORICALLY there can be no question but that the Society began as a Society of Christians, and for the most part of its life the Christian basis was accepted without demur by its members....However, a Society lives in its members and not in its history. Any discussion of what the early Quakers believed is interesting...yet the important question is what Quakers believe now, not what they believed fifty or two hundred and fifty years ago....

[Members] should not concern themselves with questions such as "What are your beliefs, my beliefs, the Society's collective beliefs...for such questions lead on to judgements of others, and the sorting of humanity into Christians and non-Christians.

It would be more productive and more Quakerly if the questions we asked ourselves were:

(a) Why do I have to have beliefs?
(b) Does it matter to me what other people believe?
(c) Is it important to me if those with whom I worship and work are exclusive Christians or not?
(d) If it matters to me, why does it matter?

This last question is...the critical issue....It is surely very important to know why the convictions of others in this respect should matter so much to us. And it is worth remembering that one reason for attaching importance to uniformity of belief is not being quite sure of oneself....I feel fairly sure Jesus himself...would have been quick to recognize and applaud other teachers whose teachings were similar to his. We need the teachings too badly to split hairs about the differences...or worry about the names we give them. — *Geoffrey Hubbard, 1974.*

"THEN if you are a Quaker you shouldn't get so angry."

"It's because I get so angry that I have to be a Quaker."

There speaks every one of us; it is because of our imperfections that we need the support and encouragement of belonging to the Society.

Now having said that Quakers are by and large rather good people, and made the necessary modest disavowal of perfection, it would be convenient to go on to a clear statement of the Quaker line on various moral issues...unmarried mothers and their children, to alcoholics, to juvenile delinquency. My weighty Friends said...that you could not have an attitude to a problem in the abstract; there were no problems, only people. Every individual has to be approached with the love which came from knowing God in yourself and seeking to find, and answer to, that of God in others...

More orthodox religions present a rigid code of beliefs and of consequent behaviour, and so enable us to identify the gap between profession and practice. The Quaker has only one fixed point, his direct experience of God's love within himself. It is to this that he turns like a magnet to the north, and in every situation this is his compass, by which he is guided. Thus it is almost impossible for anyone else to decide whether or not a Quaker is responding to a particular situation rightly, in accordance with his own inner light. The nearest one can get is to follow his path, to be as deeply concerned, and to consult one's own inner light. At that stage one tends to lose interest in checking up on other people's performance; the shortcomings of one's own behaviour are too apparent.— *Geoffrey Hubbard, 1974.*

IF WE BELIEVE in that of God in every one, we must treat all as we would be treated, with love, respect and intelligent concern, no matter what they have done or are doing. We must remember that their bad actions are not themselves; that whatever they do, they are grounded in the divinity that is the sole reality. We must try to help them move from ignorance to knowledge, from hatred to love. We may have to prevent them in their ill-doing, but if we act with love, there could be no greater service; we may hope that others may so act towards us.

If we hold a different view of human nature, believing it to be intrinsically evil, steeped in original sin, violent, "animal", imperfect, or a Manichean mixture of good and bad, our behaviour will certainly differ in dealing with unpeaceful relations. The emphasis will shift from acknowledging the divine essence in those whose actions are unpeaceful, and acting to restore them to an understanding of their true selves, to changing those actions. Depending on circumstances we would try to persuade, manipulate, or control, even to intimidate, restrain forcibly, or to kill. This would be impossible to those who recognized our shared heritage, our unity as beings made in the image and likeness of God. But to those who do not, or do so half-heartedly, the desire to alter material circumstances may legitimize such action in the name of maintaining or restoring peace.

"True justice is the harvest reaped by peace makers from seeds sown in the spirit of peace", [is found in] the passage in the Epistle of James....None can doubt that justice is the proper fruit of peace making, while materialistic greed, leading to gross inequities, is a prime source of violence.— *Adam Curle, London, 1981.*

THE MERCY of God is indeed inexpressibly great to us poor creatures, and humility, gratitude and fear ought to be our clothing, under the signal display of His kindness in sparing us this summer from the yellow fever, about which my fellow citizens were greatly intimidated in the time of its usual approach. May my soul forever bear in mind the Lord's goodness to me, a poor unworthy creature, in raising me again from the bed of languishing under that sore disease, in the year 1793. Just eleven years ago, was I seized therewith.

Many of the contemporaries of my youth being by death and otherwise removed, I seem stript and lonely, and feel in no inclination to begin a new circle, so that with regret I shall pass with any more of the few who remain, with whom I have been united in the bonds of Christian fellowship, drinking together at the one inexhaustible fountain of love and life.

That I am spared another year is indeed marvelous in my eyes. O Lord, my God! be graciously pleased to look down with an eye of compassion upon me, now in my declining years, even as Thou, in Thy adorable goodness and mercy, didst in the days of my youth, when but sixteen years of age. Thy gracious visitations of pardoning love, grace and salvation plucked my soul as a brand from the burning, cast a mantle of forgiveness and mercy over me, and with a powerful voice said unto me, *live.—Rebecca Jones, 1805.*

"Mercy and truth are met together; righteousness and peace have kissed each other."—Psalm 85:10.

MUCH OF OUR ACCEPTANCE of multitudes of obligations is due to our inability to say No. We calculated that that task had to be done, and we saw no one ready to undertake it. We calculated the need, and then calculated our time, and decided maybe we could squeeze it in somewhere. But the decision was a heady decision, not made within the sanctuary of the soul. When we say Yes or No to calls for service on the basis of heady decisions, we have to give reasons, to ourselves and to others. But when we say Yes or No to calls, on the basis of inner guidance and whispered promptings of encouragement from the Center of our life, or on the basis of a lack of any inward "rising" of that Life to encourage us in the call, we have no reason to give, except one— the will of God as we discern it. Then we have begun to live in guidance. And I find He never guides us into an intolerable scramble of panting feverishness. The Cosmic Patience becomes, in part, our patience, for after all God is at work in the world. It is not we alone who are at work in the world, frantically finishing a work to be offered to God.

Life from the Center is a life of unhurried peace and power. It is simple. It is serene. It is amazing. It is triumphant. It is radiant. It takes no time, but it occupies all our time. And it makes our life programs new and overcoming. We need not get frantic. He is at the helm. And when our little day is done we lie down quietly in peace, for all is well.— *Thomas Kelly, 1941.*

SOURCES AND REFERENCES:

1 Thomas Kelly: TESTAMENT OF DEVOTION, copyright 1941 by Harper & Row Publishers, Inc. Renewed 1969 by Lois Lael Kelly Statler, reprinted by permission of Harper & Row, Publishers, Inc. 1941, pp. 115-116.

2 Wm. Crouch: DAY BY DAY: BEING A COMPILATION FROM THE WRITINGS OF ANCIENT AND MODERN FRIENDS, Wm. H. Chase, Dennis Bros. Auburn, N.Y. 1869, p. 26,hereafter designated DBD.

3 Irwin Abrams: FRIENDS JOURNAL, hereafter designated FJ, 6/1/87, "A Word About Listening."

4 Arthur Rifkin: FJ, 6/1/87."The Healing of Death."

5 Cecil E. Hinshaw: FJ, 6/1/82. "The Born Again Experience."

6 Joseph Hoag: JOURNAL, 1860, pp. 347-349.

7 Joseph Hoag: Ibid.

8 Elizabeth Gray Vining: BEAUTY FROM ASHES, STRENGTH AND JOY FROM SORROW spoken essay, Philadelphia Yearly Mtg., Book/Publishing Committee, 1979.

9 Caroline Stephen: LIGHT ARISING, Headley Bros, London. 1908.

10 Margaret Woods: Journal, 1771-1827, London. pp. 12-15.

11 Margaret E. Wilkinson:"Wisdom: The Inward Teacher." 14th James Backhouse Lecture, Australia, 1978, © Friends Book Supplies, Canberra, Australia.

12 Elizabeth Gray Vining: FRIEND OF LIFE: THE BIOGRAPHY OF RUFUS JONES. J.P. Lippincott, New York, 1958.

13 Elizabeth Gray Vining: Ibid.

14 Daniel A. Seeger: FJ, 1/1/86. "Unity & Diversity."

15 John Barclay: DBD, p. 13.

16 James Naylor: DBD, p. 27.

17 Enoch Lewis: DBD, p. 17.

18 O. Theodore Benfey: FJ, 4/1/87, "New Paths to Follow."

19 Daniel Bassuk: FJ, 2/1/87, "The Missing Quaker Letter."

20 George Fox and Others,1660

21 Howard H. Brinton: "PEACE TESTIMONY OF THE SOCIETY OF FRIENDS," American Friends Service Committee (no date).

22 Howard H. Brinton: Ibid.

23 Howard H. Brinton: Ibid.

24 Rufus Jones: RUFUS M. JONES, by Mary Hoxie Jones, Friends Home Service Committee, London, 1955, PRESENT DAY PAPERS, 9/1914, 12/1914.

25 Larry Cargill: FJ, 6/15/86. "Moses Bailey's Lifetime Wellness Plan."

26 Peter and Carole Fingesten: FJ, 9/1/87. "Let the Silence Speak for Itself."

27 John Woolman: JOURNAL, Whittier text, p. 11, hereafter refered to as JOURNAL.

28 Thomas H. Jeavons: FJ, 4/1/87, "Between Vision And Revelation."

29 David Sands: DBD, p. 23.

30 John Woolman: JOURNAL. p. 2.

31 Rufus Jones: THOU DOST OPEN UP MY LIFE, Ed. by Mary Hoxie Jones, Pendle Hill Pamphlet # 127, Pendle Hill Publications, Wallingford, Pennsylvania, hereafter designated PHP.

32 J. M. Fry: "The Surrender of Silence", "The Communion of Life", Swarthmore Lecture. 1911, Quaker Home Service, London.

33 Margaret Woods: Ibid., pp. 476-477.

34 Rufus Jones: "Thou Dost Open Up My Life" ed. by Mary Hoxie Jones. PHP # 127, 1963.

35 John Woolman: JOURNAL, p. 8.

36 Daniel A. Seeger: FJ, 1/1/86. "Unity and Diversity in Our Spiritual Family."

37 Thomas Kelly: TESTAMENT OF DEVOTION, Harper & Row 1941, pp. 29-30.

38 Joseph Talcot: DBD,. p. 36.

39 George Fox: JOURNAL, Ed. by J. L. Nichalls.

367

40 Howard H. Brinton: THE QUAKER DOCTRINE OF INWARD PEACE, PHP # 44, 1948.

41 Howard H. Brinton: Ibid.

42 London Epistle: DBD, p .42.

43 Douglas V. Steere: DIMENSIONS OF PRAYER, Woman's Division of Christian Service, Board of Missions, the Methodist Church, 1962, hereafter designated DIMENSIONS.

44 John Woolman: JOURNAL, p. 14.

45 Thomas Kelly: REALITY OF THE SPIRITUAL WORLD, PHP # 21, 1942.

46 Thomas Kelly: Ibid., p. 114.

47 Rufus Jones: THOU DOST OPEN UP MY LIFE, ed. by Mary Hoxie Jones, PHP #127, 1963, p.5.

48 Douglas V. Steere: DIMENSIONS.

49 Thomas Chalkley: DBD, p. 54.

50 Thomas R. Kelly: REALITY OF THE SPIRITUAL WORLD, PHP # 21, 1942.

51 Reginald Reynolds: JOHN WOOLMAN AND THE 20TH CENTURY, PHP # 96, p. 24-25.

52 Ann Backhouse: DBD, p. 56.

53 Douglas V. Steere: DIMENSIONS, p. 110.

54 John Pemberton: DBD, p. 60.

55 Margaret Hope Bacon: MOTHERS OF FEMINISM: THE STORY OF QUAKER WOMEN IN AMERICA, Harper & Row, Publishers, Inc., San Francisco, 1986.

56 George Withy: DBD, p. 67.

57 Peter Donchian: FJ, 7/1/86,"What's Happening to Our Meeting for Worship?"

58 Thomas Kelly: TESTAMENT OF DEVOTION, Harper & Row, 1941, p. 74-75.

59 Thomas Evans: DBD, p. 29.

60 Elizabeth Robson, DBD, p. 70.

61 Rosalie Wahl: FJ, 12/15/80, "Here I Am, Send Me!"

62 Dorothy Hutchinson: FJ, 12/15/80, "The Right to Life".

63 Samuel Bownas: DBD, p. 71.

64 Elizabeth Watson: THIS I KNOW EXPERIMENTALLY, FGC, 1977 Rufus Jones Lecture.

65 Elizabeth Watson: Ibid.

66 Joseph John Gurney: DBD, p. 74.

67 Thomas H. Jeavons: FJ, 12/1/80, "Simplicity in Our Times".

68 Howard H. Brinton: THE QUAKER DOCTRINE OF INWARD PEACE, PHP # 44, 1946.

69 John Barclay: DBD, p. 78.

70 Elise Boulding: CHILDREN AND SOLITUDE, PHP # 125, 1962.

71 Elizabeth Fry: OBSERVATIONS ON THE VISITING, SUPERINTENDING, AND GOVERN-MENT OF FEMALE PRISONERS, "Elizabeth Fry's Advice to Visitors to Women's Prisons," 2nd ed., 1827. p. 20-24.

72 Elizabeth Fry: Ibid.

73 Margaret Hope Bacon: THE QUIET REBELS, The Story of the Quakers in America, Basic Books, Inc., 1969.

74 Robert Barclay: BARCLAY'S APOLOGY, In Modern English, ed. by Dean Freiday, Friends Book Store, main distributor, by grant from the Rebecca White Trust of the Monthly Meeting of Friends of Philadelphia,1967.

75 Donald C. Johnson: FJ, 4/1/86, "This Way to Pendle Hill."

76 Thomas Ellwood: DBD, p. 88.

77 Caroline Stephen: QUAKER STRONGHOLDS, PHP # 59, 1951.

78 Thomas Kelly: THE ETERNAL PROMISE, Friends United Press, Richmond, Ind., 1977. p. 28.

79 James Naylor: CHRISTIAN FAITH AND PRACTICE IN THE EXPERIENCE OF THE SOCIETY OF FRIENDS, published by London Yearly Meeting of the Religious Society of Friends, 1960, hereafter designated CFP, # 22.

80 Elizabeth Watson: THIS I KNOW EXPERIMENTALLY, Friends General Conference, 1977 Rufus Jones Lecture.

81 Mary Springett: DBD, p. 93.

82 Janet Scott: WHAT CANST THOU SAY?, Quaker Home Service, 1980 Swarthmore Lecture, pp. 38-39.

83 Janet Scott: Ibid., pp. 46-47.

84 John Woolman: JOURNAL, p. 18.

85 Job Scott: JOURNAL, 1831, PP. 29-31; CFP, # 54.

86 Howard H. Brinton: THE QUAKER DOCTRINE OF INWARD PEACE, PHP # 44, 1946.

87 Errol T. Elliott: forward in LET YOUR LIVES SPEAK, by Elfrida Vipont Foulds PHP, 1953.

88 D. Elton Trueblood: THE PARADOX OF THE QUAKER MINISTRY, Lecture of Indiana Yearly Meeting, 1960.

89 D. Elton Trueblood: Ibid.

90 Penns and Peningtons: DBD p. 94.

91 George Peck: SIMPLICITY; A RICH QUAKER'S VIEW, PHP # 189, 1973.

92 George Peck: Ibid.

93 Margaret Woods: Ibid., pp. 483-484.

94 Rufus Jones: FINDING THE TRAIL OF LIFE, Macmillon Publishing Co. Inc., 1926, renewed Mary Hoxie Jones 1954.

95 A. Neave Brayshaw: CFP, # 87.

96 Elizabeth Watson: THIS I KNOW EXPERIMENTALLY, FGC, Rufus Jones Lecture, 1977.

97 George Fox: CFP, # 4, 6.

98 Howard H. Brinton: QUAKER JOURNALS, Pendle Hill Pubs., 1972.

99 Fortunato Castillo: FJ, 12/1/81, "When We Are Gathered."

100 James Bowden: DBD, p. 107.

101 Caroline Stephen: QUAKER STRONGHOLDS, 1890; PHP # 59, 1951

102 Richard K. Ullmann: THE DILEMMAS OF A RECONCILER, PHP # 131, 1963.

103 Richard K. Ullmann: Ibid.

104 John Woolman: JOURNAL, p. 18.

105 A. Neave Brayshaw: CFP, #287.

106 Daniel A. Seeger: PRACTICING THE GOSPEL OF HOPE IN THE NUCLEAR AGE, Wider Quaker Fellowship, 1983.

107 Thomas Ellwood: CFP, #35.

108 Martin Cobin: THE VALUE SYSTEM OF FRIENDS, Wider Quaker Fellowship, 1970.

109 John Wilbur: JOURNAL AND CORRESPONDENCE OF JOHN WILBUR, Pub. George H. Whitney, 3 Westminister St. 1859, p. 594.

110 John Wilbur: Ibid.

111 Thomas H. Jeavons: FJ, 11/15/81, "A Friendly Notion of Discipline."

112 Elias Hicks: SERMONS OF THOMAS WETHERALD AND ELIAS HICKS, taken in shorthand by Marcus T. C. Gould, published by the The Reporter, Philadelphia, 1826, hereafter designated SERMONS, p. 118.

113 Thomas Wetherald: SERMONS.

114 Elizabeth Watson: THIS I KNOW EXPERIMENTALLY, 1977 Rufus Jones Lecture, FGC.

115 Philadelphia Yearly Meeting, FAITH AND PRACTICE, 1961, pp. 22-24.

116 Elias Hicks: SERMONS, pp. 109-111.

117 John Barclay: DBD, p. 109.

118 Caroline Stephen: QUAKER STRONGHOLDS, 1890, PHP # 59, 1951.

119 Elfrida Vipont Foulds: LET YOUR LIVES SPEAK, PHP, 1953.

120 Elfrida Vipont Foulds: Ibid.

121 Elias Hicks: JOURNAL OF THE LIFE AND RELIGIOUS LABORS OF ELIAS HICKS, pub. by Isaac T. Hopper, New York, 1832, hereafter designated JOURNAL, p. 16.

122 Calvin Keene: FJ, "The Use of Silence," 7/1/81.

123 Calvin Keene: Ibid.

124 Elias Hicks: JOURNAL, p. 162.

125 Rufus Jones: FINDING THE TRAIL OF LIFE, MacMillan Pub. Co. 1926, renewed Mary Hoxie Jones 1954, pp. 78, 100.

126 Jonathan Hutchinson: DBD, p. 241.

127 Martin Cobin: WIDER QUAKER FELLOWSHIP, address to Southern Appalachian Association of Friends, 1970.

128 George Fox: JOURNAL, pp. 150-156.

129 Robert Barclay: BARCLAY'S APOLOGY In Modern English, ed. by Dean Freiday, p. 295-296.

130 Thomas Kelly, TESTAMENT OF DEVOTION, "The Simplification of Life," Harper & Row, 1941.

131 John Conron: DBD, p. 112.

132 Virginia W. Apsey: FJ, 3/1/87, "Worry, Trust, and Faith."

133 Henry J. Cadbury: THE CHARACTER OF A QUAKER, PHP # 103, 1959.

134 Josephine Whitney Duveneck: LIFE ON TWO LEVELS, reprinted with permission from Tioga Publishers, Box 50490, Palo Alto, Calif, 94303, 1978, chapters 34, 38.

135 Thomas R. Kelly: TESTAMENT OF DEVOTION, "The Simplification of Life," Harper & Row, 1941.

136 John Woolman, JOURNAL, pp. 36-37.

137 Wolf Mendl: THE STUDY OF WAR AS A CONTRIBUTION TO PEACE, PHP # 247. 1983.

138 James I'Anson, JOURNAL OF FRIENDS HISTORICAL SOCIETY, xilviii, p. 57.

139 Patience Schenck: FJ, 3/1988, "Courage and Spiritual Leadings."

140 George Howland: DBD, p. 120.

141 Thomas Kelly: THE ETERNAL PROMISE, Friends United Press, 1977, pp. 37-38. Harper & Row, 1966.

142 D. Elton Trueblood: THE PEOPLE CALLED QUAKERS, Harper & Row, 1966, Friends United Press, 1971, pp. 197, 203.

143 William Penn: CFP, # 227, 395.

144 Elias Hicks: JOURNAL, p. 157.

145 George H. Gorman: THE AMAZING FACT OF QUAKER WORSHIP, Swarthmore Lecture 1973, Quaker Home Service 1979, pp. 20-21.

146 Kenneth Boulding, MENDING THE WORLD, PHP # 266, 1986.

147 Elizabeth Gurney, DBD, p. 127.

148 Christopher Holdsworth: STEPS IN A LARGE ROOM: A Quaker Explores The Monastic Tradition, Swarthmore Lecture 1985, pp. 25-26.

149 George Fox: JOURNAL, pp. 169-170.

150 Wallace Cayard: FJ, 8/1/87, HOW I HAVE CHANGED IN TALKING ABOUT GOD.

151 George Peck: SIMPLICITY: A Rich Quaker's View, PHP # 189, 1973.

152 Margaret Woods: Ibid., pp. 11-12.

153 Kenneth E. Boulding: MENDING THE WORLD, PHP # 266, 1986.

154 John Greenleaf Whittier: Letter in "The Friends Review, CFP # 70.

155 George Peck: SIMPLICITY: A RICH QUAKER'S VIEW, PHP # 189, 1973.

156 Joseph John Gurney: MEMOIRS OF JOSEPH JOHN GURNEY, by Joseph Braithwaite, 1859, vol. I pp. 94-97.

157 Joseph John Gurney: Ibid.

158 William Taber: FJ, 3/1988, ON MINISTERING TO THE MEETING FOR BUSINESS.

159 John Greenleaf Whittier: Circular letter "To the Members of the Society of Friends", and "Anniversary Poem", both appearing in JOHN GREENLEAF WHITTIER, A PORTRAIT IN PARADOX, by Edward Wagenknecht, New York Oxford University Press.

160 Kenneth Boulding: MENDING THE WORLD, PHP # 266.

161 Levi Coffin: JOURNAL, 1880, pp. 147-150.

162 Edward Stabler: JOURNAL, 1846, pp. 109-110.

163 Thomas Wetherald: SERMONS, pp. 32-33.

164 Douglas V. Steere: PRAYER IN THE CONTEMPORARY WORLD, PHP # 907, 1966.

165 Elias Hicks: JOURNAL, p. 340.

166 Rufus Jones: FINDING THE TRAIL OF LIFE, MacMillan Pub. Co., 1926, pp. 38-39, 60.

167 John Greenleaf Whittier: JOHN GREENLEAF WHITTIER, A PORTRAIT IN PARADOX, by Edward Wagenknecht, New York Oxford University Press, pp. 20, 23.

168 Pieter Byhouwer: FJ, 5/15/1971, "The Conduct of Business."

169 Paton B. Crouse: FJ, THE RIGHT ORDERING OF MEETINGS FOR BUSINESS, 1/15/71, Queries from San Francisco Meeting.

170 George Fox: INSTITUTION OF THE DISCIPLINE, Vol. 1, appearing in OHIO CONSERVATIVE FRIENDS REVIEW, # 9.

171 Thomas Chalkley: JOURNAL, 1754, pp. 124-5, 366-7, 207-8.

172 Howard K. Brinton: QUAKER JOURNALS; VARIETIES OF RELIGIOUS EXPERIENCE AMONG FRIENDS, PHP, 1972, Wallingford, Penn.

173 Stuart Banister: then of Indiana, later of Ohio, Letter to editor, 1984.

174 Mary Capper: DBD, p. 132.

175 Mary Capper: DBD, p. 133.

176 John L. P. Maynard: OHIO CONSERVATIVE FRIENDS REVIEW, Issue No. 5, Book & Children's Literature Committee of Ohio Yearly Meeting of the Religious Society of Friends.

177 Susan Smith: Letter to editor, 7/29/84.

178 John L. P. Maynard: (15th St. Mtg.) "Untitled", OHIO CONSERVATIVE FRIENDS REVIEW, Issue # 5,

179 Christopher Holdsworth: STEPS IN A LARGE ROOM: A Quaker Explores the Monastic Tradition, Swarthmore Lecture 1985, Quaker Home Service, London, pp. 29-30.

180 John Woolman: JOURNAL, pp. 41-42.

181 Richard K. Ullmann: DILEMMAS OF A RECONCILER, PHP # 131. 1963.

182 Thomas Jeavons: FJ, "Changing Hearts As Well As Minds", 3/1/1982.

183 George Whitehead: DBD, p. 135.

184 Thomas Kelly: THE ETERNAL PROMISE, Harper & Row, 1966, Friends United Press, 1977, p. 40-41.

185 J. Howard Binns: OHIO CONSERVATIVE FRIENDS REVIEW, issue # 5, "Memories of Meeting."

186 J. Howard Binns: Ibid.

187 Mary Proude: DBD, p. 137.

188 Mary Proude: DBD, p. 138.

189 Mary Proude: DBD, p. 139.

190 Daniel A. Seeger: PRACTICING THE GOSPEL OF HOPE IN THE NUCLEAR AGE, Wider Quaker Fellowship, 1983.

191 Douglas V. Steere: DIMENSIONS OF PRAYER, Woman's Division Christian Service, Board of Missions, the Methodist Church, pp. 55-56.

192 George Fox: JOURNAL, pp. 181-183.

193 Isaac Penington: DBD, p. 142, CFP # 362, 404.

194 Thomas Jeavons: FJ, 3/1/82, "Changing Hearts As Well As Minds."

195 Christopher Holdsworth: STEPS IN A LARGE ROOM, Quaker Home Service, London, Swarthmore Lecture, 1985.

196 Errol T. Elliot: QUAKERS ON THE AMERICAN FRONTIER, Friends United Press, 1972, p. xviii-xix.

197 William Dewsbury: CFP # 30.

198 Adam Curle: TRUE JUSTICE, Quaker Peace Makers and Peace Making, Quaker Home Service, Swarthmore Lecture, 1981. p. 21.

199 Douglas V. Steere: PRAYER IN THE CONTEMPORARY WORLD, PHP # 907, 1966.

200 Phillips P. Moulton: VIOLENCE: OR AGGRESSIVE NONVIOLENT RESISTANCE?, PHP # 178, 1971.

201 John Barclay: DBD, p. 144.

202 Unknown: PLAYING MEETING, Ohio Conservative Friends Review, issue # 9.

203 Unknown: Ibid.

204 W. Russell Johnson: QUAKER RELIGIOUS THOUGHT: Vol. XI, No.1, "Hope."

205 John Greenleaf Whittier: quotations appearing in JGW, A PORTRAIT IN PARADOX, New York Oxford University Press, pp. 33, 122, 193.

206 John Woolman: JOURNAL , pp. 42-43.

207 Dwight Ericsson: FJ, 1/1988, SILENCE.

208 Cyrus Pringle: THE CIVIL WAR DIARY OF CYRUS PRINGLE, PHP # 122, 1962.

209 Douglas V. Steere: PRAYER IN THE CONTEMPORARY WORLD, PHP # 907, 1966.

210 Edward Burrough: DBD, p. 146, CFP # 177.

211 George Fox: DBD, p. 147.

212 Errol T. Elliott: QUAKER PROFILES FROM THE AMERICAN WEST, Friends United Press, Richmond, Ind., 1972, p. 106, 108-109.

213 Isaac Penington: CFP # 222.

214 Ross Flanagan: FJ, 1/1/1981, "Keeping Our Eyes On The Prize."

215 Ross Flanagan: Ibid.

216 Margaret Fell Fox: WORKS: A BRIEF COLLECTION OF REMARKABLE PASSAGES, London 1710, pp. 534-35., published in Early Quaker Writings 1650-1700, ed. by Hugh Barbour and Arthur O. Roberts, William B. Eerdmans Pub. Co. Grand Rapids, Michigan, p. 565.

217 Caroline Stephen: QUAKER STRONGHOLDS, 1890, PHP # 59, printed 1951.

218 Thomas Kelly: THE ETERNAL PROMISE, Friends United Press, 1977, pp. 47-48.

219 George Fox: DBD, 151.

220 Levi Coffin: REMINISCENCES, Robert Clark Company, 1898, pp. 107-108.

221 Levi Coffin: Ibid, pp. 108-110.

222 Elizabeth Watson: FJ, 5/1/1980, "Ask Not Good Fortune."

223 George Fox: DBD, p. 150.

224 John Woolman: JOURNAL, pp. 46-47.

225 William Penn: FRUITS OF A FATHERS'S LOVE, 1726, NO CROSS, NO CROWN, 1682, (Chapter 4, section 13).

226 Phillips P. Moulton: VIOLENCE, OR AGGRESSIVE NONVIOLENT RESISTANCE?, PHP # 178, 1971.

227 Mary Penington: DBD, 157.

228 Mary Penington: DBD, 158.

229 Daniel A. Seeger: THE GOSPEL OF HOPE IN THE NUCLEAR AGE, 1983, Wider Quaker Fellowship.

230 George Fox: DBD, 162.

231 Paul Niebanck: FJ, 1/1/81, "Commitment To The Unknown."

232 John Greenleaf Whittier: WHITTIER, M. A. Donohue & Co., Chicago, Ill., 1857.

233 Henry J. Cadbury: THE QUAKER PEACE TESTIMONY, An Anthology compiled by Jos. S. Rowntree, M.A., 1938, revised by Helen Byles Ford, 1949, Friends' Peace Committee, Friends House, London.

234 Reginald Reynolds: JOHN WOOLMAN AND THE 20TH CENTURY, PHP # 96, 1958.

235 George H. Gorman: THE AMAZING FACT OF QUAKER WORSHIP, Swarthmore Lecture 1973, Quaker Home Service 1979, pp. 20-23.

236 George H. Gorman: Ibid., pp. 23-24.

237 Levi Coffin: REMINISCENCES, Robert Clark Company, 1898, pp. 267-268.

238 Christopher Holdsworth: STEPS IN A LARGE ROOM: A Quaker Explores the Monastic Tradition, Quaker Home Service, Swarthmore Lecture, 1985, pp. 49-50.

239 Christopher Holdsworth: Ibid., pp. 50-51.

240 John Banks: JOURNAL OF THE LIFE, LABOURS, TRAVELS, AND SUFFERINGS...JOHN BANKS, J. Sowle, in White-Hart-Court in Gracious-Street, 1712.

241 Isaac Penington: SELECT SERIES, John Barclay, 1837, pp. 172-173.

242 Francis Howgill: THE INHERITANCE OF JACOB DISCOVERED, AFTER HIS RETURN OUT OF EGYPT, Printed for Giles Calvert At the Back Spreadeagle at the West End of Pauls, 1656.

243 Dwight Ericsson: FJ, 1/1/1988, "Silence."

244 Margaret Woods: Ibid. pp., 222-223.

245 Thomas Kelly: TESTAMENT OF DEVOTION, Harper & Row, 1941, pp. 34-35.

246 William O. Brown: TRANSCENDENCE IN THE PURSUIT OF WHOLENESS, Illinois Yearly Meeting, 1978 Jonathan Plummer Lecture.

247 William O. Brown: Ibid.

248 Elizabeth Gray Vining: A QUEST THERE IS, PHP # 246, 1982.

249 John Woolman: Journal, pp.50-51.

250 Howard H. Brinton: QUAKER EDUCATION IN THEORY AND PRACTICE, PHP # 9, 1949, reprinted THE NATURE OF QUAKERISM, PHP # 47, 1962.

251 John Woolman: DBD, p. 181.

252 Howard H. Brinton: QUAKER EDUCATION IN THEORY AND PRACTICE, PHP # 9.

253 Janet Scott: WHAT CANST THOU SAY?, Quaker Home Service, London, Swarthmore Lecture, 1980, p. 13.

254 George Fox: Epistle 47, 219, 319.

255 Sylvia Messner: "Our Eternal Source," FJ, 4/15/80.

256 James Parnell: DBD, p. 186.

257 James S. Best: FJ, 4/15/80, "Light Unto My Feet."

258 Christopher Holdsworth: STEPS IN A LARGE ROOM, Quaker Home Service, Swarthmore Lecture 1985, p. 54.

259 Christopher Holdsworth: Ibid., pp. 55-56.

260 Job Scott: DBD, p. 198.

261 John Greenleaf Whittier: JOHN GREENLEAF WHITTIER: A PORTAIT IN PARADOX, New York Oxford University Press, 1967, p. 182, 140.

262 Caroline Stephen: QUAKER STRONGHOLDS, 1890, abridgement, PHP # 59, 1951.

263 Martin Cobin: FROM CONVINCEMENT TO CONVERSION, PHP # 134, 1964.

264 John Woolman: JOURNAL, p. 61.

265 Martin Cobin: FROM CONVINCEMENT TO CONVERSION, PHP # 134, 1964.

266 John Woolman: DBD, p. 199.

John Greenleaf Whittier: POEMS,"The Preacher".

267 Deb Sawyer: FJ, 3/15/87, "Creating A Nonviolent Society."

268 Lucretia Mott: quotes taken from VALIANT FRIEND, by Margaret Hope Bacon, Walker & Company, New York, 1980.

269 Margaret Hope Bacon: VALIANT FRIEND, Walker & Company, New York, 1980, pp. 230-231. Lucretia Mott quotation taken from same, p. 220.

270 Margaret Woods: Ibid. pp., 472-473.

271 Elizabeth L. Comstock: LIFE AND LETTERS OF ELIZABETH L. COMSTOCK, Headly Brothers, London, John C. Winston, Philadelphia, 1895, pp. 2-3.

272 Elizabeth L. Comstock: Ibid., pp. 92-93.

273 Elizabeth L. Comstock: Ibid., pp. 95-97.

274 John Greenleaf Whittier: POEMS: "First Day Thoughts," 1857.

275 Carol Urner: "A Modern Lazarus", FJ, 4/1/1985.

John Greenleaf Whittier: POEMS: "Lines Inscribed to Friends Under Arrest for Treason against the Slave Power."

276 John Woolman: JOURNAL, pp. 63-65.

277 Gene Knudsen-Hoffman: FJ, 10/1/1981, "Reflections on Speaking Truth to Power."

278 Caroline Stephen: LIGHT ARISING, Headley Bros, London, 1908.

279 Lewis Benson: FJ, 4/1/1985, "The Concern Of The New Foundation Movement."

280 Daniel A. Seeger: THE SEED AND THE TREE: A REFLECTION ON NONVIOLENCE, 1986, PHP # 269.

281 Daniel A. Seeger: Ibid.

282 Elizabeth L. Comstock: Life & Letters, Headly Bros., London, John C. Winston, Philadelphia, 1895, p. 107.

283 Brinton Turkle: FJ, 12/1/81, TRUSTING DIVINE CHAOS: AN INTERVIEW WITH BRINTON TURKLE, by Shirley Ruth.

284 Bill Ashworth: ROGUE VALLEY FRIENDS, 12/1986.

285 Bill Ashworth: Ibid.

286 Advices and Queries: London Yearly Meeting of the Religious Society of Friends, 1964.

287 Advices and Queries: Ibid.

288 Jonathan Hutchinson, DBD, p. 211.

289 Dwight Spann-Wilson: FJ, 3/15/81, "How Important is the Justice Testimony?"

290 Robert Barclay: BARCLAY'S APOLOGY IN MODERN ENGLISH, edited by Dean Freiday, 1967, pp. 330, 331.

291 Vince Oredson: ROGUE VALLEY FRIENDS, "Clerks Corner," 4/1986.

292 Advices & Queries, London Yearly Meeting of the Religious Society of Friends, 1964.

293 Elizabeth Taber King: DBD, p. 215.

294 George Dillwyn: DBD. p. 216.

295 Thomas Kelly: TESTAMENT OF DEVOTION, Harper & Row, 1941, pp. 114-115.

296 Advices & Queries, London Yearly Meeting of the Religious Society of Friends, 1964.

297 Elizabeth Comstock: LIFE & LETTERS, Headley Brothers, London, 1895, pp. 126-127, 151.

298 Peace Pilgrim: FJ, ll/15/1980, "One Pilgrim"s Path", by Robert Horton.

299 John Woolman: JOURNAL, pp. 65-66.

300 Shirley Dodson: FJ, 9/1/1980, "Theology For Each Of Us."

301 Margaret Woods: Ibid. pp., 22-23.

302 Daniel A. Seeger: THE SEED AND THE TREE, PHP #269, 1986.

303 John Greenleaf Whittier: "COMPLETE POETICAL WORKS OF WHITTIER, "The Eternal Goodness," Riverside Press, 1848

304 Howard H. Brinton: THE INWARD DOCTRINE OF PEACE, PHP # 44, 1948.

305 William Penn: A COLLECTION OF THE WORKS OF WILLIAM PENN, London, 1726, Vol. I, 219.

306 Elise Boulding: BORN REMEMBERING, PHP # 200, 1975.

307 George Peck: SIMPLICITY: A RICH QUAKER'S VIEW, 1973, PHP # 189.

308 William Penn: NO CROSS, NO CROWN, WORKS, I, pp. 295-296.

309 Leila Ward: HERE AND NOW, SOME EXPERIENCES CONSIDERED, Quaker Home Service, London, 1980.

310 Peter Fingesten: FJ, 7/1/85. "On Contemplation."

311 Richard Shackleton: DBD, p. 219.

312 Elise Boulding: BORN REMEMBERING, PHP # 200, 1975.

313 London Yearly Meeting: Advices & Queries, 1964.

314 William Penn: SOME FRUITS OF SOLITUDE, WORKS, I, 843-844.

315 Daniel A. Seeger: THE SEED AND THE TREE: A REFLECTION ON NONVIOLENCE, 1986, PHP # 269.

316 London Yearly Meeting: Advices & Queries, 1964.
   Elise Boulding: BORN REMEMBERING, PHP # 200, 1975.

317 Thomas Kelly: REALITY OF THE SPIRITUAL WORLD, 1942, PHP # 21.

318 William Penn: SOME FRUITS OF SOLITUDE, WORKS, I, 850-851.

319 Elizabeth Watson: GUESTS OF MY LIFE, Celo Press, 1979, pp. 38, 51-52.

320 John Woolman: JOURNAL, pp. 70-71.

321 Thomas H. Jeavons: FJ, 3/1/1984, "If God Already Knows, Why Ask?"

322 Elizabeth Gurney: DBD, p. 229.

323 Janet Scott: WHAT CANST THOU SAY?, Quaker Home Servce, Swarthmore Lecture, 1930, pp. 41-42.

324 Thomas Kelly: REALITY OF THE SPIRITUAL WORLD, PHP # 21, 1942.

325 William Taber: FJ, 2/1/1984, "Toward A Broader Quaker Message."

326 William Taber: Ibid.

327 John Woolman: JOURNAL, pp. 76-77.

328 John Woolman: Ibid., pp. 77-78.

329 John Greenleaf Whittier: COMPLETE POETICAL WORKS, Riverside Edition, 1848.

330 Paul A. Lacey: LEADING AND BEING LED, PHP #264, 1985.

331 Richard Shackleton: DBD, p. 111.

332 Elizabeth Watson: GUESTS OF MY LIFE, Celo Press, 1979, pp. 137, 181.

333 Josephine Whitney Duveneck: LIFE ON TWO LEVELS, reprinted with permission from Tioga Publishers, Box 50490, Palo Alto, Calif., 1978, chapters 34, 38.

334 Douglas V. Steere: FJ, 5/15/82, "Some Dimensions of the Quaker Decision-making Process."

335 John Woolman: JOURNAL, pp. 81-82.

336 Rufus Jones: FINDING THE TRAIL OF LIFE, MacMillan Pub. Co. 1926, renewed by Mary Hoxie Jones, 1954, pp. 120-123.

337 William Penn: A BRIEF ACCOUNT OF THE RISE AND PROGRESS OF THE PEOPLE CALLED QUAKERS, WORKS, I, 891-892, WORKS ,I, 842-843, 213,-214.

338 Hannah Whitall Smith: THE UNSELFISHNESS OF GOD, 1903, pp. 289-290, A RELIGIOUS REBEL: THE LETTERS OF H.W.SMITH, ed. by Logan Pearsall Smith, 1949. CFP, #77, 78, 519.

339 Anne Farrer Scott: FJ, 1/1/1982, "Fishing in Troubled Waters."

340 Richard D. Cooper: FJ, 1/1/1982, "A Second Gift of Life."

341 Thomas Chalkley: DBD, p. 252.

342 Jonathan Dymond: DBD, p. 269.

343 London Yearly Meeting: "Advices and Queries," 1964.

344 Isaac Penington: CFP, "To the Reader", # 362, # 222.

345 Ross Flanagan, FJ, 5/1/1982, "On Regaining My Trust In God".

346 John Crook: DBD, p. 280.

347 Elden H. Mills: QUAKER LIFE, 1/1981, "The Quaker Face."

348 George H. Gorham: THE AMAZING FACT OF QUAKER WORSHIP, Quaker Home Service, London, 1979.

349 Thomas Story: DBD, p. 365.

350 Margaret Woods: Ibid., pp. 85-86.

351 Betty-Jean Seeger: FJ, 7/1/1982, "Seeking, Finding, & Affirming."

352 Peace Pilgrim: FJ, 11/15/80, "Steps Toward Inner Peace: From a Discourse by Peace Pilgrim", by Robert Horton.

353 Katherine Green-Ellison: FJ, 5/1/1982, "Cut Off From God."

354 John Woolman: JOURNAL, pp. 132-133.

355 Alfred LaMotte: FJ, 7/1/1982, "Are You Here?"

356 Thomas Scattergood: DBD, p. 331.

357 Elizabeth Watson: FJ, 4/1/1981, "Clearness For Marriage."

358 Ruth Morris: FJ, 5/1/1981, "Loving Farthest Out."

359 Barry Morley: FJ, 5/1/1981, "Let There Be Light."

360 Vickie Aldrich: FJ, 8/1/1980, "Some Quaker Roots".

361 Geoffrey Hubbard: QUAKER BY CONVINCEMENT, Quaker Home Service, London, 1985, pp. 217-218.

362 Geoffrey Hubbard: Ibid., pp. 122-123.

363 Adam Curle: TRUE JUSTICE: QUAKER PEACE MAKERS AND PEACE MAKING, Quaker Home Service, London, Swarthmore Lecture, 1981, pp. 100-101.

364 Rebecca Jones: DBD, p. 346.

365 Thomas Kelly: TESTAMENT OF DEVOTION, Harper & Row, 1941, pp. 123-124.